Windows™ 3
QuickStart

Ron Person
Karen Rose

que ®
CORPORATION
LEADING COMPUTER KNOWLEDGE
CARMEL, INDIANA

Windows™ 3 QuickStart.
Copyright© 1990 by Que® Corporation.

Library of Congress Catalog No.: LC 90-62960

ISBN 0-88022-610-2

93 92   6   5

Interpretation of the printing code: the rightmost double-digit number is the year of the book's printing; the rightmost single-digit number, the number of the book's printing. For example, a printing code of 90-1 shows that the first printing of the book occurred in 1990.

Windows 3 QuickStart is based on Microsoft Windows 3.

About the Authors

Ron Person has written more than 12 books for Que Corporation, including *Using Excel: IBM Version*; *Excel Tips, Tricks, and Traps*; *Using Word for Windows*; *Using Microsoft Windows 3*, 2nd Edition; and *Using 1-2-3 Release 3*. Ron is the principal consultant for Ron Person & Co. In addition to corporate consulting and conducting seminars, he teaches at University of California, Berkeley Extension, and Sonoma State University. He has an M.S. in physics from The Ohio State University and an M.B.A. from Hardin-Simmons University.

Karen Rose is a senior trainer for Ron Person & Co. She has written five books for Que Corporation, including *Using Microsoft Windows 3,* 2nd Edition; *Using Word for Windows;* and *Using WordPerfect 5*. Karen teaches desktop publishing and design for University of California, Berkeley Extension, and Sonoma State University. She previously owned Write on Target, a corporate newsletter publishing business using desktop publishing technologies.

Ron Person & Co., based in San Francisco, consults and trains nationwide in Excel, Word for Windows, and other strategic Windows and OS/2 Presentation Manager applications. Ron Person & Co. does consulting and development in financial, marketing, and executive information systems based on Windows and Presentation Manager applications. The firm trains a spectrum of courses tailored to users, trainers, and developers.

For more information about consulting, training, on-site seminars, or support materials from Ron Person & Co., write or call:

Ron Person & Co.
P.O. Box 5647
Santa Rosa, CA 95402
(415) 989-7508
(707) 539-1525

Publishing Director

David P. Ewing

Acquisitions Editor

Terrie Lynn Solomon

Product Director

Kathie-Jo Arnoff

Production Editor

Ginny Noble

Editors

Martha Karatz
Nancy Sixsmith

Editorial Assistant

Stacey Beheler

Technical Editor

Dana Schmeller

Technical Support

Tim Stanley
Jerry Ellis

Book Design and Production

Denny Hager
William Hartman
Betty Kish
Sarah Leatherman
Joe Ramon
Dennis Sheehan
Mary Beth Wakefield

Indexer

Sherry Massey

Composed in Garamond by

William Hartman, Hartman Publishing

Acknowledgments

Windows 3 QuickStart was created through the work and contributions of many professionals. We want to thank the people who helped make this book possible.

Thanks to all at Microsoft for their energy and clear vision of the future. Working with the professionals at Microsoft energizes and invigorates us. You make a major difference in people's lives.

Tanya van Dam for providing information and software coordination with Microsoft. She kept us up-to-date and well informed. Through our years of beta testing software and meeting book deadlines, she's been a graceful professional.

The product managers, sales people, analysts, and technical support at Microsoft for their assistance and support with our books and consulting.

Thanks to all at Que Corporation for their professional attitudes and high energy. You're a great group of people who produce the highest-quality computer books. From our vantage point behind the desks on the business battlefront, we see how much people depend on Que books to get work done. Thank you from them and from us.

Dave Ewing, Publishing Director, for his knowledge of the industry and his development of a Windows book product line.

Terrie Lynn Solomon, Acquisitions Editor, for standing by us through a suite of Windows books and for guiding us through the meteoric rush of deadlines.

Kathie-Jo Arnoff, Product Development Specialist, for her clear vision and knowledge in designing books. Her design of the *QuickStart* books makes computer use more accessible to everyone.

Ginny Noble, Production Editor, for being easy to work with and for her diligence and smooth-flowing style. Her editing and questions enhanced the book.

Stacey Beheler for tracking and coordinating our paper and diskette volleys with Que.

Dana Schmeller for her conscientious technical edit on yet another of our Windows books. Her queries and in-depth review gave us confidence. Should an error have missed us all, however, the responsibility still lies with us.

Bill Hartman of Hartman Publishing for the layout and typesetting of *Windows 3 QuickStart* in Aldus PageMaker, a desktop publishing application. His expertise gave us the high quality and fast turnaround time demanded by a rapidly changing industry.

Thanks to the manufacturers who helped us with their knowledge, time, and products. Combining these products under Windows 3 brings a new level of productivity to more people.

Microsoft Corporation for Windows, Word for Windows, and Excel for Windows.

Hewlett-Packard for the Microsoft Z1A font cartridge used in most of the examples and figures.

Polaris Software for Pack*Rat*, a personal information system that links data directly into Word for Windows or Excel.

Aldus Corporation for PageMaker, the page-layout software used to create books, newsletters, and other publications.

Future Soft Engineering for DynaComm, the Windows and Macintosh communication program that crosses platforms with a wide range of protocols.

Precision Software for its relational Windows database, SuperBase 4, that runs and links to other Windows applications.

Pioneer Software for its dBASE query-and-edit application Q+E. With it, linking Windows applications to dBASE files is easy.

Roykore for its ABC Flowcharter that enables users to create flow charts or organization charts as they work in other applications.

Trademark Acknowledgments

Que Corporation has made every attempt to supply trademarks about company names, products, and services mentioned in this book. Trademarks indicated below were derived from various sources. Que Corporation cannot attest to the accuracy of this information.

1-2-3 and Lotus are registered trademarks of Lotus Development Corporation.

Aldus and PageMaker are registered trademarks of Aldus Corporation.

Amí is a trademark of Samna Corporation.

COMPAQ and COMPAQ Deskpro 286 are registered trademarks of COMPAQ Computer Corporation.

CompuServe Information Service is a registered trademark of CompuServe Incorporated and H&R Block, Inc.

dBASE and MultiMate are registered trademarks of Ashton-Tate Corporation. dBASE IV is a trademark of Ashton-Tate Corporation.

DynaComm is a registered trademark of Future Soft Engineering, Inc.

EPSON is a registered trademark of Epson Corporation.

Helvetica and Times are registered trademarks of Allied Corporation. Linotronic is a trademark of Allied Corporation.

HP and LaserJet are registered trademarks of Hewlett-Packard Co.

IBM, IBM PC, IBM PC AT, OS/2, and PS/2 are registered trademarks of International Business Machines Corporation.

Micrografx is a registered trademark of Micrografx, Inc., and Micrografx Designer is a trademark of Micrografx, Inc.

Microsoft, Microsoft Excel, Microsoft Windows Write, Microsoft Project, Microsoft Word, and MS-DOS are registered trademarks of Microsoft Corporation. Windows is a trademark of Microsoft Corporation.

Norton Utilities is a trademark of Peter Norton Computing.

Pack*Rat* is a trademark of Polaris Software.

Paintbrush is a trademark of Zsoft Corporation.

PostScript is a registered trademark of Adobe Systems Incorporated.

Quicken is a registered trademark of Intuit.

SideKick is a registered trademark of Borland International, Inc.

SuperBase is a registered trademark of Precision Incorporated.

Vopt is a trademark of Golden Bow Systems.

WordPerfect is a registered trademark of WordPerfect Corporation.

Contents at a Glance

Table of Contents

Introduction

Welcome to *Windows 3 QuickStart*. Whether you are a novice with computers or are familiar with non-Windows programs, this *QuickStart* is one of the easiest and fastest ways to master the Windows revolution.

You will find that Windows 3 makes personal computers more accessible, even to first-time computer users, and moves everyone farther up the productivity curve. Controlled studies, surveys, and the experience of thousands of students have shown that Windows programs help new users learn more quickly and experienced users become more productive. And besides increasing productivity, Windows and Windows programs are more fun to use.

Who Should Use This Book?

Consider *Windows 3 QuickStart* your personal instructor. Because the step-by-step instructions include only the most important concepts, your learning isn't obstructed by clouds of side issues. The numbered steps and concise explanations get you into the program and through your work without much page turning, rereading, or index flipping.

What you learn in *Windows 3 QuickStart* carries over to Windows programs such as Microsoft Excel, Word for Windows, and Aldus PageMaker. The *QuickStart* not only gets you going quickly but also gives you a head start on learning any Windows programs.

If you're an experienced personal computer user but are not familiar with Windows, you will find *Windows 3 QuickStart* an excellent way to come up to speed quickly. When you need more detailed information, you can turn to the Help menu found in Windows programs and to Que's line of Windows books, including *Using Microsoft Windows 3*, 2nd Edition; *Using Excel: IBM Version*; and *Using Word for Windows*.

How To Use This Book

Each chapter follows the same style. New commands or procedures are first described briefly, and then numbered steps guide you through the required mouse actions or keystrokes. The numbered steps make it easy for you to follow the procedures without losing your place. Throughout the procedures, illustrations are provided to show how the screen (or a similar program's screen) should appear. Some procedures are followed by short notes that describe important tips or cautions in using basic features of the program.

Many of the free programs that come with Windows will help you understand how other Windows programs operate. In this book, the most important chapters for learning about different types of Windows programs and for learning how to work with multiple programs are these:

Chapter	*Purpose*
Chapter 1 An Overview of Windows	Gives you the big picture about how Windows operates
Chapter 3 Operating Windows	Shows how to use Windows menus and dialog boxes
Chapter 9 Using Windows Write	Explains how to enter and edit text in any Windows program while you use a simple word processor
Chapter 10 Using Windows Paintbrush	Shows how to draw with a bit-mapped drawing program
Chapter 13 Running Non-Windows Programs	Explains how to run one or more non-Windows (DOS) programs under Windows
Chapter 14 Integrating Programs	Explains how to run multiple programs and pass data between them

As you use *Windows 3 QuickStart*, you may want to do the following:

- *Skim* through a descriptive chapter to learn about features that could be useful at a later time.
- *Scan* the Table of Contents at the front of the book when you aren't sure what you are looking for.
- *Search* for a specific word in the Index at the back of the book when you know exactly what word or command you need to learn about.
- *Experiment* with ideas you find in this book.
- *Guide* yourself as you work with the Help information found in the Help menu of all Windows programs.

How This Book Is Organized

Windows 3 QuickStart shows you how to operate Windows and the free programs that come with it. The book contains chapters on sharing data between programs designed for Windows, including Microsoft Excel, Word for Windows, and Aldus PageMaker, as well as between such DOS programs as Lotus 1-2-3 and WordPerfect.

Chapter 1, "An Overview of Windows," illustrates how Windows can improve your work and helps you decide what features are most important to the way you work.

Chapter 2, "Getting Started," explains how to start Windows and describes its capabilities on different computer systems.

Chapter 3, "Operating Windows," covers the important concepts used in all Windows programs. You learn how to control window sizes, operate menus, select from the choices in dialog boxes, and enter and edit data. What you learn in this chapter applies to all Windows programs.

Chapter 4, "Grouping Programs and Documents," explains how to use the Program Manager to keep related programs and documents together so that they are easy to find and use.

Chapter 5, "Managing Files," explains how to use the File Manager to copy and erase files, create directories, and format diskettes—all the disk-maintenance problems that were tough and time-consuming under DOS but are now easy under Windows.

Chapter 6, "Customizing Your Work Area," shows how to customize Windows with your own color schemes and "draw it yourself" desktop patterns. The chapter even discusses more mundane topics, such as how to add a new printer.

Chapter 7, "Controlling the Printer," describes how Windows programs store print jobs in a spooler while they are waiting to print. This feature enables you to keep working in Windows while the Print Manager manages printing.

Chapter 8, "Using the Clipboard To Copy and Paste," illustrates how to copy and paste your work. You learn also how to view what is in the Clipboard and save the contents to paste later.

Chapter 9, "Using Windows Write," does two things at once. It shows you how to use an executive word processor and how to enter and edit text in any Windows text-oriented program.

Chapter 10, "Using Windows Paintbrush," describes an enjoyable and colorful Windows program that introduces you to drawing in Windows. Paintbrush works the same way, with a similar toolbox, as many of the powerful drawing, design, and drafting programs designed for Windows.

Chapter 11, "Using Desktop Accessories," reviews the personal productivity programs that come free with Windows, including the Clock, Calculator, Calendar, Cardfile database, Terminal, and Notepad. These small pop-up programs are convenient to use while you use other Windows programs.

Chapter 12, "Creating Macros," shows you how to make recordings that duplicate your keystrokes and mouse actions—a great way to eliminate repetitive tasks.

Chapter 13, "Running Non-Windows Programs," explains how to run multiple non-Windows programs, such as Lotus 1-2-3 and WordPerfect, and how to customize Windows so that your non-Windows programs run efficiently.

Chapter 14, "Integrating Programs," brings you into the next generation of personal computers. You'll learn how to run multiple programs and how to copy and paste data and graphics from one program to another. You'll even learn how to link Windows programs together so that they pass data automatically.

Appendix A, "Installing Windows 3," helps you install Windows and its desktop programs.

Appendix B, "Summary of Windows Commands," lists the most important operating commands in Windows and a few of the free programs.

Where To Find More Help

You can get additional information about Windows and products designed for Windows from Que, the leading publisher of personal computer books for business. Some of the Windows and Windows application books available through Que are these:

Using Microsoft Windows 3, 2nd Edition

Using Word for Windows

Using Excel: IBM Version

Excel QuickStart

Excel Tips, Tricks, and Traps

Excel Business Applications: IBM Version

Using PageMaker: IBM Version

When you want books that help you get started quickly or that increase your productivity with Windows products, outside Indiana, contact Que at 1-800-428-5331. In Indiana, call 317-573-2500.

For corporate consulting and training on major Windows and OS/2 applications, such as Microsoft Excel and Word for Windows, contact Ron Person & Co.:

Ron Person & Co.
P.O. Box 5647
Santa Rosa, California 95402
415-989-7508
707-539-1525

Conventions Used in This Book

With Windows, you can use the mouse, the keyboard, or shortcut keys for most operations. Throughout the chapters, keyboard and mouse techniques are provided.

To select menu options by typing underlined letters or pressing shortcut keys, you may need to use key combinations. In this book, a key combination is joined by a comma or a plus (+) sign:

Combination	Keystrokes
Alt, *letter*	Press the Alt key, release it, and then press the letter key.
Alt+*letter*	Hold down the Alt key, press the letter key, and then release both keys.
Ctrl+Ins	Press and hold down the Ctrl key while you then press the Ins key.

When you use the mouse to operate Windows, you can perform four kinds of actions:

Action	Explanation
Click	Place the on-screen pointer on the item you want to affect, and click the left mouse button.
Double-click	Place the on-screen pointer on the item you want to affect, and click the left mouse button twice in rapid succession.
Drag	Place the on-screen pointer on the item you want to affect, and hold down the left mouse button as you move the mouse.
Shift+Click	Hold down the Shift key as you click on the item.

Text that you are instructed to type appears in **boldface**. Text that is displayed on-screen, such as prompts and messages, appears in a special typeface.

An Overview of Windows

Windows is leading a revolution in personal computers. The Windows revolution makes people more productive with less work, yet Windows is easier to learn and use. This chapter shows you why Windows is fueling this revolution.

Windows is an *environment* surrounding DOS, the *Disk Operating System*. DOS enables computer programs to run on your computer. Before Windows, computer operators were faced with remembering difficult DOS commands. Operators also had to learn such programs as Lotus 1-2-3 and WordPerfect, which shared no common menu structure or operating techniques. Much practice was necessary to become proficient in DOS-based programs, and hard work was required to master the power that was hidden inside.

Windows eliminates these problems. It masks DOS, doing away with arcane DOS commands and improving the way DOS uses memory. Programs designed specifically for Windows—such as Microsoft Excel, Aldus PageMaker, and Word for Windows—share common menus and operate the same way. Learning one program, therefore, helps you learn other Windows programs. And because pull-down menus and pop-up dialog boxes make all options available to beginners and experts, Windows programs are more accessible to all users—everyone moves up the productivity curve.

Understanding the advantages of Windows

Learning how Windows adds features to non-Windows programs

Identifying the Windows features that will be helpful to you

1

Key Terms in This Chapter

Desktop	The screen background area on which windows and icons containing programs are displayed.
Document	The data on which a program works. A document may be the data in a spreadsheet, a letter in a word processor, or a chart in a drawing program.
DOS	The Disk Operating System that coordinates hardware and software actions. DOS is a foundation underneath Windows.
Environment	The collection of objects, commands, and rules composing the work space in which Windows and Windows programs work.
Graphical user interface (GUI)	A visual environment that helps people control computer programs more easily and with more consistency.
Icon	A pictorial representation of a command, program, or document.
Window	A rectangular area on-screen that encloses one specific program or one specific document.

Learning Faster with Windows

People are visual creatures. Most of what we learn comes through our sight. We remember best what we put in a unique location, not what we tag with a text name.

Windows programs use what is technically known as a *graphical user interface*, or GUI for short. A GUI takes advantage of the visual way that people are used to working and that most people prefer to work.

Like the programs designed for Windows, a GUI uses pull-down menus. Many of these menus are the same—and are in the same locations—in different Windows programs.

8

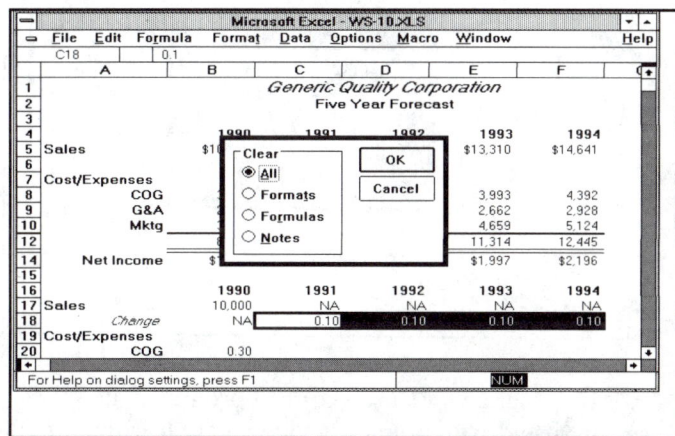

For example, when you choose Edit from the menu bar in an Excel window, the Edit pull-down menu appears.

Selecting a command on a pull-down menu from a Windows program produces a dialog box if the command requires additional information.

All choices or options for the command are visible in the dialog box.

You don't need to move down through ten or twelve layers of menus, as some non-Windows programs require. Because all your choices or options are immediately visible, a beginner and an expert have the same access to the program's features. Windows programs make their power accessible, not hidden beneath layers of menus.

Windows also uses *icons*, or small pictures, to represent items you can quickly identify. For example, the simple drawing program that comes with

1

Windows, called Windows Paintbrush, contains a memorable toolbox that needs little explanation.

The toolbox on the left side of the Paintbrush program contains icons that represent the drawing tools.

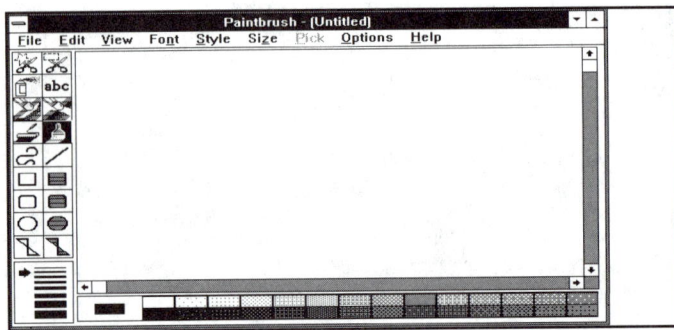

The Program Manager makes it obvious which icon to select to start different programs.

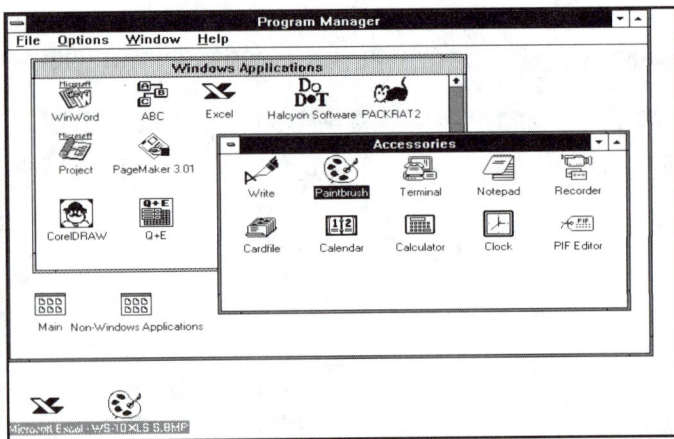

With Windows and Windows programs, you can control programs the way you prefer. You can use a mouse-driven pointer while you are learning or drawing, use touch-typing while doing data entry, or use shortcut keys for speed. Many people first learn with the mouse and then use both the mouse and the keyboard as they become two-handed masters.

Sharing Operating Methods

Learning one Windows program helps you learn other Windows programs. Not only are the operating methods the same in different Windows programs, but also many of the menus and commands are identical.

1

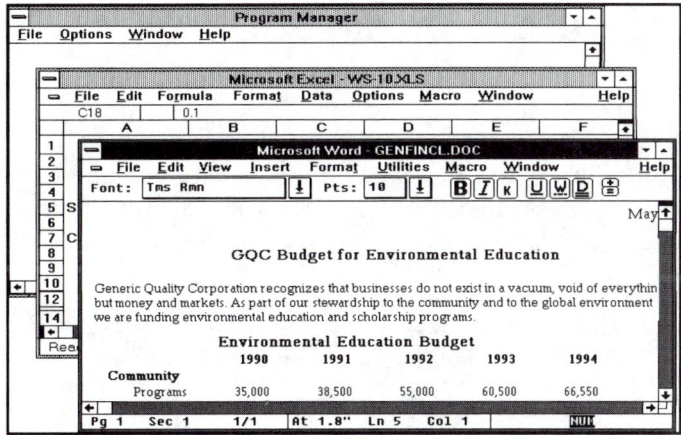

Many menus and commands—such as **File**, **Edit**, **Format**, **Window**, and **Help**—are in the same locations and perform the same operations in different Windows programs.

Using the Windows Desktop

The Windows desktop, which runs multiple programs, is a metaphor for the desktop on which you're used to working. Each Windows program can fill the screen or fit into a window. Non-Windows programs must fill the screen, unless you are running Windows on an 80386 computer.

Running programs in separate windows enables you to see what is happening in other programs and to switch to other programs quickly.

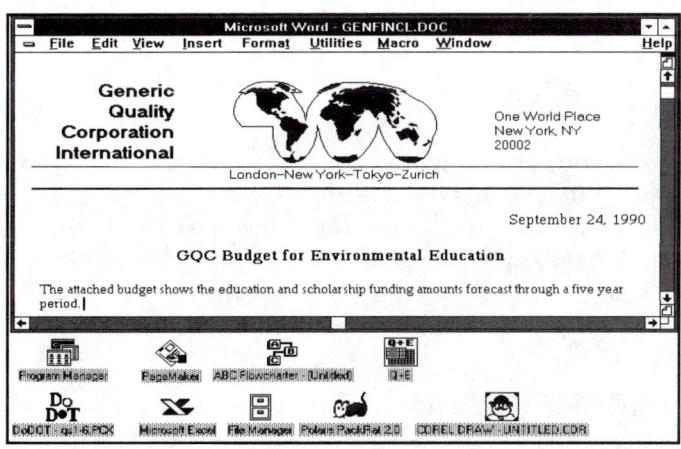

When you want to save space on the desktop, you can shrink a program's window so that it becomes an icon at the bottom of the desktop.

11

1

Running Multiple Programs at One Time

You can load multiple programs in Windows and quickly switch from one program to another—even if they are a mix of Windows and non-Windows programs. If you run Windows on an 80386 computer, you can even request that programs you aren't currently working in continue to run in background windows.

For example, you can run 1-2-3, Quicken, and Excel—all at the same time.

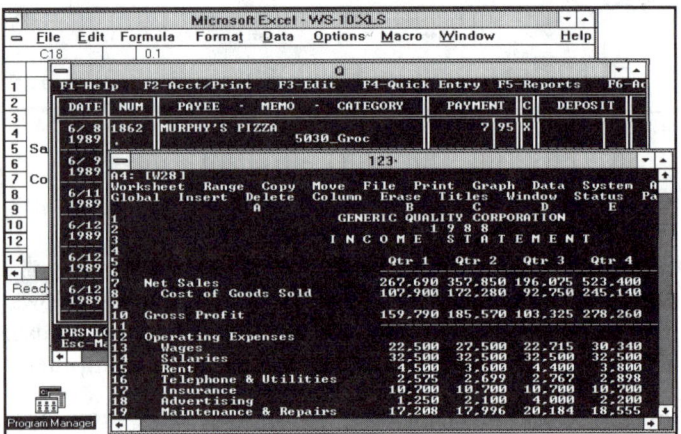

Copying and Pasting Text and Graphics between Programs

Windows makes it easy to copy text or graphics from one program to another. You can copy and paste text, numbers, or graphics between programs designed for Windows. You can even capture an image of the screen and paste it into Windows programs. If you are using non-Windows programs, you can still copy and paste text and numbers between programs, saving typing time and eliminating the chance for typing errors.

Many Windows programs can be linked together so that changes to one program's data automatically transfer to the data in other linked Windows programs. Therefore, separate programs from different manufacturers can work together and share data as though they were a single program.

1

For example, the program PackRat is a personal information manager that stores names, addresses, phone numbers, appointments, and notes. Word for Windows is a high-performance word processor.

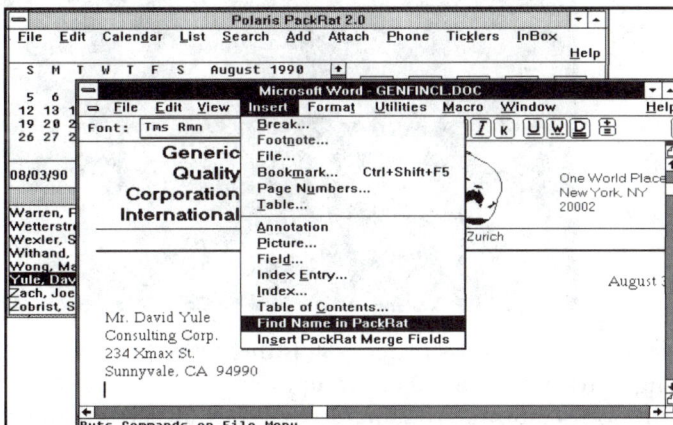

Although these two programs are made by different companies, you can write letters in Word for Windows and let PackRat retrieve the name and address from its database of people you contact.

Using the copy and paste capabilities of Windows, you can integrate text, graphics, and captured computer screens into a single document like this training tutorial in Aldus PageMaker.

Running Non-Windows (DOS) Programs under Windows

You don't have to leave behind non-Windows programs, such as Lotus 1-2-3 and WordPerfect, when you run Windows. Although these programs were designed to run under DOS, Windows adds new capabilities to them.

1

You can run Lotus 1-2-3 and WordPerfect at the same time and even copy and paste text and numbers between them.

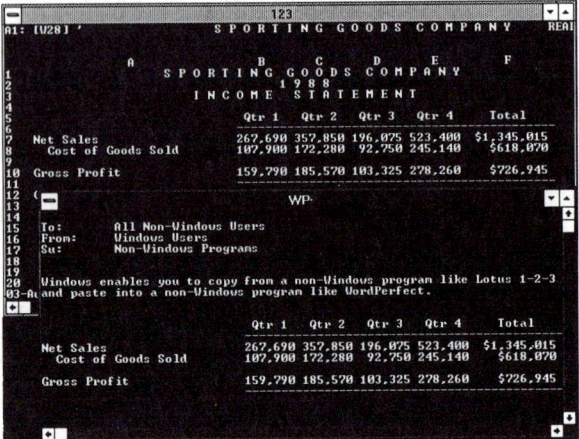

Remember that the active non-Windows program fills the entire screen— unless you are running Windows on an 80386 computer. On an 80386 computer, you can run non-Windows programs so that they fill the screen or fit into a window.

Making Better Use of Memory

Programs designed for DOS 4.0 and earlier were restricted to using no more than 640K of memory. Such programs either left out features to stay small or were slow because they continually had to retrieve pieces of the program from disk.

Windows breaks that 640K memory limit. Programs designed for Windows aren't restricted to using 640K. That means faster operation for large programs and almost unlimited memory for data. In fact, if you run Windows on an 80386 computer, information that doesn't fit into memory spills over onto your hard disk—making it an extension of memory.

Getting Help When You Need It

Windows programs are easy to use because they offer an extensive Help feature. Word for Windows, for example, includes almost 200 pages of Help information that is on the hard disk and available to you while you work.

Many Windows programs contain help about commands and procedures, such as how to create a form letter.

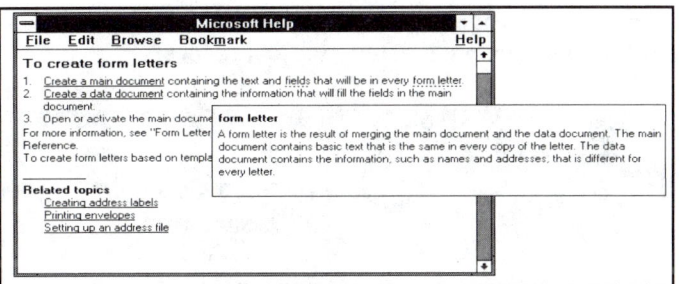

Selecting under-
lined words or
phrases in the
Help window
gives you a defi-
nition or takes
you to another
Help window.

Help files in many Windows programs use a feature known as *hypertext*.
Hypertext enables you to jump quickly from one Help topic to another. For
instance, if you are looking at a Help file in Word for Windows that shows
how to build a mailing list, you might see the command <u>File Print Merge</u>
underlined in the explanation. Clicking the mouse on the underlined
command takes you immediately to a window that explains what File Print
Merge is. You also can backtrack to an earlier action, search for help by key
words, and print the Help information.

Taking Advantage of Windows Features and Programs

In addition to providing the features already discussed, Windows comes with
programs and tools that make using your computer easier.

The Program Manager displays icons that represent the programs and data
documents you work with most frequently.

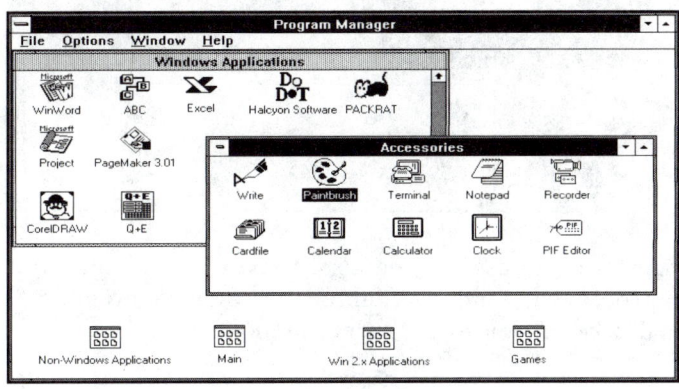

You can group
your programs
together and
start them by
choosing an icon
in the Program
Manager instead
of searching for a
program file
name on your
hard disk.

15

An Overview of Windows

1

Using the File Manager is much easier than using arcane DOS commands for organizing your hard disk and copying, erasing, or moving files.

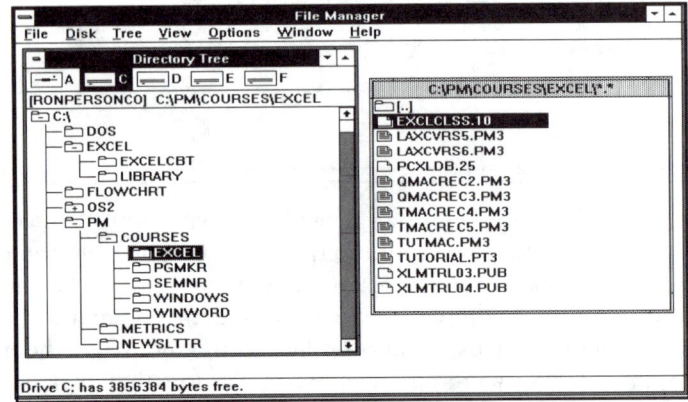

The File Manager displays a tree-like structure that shows how files and subdirectories are arranged on your hard disk.

Using the Control Panel, you can customize many features within Windows, such as the desktop background, colors, printer connections, and mouse operation.

Customizing the desktop background and window colors can make your computer a little more friendly and a lot more personal.

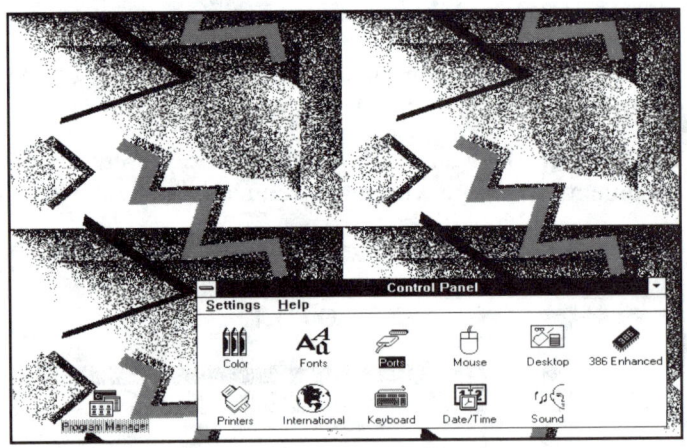

Windows provides many other accessory programs. These include Windows Write (a simple word processor), Windows Paintbrush (a drawing program), and Windows Terminal (a communication program). Another program included with Windows and described in this book is the Print Manager. It enables you to continue working in a Windows program while the Print Manager controls the printer and a list of documents to be printed.

1

Summary

Now you've seen why Windows is causing a revolution in the way people use personal computers. Windows adds features to non-Windows programs and makes Windows programs easier to use, which means that advanced programs are more accessible to everyone. Generally, Windows makes your personal computer more enjoyable to use.

This chapter covered the following important points:

- Windows provides consistent menus and operations in Windows programs.
- You can copy and paste text and graphics between Windows and non-Windows programs.
- You can load or run multiple programs at the same time.
- You can customize your work area to fit the way you like to work.
- The Program Manager and File Manager enable you to manage your programs and hard disk more easily.

Now that you are familiar with what Windows can do for you, put it to work. Chapter 2 shows you how to get started. If you are totally new to Windows, you will want to read Chapter 3, "Operating Windows." What you learn in that chapter applies to all Windows programs.

Once you have learned the basic concepts of operating Windows programs, you will want to learn about the Program Manager in Chapter 4 and the File Manager in Chapter 5. From there, take a look at the Table of Contents and explore topics that look interesting.

Getting Started

If you are new to personal computers or if you are new only to Windows, this chapter helps you get started. It shows you step-by-step how to start and exit Windows. You learn about the different parts of the Windows display and the purpose of the mouse or the keyboard in Windows. The Help feature is discussed in Chapter 3, "Operating Windows."

If you have any experience with personal computers or with Windows, some of this material may be familiar to you. Once you feel comfortable with the parts of the Windows environment, you can move to the next chapter to learn some basic Windows operations. Chapter 3 supplies detailed instructions for starting programs, controlling windows, and using pull-down menus and dialog boxes.

Starting Windows

Understanding the Windows desktop

Understanding the parts of a window

Using the keyboard

Closing documents, programs, and windows

2

Key Terms in This Chapter

Program window   A window that contains a Windows or non-Windows program. Multiple program windows can be open at one time.

Document window   A window that contains a document and is displayed within a program window. Some programs let you open multiple document windows.

Control menu   A menu that appears as a hyphen or a long bar at the top left of each program or document window and enables keyboard users to move, size, or close windows.

Mouse pointer   An on-screen pointer that moves as you move the mouse on your desk. You use the mouse pointer to select text or objects and then choose a menu command by pressing a mouse button.

Program Manager   A Windows program that helps you group other programs and documents together so that they are easy to find and start.

Starting Windows

This section shows you how to start Windows from your hard disk. Before you start Windows, you must install it. Refer to Appendix A for instructions on how to install Windows for the printers and display you use.

Follow these steps to start Windows from the hard disk in your computer:

1. Check to be sure that the drive door is open for the floppy drive(s).
2. Turn on your computer.
3. If necessary, respond to the prompts for date and time.
4. When the `C>` prompt appears, type **win** and press ⏎Enter.

If you have followed the Windows on-screen installation instructions and let the installation process modify your AUTOEXEC.BAT file, you can use the preceding instructions to start Windows from any directory on your hard disk.

Note: Windows cannot be run from a diskette-only system unless that system is on a network.

Starting Windows in Different Modes

Unless you indicate otherwise during start-up, Windows runs in the mode that best fits your computer's configuration. You may, however, have a reason for wanting Windows to start in another mode. If, for example, you want to run Windows 2.X programs, you must force Windows to run in real mode. If you run only Windows programs on an 80386 computer with 1M to 2M of extended memory, you will get a performance improvement by running in standard mode. Above 2M, you should run in 386-enhanced mode on 80386 computers for the best performance.

Note: Windows 2.X programs may not run under Windows 3.0. If you are not sure whether a Windows program is made for Windows 3.0, start the program under Windows 3.0. A warning box is displayed if the program was made for the earlier Windows. If this happens, you can run the program by starting Windows in real mode. Contact the program's manufacturer for the Windows 3.0 updated version.

To start Windows in a specific mode, type one of the following lines at the DOS prompt:

win /r	(to start in real mode)
win /s	(to start in standard mode)
win /3	(to start in 386-enhanced mode)

For example, to start an 80386 computer with at least 1M of extended memory in standard mode, type **win /s**.

You can see in which mode your computer is running by opening the Program Manager and choosing the **Help** About Program Manager command. The Program Manager is described in Chapter 4, "Grouping Programs and Documents."

2

Starting a Program along with Windows

You can start a program when you start Windows. For instance, to start Windows in standard mode and simultaneously start Word for Windows, which is located in the C:\WINWORD directory, type the following at the DOS prompt:

    win /s c:\winword\winword.exe

Then press Enter. The win /s portion of this command starts Windows in standard mode, and the rest of the line tells Windows which program to run and where it is located.

You can start a Windows program and also load one of its documents when you start Windows. For example, to start Windows in 386-enhanced mode and to start Excel with the BUDGET.XLS worksheet loaded, type the following line at the DOS prompt:

    win /3 c:\excel\budget.xls

In this example, the BUDGET.XLS worksheet is located in the C:\EXCEL directory. Because Files ending with XLS are *associated* with Excel, the Excel program starts and then loads the BUDGET.XLS file. In Chapter 5, "Managing Files," the discussion of the File Manager describes how to associate data files with a program.

Understanding the Windows Desktop

Windows programs run on a screen background known as the *desktop*. The programs and their documents appear on-screen, like reports lying on your desktop. Your Windows desktop may contain multiple Windows or non-Windows (DOS) programs. Each program appears in its own window or fills the screen.

Two types of windows appear on the desktop. A *program window* contains the program itself. The menu bar that controls the program is always at the top of the program window and underneath the title bar. In Windows, you can have several program windows open at one time. (A non-Windows program must fill the screen when Windows is in real or standard mode.) A *document window* may appear within some program windows. Document windows contain the data or document on which the program works.

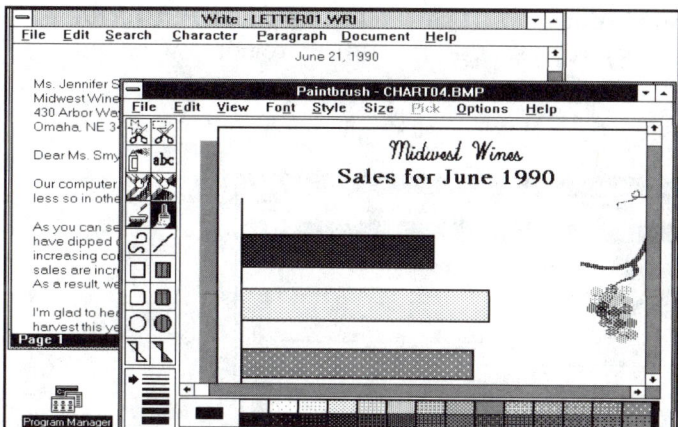

Some Windows programs, such as Windows Write and Windows Paintbrush, display a single document at a time within the program's window.

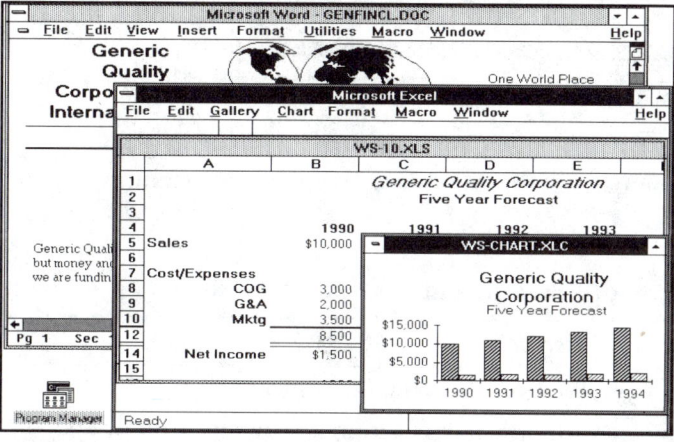

Programs like Microsoft Excel and Word for Windows can have more than one document window, enabling you to work on multiple letters, worksheets, charts, or databases at once.

Understanding the Parts of a Window

A window is built from parts that enable you to change the window by moving, sizing, or scrolling it. You must know what the parts of a window are called in order to understand directions given later in this book.

Illustrated in this section are the different parts of a program (or document) window. The window elements are the same for all Windows programs. In this example, the Word for Windows program is on the upper portion of the Windows desktop. The smaller window, internal to the Word for Windows window, contains a single document. The small icons—miniature pictures—at the bottom of the screen represent programs that are not in windows.

2

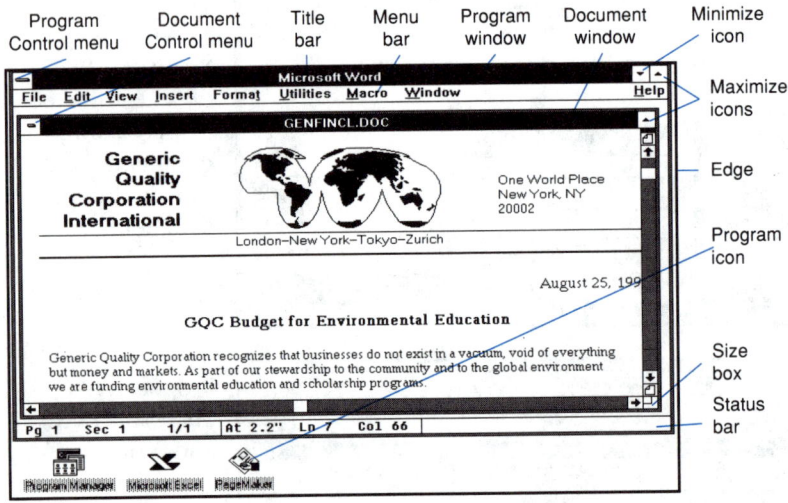

Table 2.1 describes the parts of the window shown in the illustration.

Table 2.1
The Parts of Program and Document Windows

Window Part	Description
Program window	A window that contains a program
Document window	A window that is within a program window and contains the data document being worked on
Program icon	A program window reduced to an icon
Program Control menu	A menu that controls a program window's size and, location
Document Control menu	A menu that controls a document window's size and location
Title bar	A bar containing a program or document title
Menu bar	A bar containing a program's pull-down menus

Table 2.1—(continued)

Window Part	Description
Status bar	A bar containing menu descriptions or prompts to action
Maximize icon	An icon used to increase a window to a full screen
Minimize icon	An icon used to shrink a program window to a pictorial representation (icon) at the bottom of the screen
Edge	A window edge that can be moved by the mouse to resize a window
Size box	A moveable corner used to resize two window edges

If a document window fills the inside of a program window, or if a program window fills the screen, a different set of sizing icons appears at the top right corner of the program window. This next example shows the same document, but the Word for Windows program window fills the screen, and the document window fills the inside of the Word window.

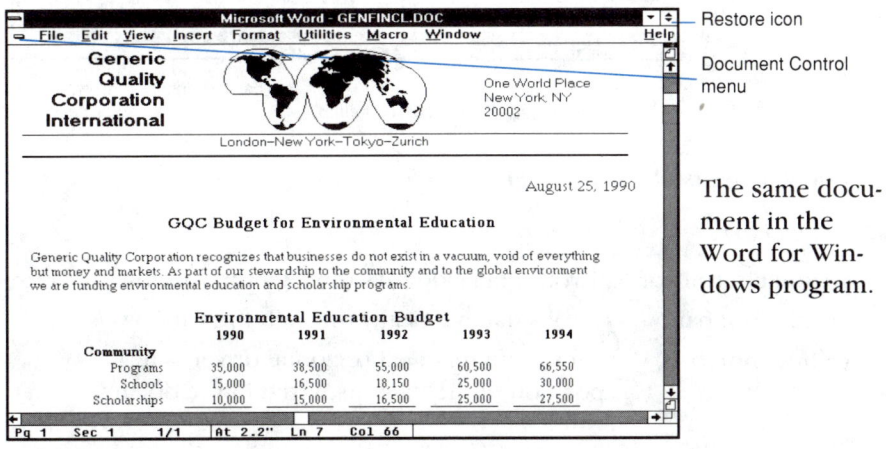

Restore icon

Document Control menu

The same document in the Word for Windows program.

Note: When a document window fills the inside of a program window, the document Control menu changes its location from the top left corner of the document window to a position left of the **F**ile menu.

2

Now notice the parts of the window:

Window Part	Description
Document Control menu	Positioned left of the **File** menu when the document fills the program window; controls the document window's size and location
Restore icon	Restores the full-screen program into the window it previously occupied

You can scroll a data document within its window so that you can see more information than is immediately visible.

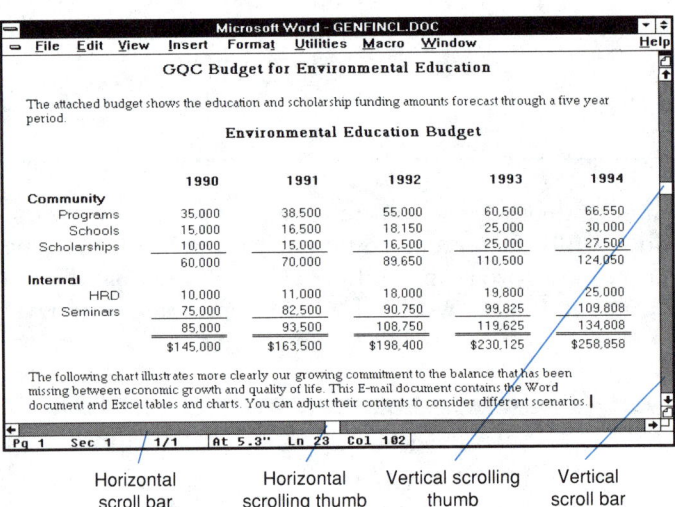

Horizontal scroll bar   Horizontal scrolling thumb   Vertical scrolling thumb   Vertical scroll bar

The following parts of a window are used for scrolling:

Window Part	Description
Horizontal scroll bar	Scrolls data sideways through the window
Vertical scroll bar	Scrolls data vertically through the window
Scrolling thumb	Shows the relative horizontal or vertical position of the data displayed in the document window

Understanding the Program Manager

When Windows starts, it displays the Program Manager, which contains group windows and group icons. Each of these groups contains a collection of programs or data you use to get a specific type of work done. When you group work-related programs and data together, starting programs and their associated data documents is easier. You can start a program by choosing the icon that represents the program.

The Main group is a collection of programs that comes with Windows. Inside the Main group window are program item icons that represent a program, or a program and an associated data document. Activating a program item icon, as explained in Chapter 4, starts the program for that icon and loads an associated data document if one has been defined.

Programs that are already running are displayed in their own windows or as icons at the bottom of the screen.

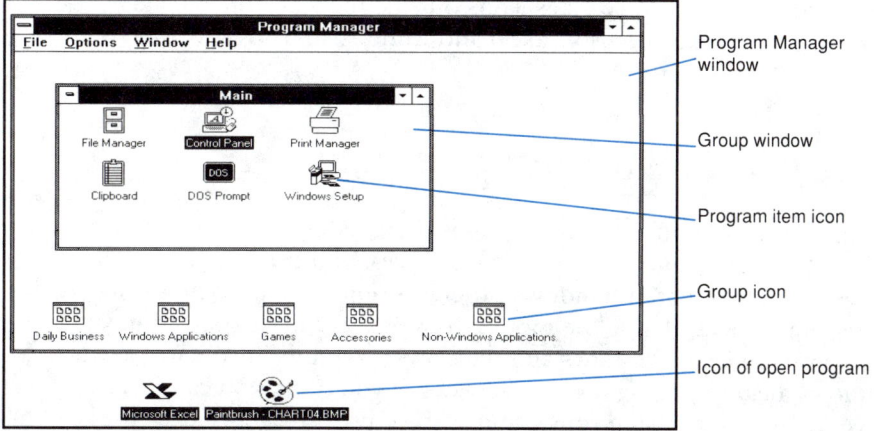

Program Manager window

Group window

Program item icon

Group icon

Icon of open program

Note the following parts of this window:

Window Part	Description
Program Manager window	A program window containing group windows and group icons
Group window	A document window that is within the Program Manager and contains program item icons
Group icon	A small representation of a group window
Program item icon	An icon that starts a Windows or non-Windows program and an associated data document

Other groups that come with Windows are shown as group icons at the bottom of the Program Manager window. The Accessories group contains small desktop programs, including an executive word processor, a calculator, a clock, and a calendar. The Games group contains two games. You may see other group icons within the Program Manager window that were added during installation or by a previous Windows operator. Programs that are already running are displayed as icons outside the Program Manager window, such as the Microsoft Excel and Paintbrush icons shown in the preceding illustration.

Using the Mouse

You can control Windows and programs designed for Windows with the mouse, keyboard, function keys, shortcut keys, or a combination of these. A few graphically oriented Windows programs require a mouse for drawing or positioning objects. Using the mouse, however, is the easiest and most natural way to learn Windows and Windows programs. If you are new to Windows, begin by using the mouse; later, if you want, you can make a transition to touch-typing your commands or pressing shortcut keys (key combinations).

Note: Do not feel that you must use either the mouse or the keyboard exclusively. Use them together for more efficiency and productivity.

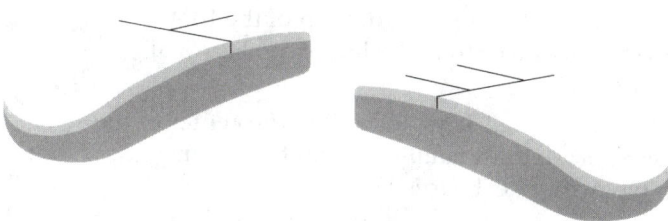

The mouse you are using has two or three buttons; you can use either type of mouse with Windows.

2

The mouse serves two purposes: to make selections from pull-down menus and pop-up dialog boxes; and to select text or objects you want to delete, move, or modify.

Hold the mouse in a relaxed but firm grip with two fingers resting on the buttons, the head under your palm, and the tail (wire) pointing in the same direction as your fingers. When you press a mouse button, do not move the mouse. Just relax and comfortably click on the button.

Do not choke the mouse. Relax!

As you move the mouse on your desktop, a pointer on the Windows screen moves accordingly. The pointer is often shaped like an arrowhead but may change shape depending on the pointer's location on-screen. If you find that you aren't moving the pointer accurately when you use the mouse, check how you are holding the mouse. Make sure that the tips of your fingers are on the buttons and that the wire runs parallel to your fingers.

Note: The left mouse button is usually the only button that you press. If you are left-handed, refer to Chapter 6, "Customizing Your Work Area," for an explanation of how to customize Windows for use of the right mouse button.

Using the Keyboard

With Windows and Windows programs, you can use the keyboard for typing, choosing menus and commands, and selecting options from pop-up dialog boxes. In addition, many Windows programs have shortcut keys (key combinations) that reduce multiple-keystroke or mouse-keystroke combinations.

Windows uses the following areas of the keyboard (there may be slight variations on your keyboard):

2

- The function keys, labeled F1 to F12 at the top of the IBM Enhanced Keyboard (or F1 to F10 at the left of the Personal Computer AT keyboard).
- The alphanumeric, or "typing," keys, located in the center of the keyboard. (These keys are most familiar to you from your experience with typewriter keyboards.)
- The numeric and cursor-movement keys, found at the right side of the keyboard.

Personal Computer AT keyboard

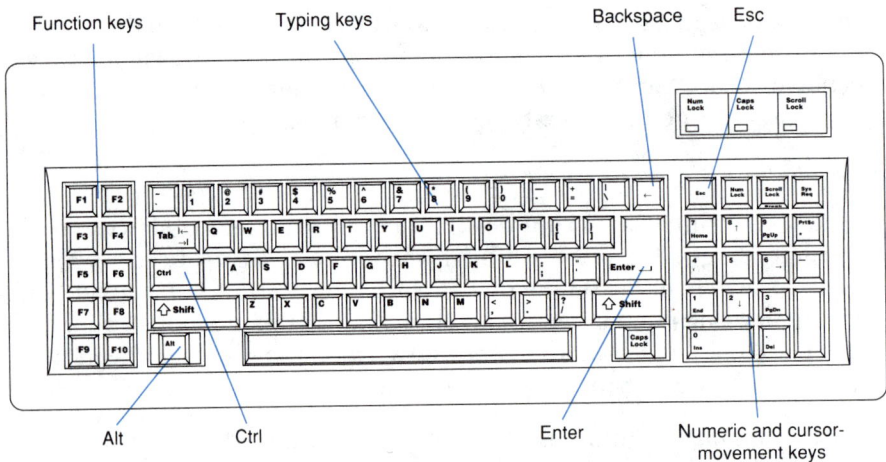

Enhanced Keyboard (PS/2 computers and others)

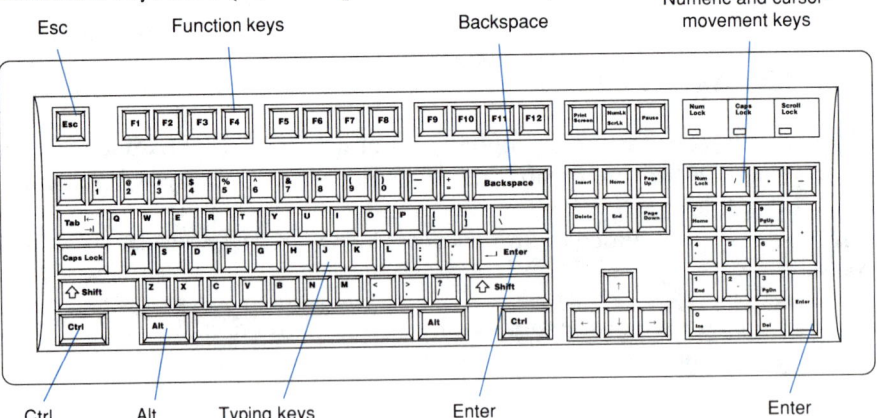

Function Keys

Many Windows programs use function keys in combination with other keys. In some programs, each function key can carry out four tasks when used by itself or with another key. In Windows, the function keys or their combinations provide shortcuts for commands you can choose from the menu. Use these commands from the menus as you are learning or with infrequently used commands. Use shortcut keys once you become experienced.

The keys you use in combination with the function keys are these:

Shift

Alt

Ctrl (Control)

Key combinations are shown in this book with a plus (+) sign between the keys—for example, Alt+F4. To use this combination, you hold down the Alt key as you press the F4 function key. Once you have pressed the function key, release both keys.

Note: In many Windows programs, shortcut keys are shown on the right side of pull-down menus next to the commands they duplicate.

Keys that should be pressed in a specific order but not held down during the key sequence are shown with the keys separated by commas—for example, Alt, T, and then P.

Alphanumeric Keys

The alphanumeric keys work similarly to those on a typewriter. A critical but easily overlooked difference between typing with a typewriter and typing in a computer program is that you do not need to press the Enter key to end lines at the right margin. When you type text and reach the end of a line, the text automatically "wraps" to the next line.

You can use the Enter key as a carriage return. You press Enter to insert blank lines in your text, such as the lines that separate paragraphs. You can use the Enter key to complete commands or dialog boxes you have selected in Windows programs.

2

2

The Shift, Alt, and Ctrl keys are part of the alphanumeric keyboard. The Shift key creates uppercase letters and other special characters, just as it does on a typewriter keyboard. Shift, Alt, and Ctrl are used also with the function keys as shortcut key combinations that duplicate menu commands. The Alt key pressed by itself activates the menu bar.

Movement Keys

The *insertion point* is the blinking vertical line in Windows programs that marks the location on the screen where the next character you type will appear. In non-Windows programs, the insertion point is called a *cursor* and appears as a blinking underline character or an inverse-video (highlighted) character.

Use the keys marked with arrows at the right of the keyboard to control the movement of the insertion point or cursor. When you press an arrow key, the insertion point or cursor moves, if possible, in the direction indicated by the arrow on the key.

Direction keys also are located on the number keys on the numeric pad at the far right side of the keyboard. When the Num Lock key is activated (indicated by a light on some keyboards), pressing keys on the numeric pad produces numbers. You press the Num Lock key to alternate between numbers and direction keys on the numeric pad.

Note: Windows enables you to customize the flashing rate and the movement rate of the insertion point. See Chapter 6, "Customizing Your Work Area," for the procedures to make these changes.

Closing Documents, Programs, and Windows

When you close a document window, program window, or Windows itself, you clear open data documents from the computer's electronic memory. If you need to use these documents again, you must make a magnetic recording of them on a diskette or your hard disk. (You can later open these magnetic recordings, called *files*, and your documents will reappear on-screen.)

Note: Windows programs ask whether you want to save changes to documents when you close the windows containing those documents. When working with non-Windows programs, be careful; some programs close immediately without asking whether you want to save changes to the document. In these non-Windows programs, you must remember to save the document before exiting the program.

Closing a Document Window

Some Windows programs, such as the File Manager, Word for Windows, and Excel, can contain more than one open document window. Excel is used in the following illustrations to show how to close document windows. To close the topmost document window, follow these steps:

1. Put the tip of the mouse pointer on the document Control menu and click on the button; then click on the Close command.

   Or press ⌊Alt⌋ ⌊-⌋ (hyphen), and then ⌊C⌋.

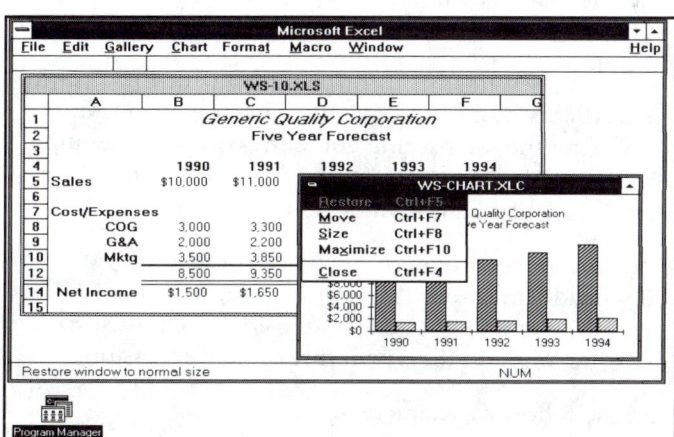

In this example, the document Control menu is pulled down in the topmost document window.

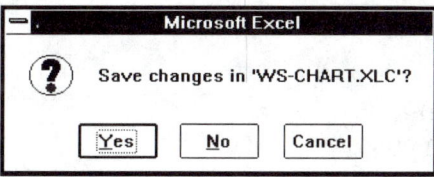

If the document has changed since it was opened, a dialog box appears before the document closes.

2

2. Click on the **Yes** button to save and then close the document, the **No** button to close without saving, or the Cancel button to ignore the **Close** command.

   Or press Y to save and then close the document, N to close without saving, or Esc to cancel the **Close** command.

If the document has previously been saved, it will be saved under the same name.

If the document has not been saved, another dialog box appears, prompting you to type a new file name.

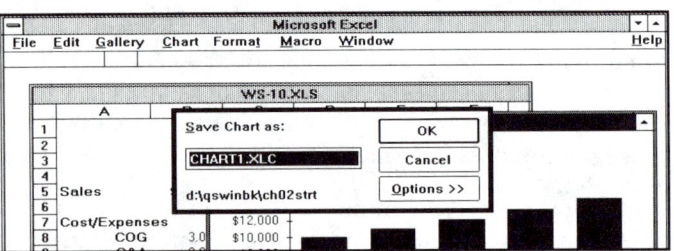

A default file name, such as CHART1.XLC, may appear. You can type a new file name over the default file name. Use the Del (Delete) or Backspace key to correct errors in typing.

A file name consists of a root name of one to eight characters. When you name a file, you must observe the file-naming guidelines of your operating system (MS-DOS or PC DOS). After you name and save a file, the file name appears in the title bar of the document's window.

File names for some non-Windows programs include a three-letter extension after the root name. If you add an extension, you must separate it from the root name by a period (.). If you do not add an extension, do not use a period. Most Windows programs add their own three-letter extension.

File names can contain the following characters:

Letters	a to z
	A to Z
Numbers	0 to 9
Symbols	- (hyphen)
	_ (underscore)
	! (exclamation point)

2

Use the - or _ instead of a blank space. Use the ! as the first character to make a file name appear first in a list of file names.

File names cannot contain the following:

Blank spaces (use the - or _ instead)

Some symbols (such as \)

More than one period

These file names are valid:

BDGT_JUN.XLS

!PROPSL.DOC

LTR0812.DOC

However, the following file names are invalid:

BDGT JUN.XLS (blank space used)

\PROPSL.DOC (backslash used)

LTR08.12.DOC (extra period used)

Closing a Program Window

When you close a program's window, you are closing also any document windows within it. When you close a Windows program, you are prompted to save documents that have been changed.

Note: Closing the Program Manager window exits Windows.

PageMaker is used in the following illustrations to show how to close a program window. To close the topmost program in Windows, follow these steps:

1. Put the tip of the mouse pointer on the program Control menu, click on the button, and then click on the Close command.

   Or press Alt, the space bar, and then C.

2

The program Control menu is a square icon at the left end of the title bar on all Windows programs.

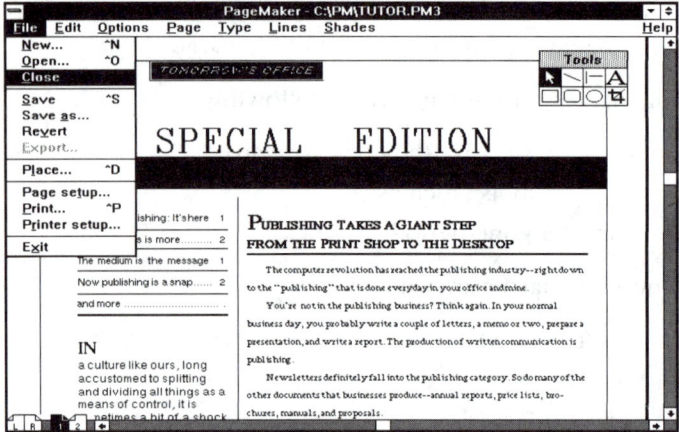

If documents have changed since they were opened, a dialog box appears for each document.

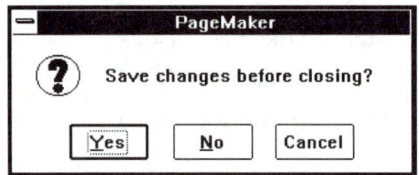

2. Click on the **Yes** button to save and then close the document, the **No** button to close without saving, or the Cancel button to ignore the **Close** command.

   Or press [Y] to save and then close the document, [N] to close without saving, or [Esc] to ignore the **Close** command.

If the document has previously been saved, it will be saved under the same name. If the document has not been saved, you will be prompted to enter a file name for the document. The preceding section describes valid file names.

You close windows containing non-Windows programs by saving any documents that have changed and then exiting the non-Windows program. When you exit the non-Windows program, its window will close. Chapter 13, "Running Non-Windows Programs," contains more information on running and exiting non-Windows programs.

Exiting Windows

Windows is under the control of the Program Manager. When you close the Program Manager window, you exit Windows.

Follow these steps to exit Windows:

1. Exit all non-Windows programs, using their normal exit or quit procedures.

2. If the Program Manager window is visible, click on it to make it the topmost window.

   Or press Alt + Tab↹ until the Program Manager is in the topmost window.

3. Click on the program Control menu and then click on the Close command.

   Or press Alt, the space bar, and then C.

4. If documents in open programs have changed, you will be prompted to save the changes before exiting Windows. As explained in the preceding sections, you may be asked to type a file name for documents that have not previously been saved.

5. When the Exit Windows dialog box appears, click on OK to exit Windows, or click on Cancel to return to Windows.

   Alternatively, press ↵Enter if you want to exit Windows. Or press Esc to cancel and return to Windows.

The Save Changes check box in the Exit Windows dialog box is used to save the position of groups in the Program Manager.

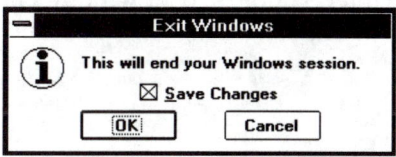

The Exit Windows dialog box.

Summary

This chapter helped you get Windows started, described the different parts of a window, and showed you how to quit Windows and its programs.

The following important points were covered in the chapter:

- The program Control menu is a square icon to the left of the program's title bar. The program Control menu controls the program window and is used for exiting the program.

- The document Control menu is a square icon to the left of a document window title. If a document window fills the program window, the document Control menu appears as a hyphen or a long bar to the left of the **File** menu. The document Control menu controls the document window.

- The menu bar is always below the title bar in Windows programs. A menu pulls down from the menu bar when you click on a menu name with the mouse, or when you press Alt and then press the underlined letter in the menu name.

- You start Windows by typing **win** at the DOS prompt and then pressing Enter.

- You exit Windows by quitting non-Windows programs and clicking on the program Control menu of the Program Manager. When you then choose the **Close** command, you are asked whether you want to save documents which have changed in Windows programs that are still open.

Now move to Chapter 3 to learn how to operate Windows and Windows programs. What you learn in Chapter 3 applies to all Windows programs; you will then have a good head start in understanding any new Windows program you use.

Operating
Windows

3

Compared with most DOS character-based
programs, Windows programs are easier and more
natural to learn and operate. With Windows programs,
you benefit from decreased learning time, fewer
mistakes, and an easier transition from one Windows
program to another. In fact, studies show that
operators with graphical interfaces such as Windows
use three times as many programs in their daily work
as operators with character-based programs. Windows
programs can make you more efficient, productive,
and valuable at work.

> What you learn in this chapter will help you to
> operate any Windows program. The skills you
> learn here carry over to other programs.

This chapter shows the three methods of controlling
Windows and Windows programs: the mouse, the
keyboard, and shortcut keys (key combinations). The
mouse is the primary method because it makes
learning new programs easier. The keyboard works
well for touch-typists in choosing commands or
entering data. And shortcut keys improve everyone's
speed.

**Working with the
mouse and the
keyboard**

**Controlling menus
and dialog boxes**

Editing text

**Controlling positions
and sizes of windows**

Switching programs

Getting help

Key Terms in This Chapter

Pointer   The on-screen symbol that moves under mouse control and is used to select items and commands.

Mouse button   The button on the mouse that, when pressed, selects the item on which the pointer is located.

Dialog box   A window that contains options. The window appears when a command needs additional information before it can be executed.

After learning how to choose menus, to select commands from the menus, and to select options from pop-up dialog boxes, you learn how to control the location, size, and status of windows that contain programs.

Finally, you learn how to use one of the most important features of Windows programs: the Help commands.

Working with the Mouse and the Keyboard

Most Windows programs work equally well under mouse or keyboard control. The mouse makes learning and searching through program menus easier. A mouse is also invaluable in using graphics programs. In time, you will find that using the mouse and the keyboard together is the fastest and most efficient way to work.

Using the Mouse

The mouse pointer can change appearance on-screen. Usually, the mouse pointer appears as an arrow or an I-beam. Other pointer shapes are described throughout the chapter. The basic shapes of the mouse pointer are these:

Mouse Shape	Use
Arrow pointer	Selects or chooses menus, commands, or options
I-beam	Moves the insertion point (cursor) or selects text to be edited
Hourglass	Waits while the program works

Ordinarily, you press the left button on the mouse for most tasks. If you prefer to press the right button, however, you can use the customizing features described in Chapter 6, "Customizing Your Work Area," to make the modification.

There are four types of mouse actions:

Action	Meaning
Click	Put the mouse pointer on an item and press the left mouse button.
Drag	Put the mouse pointer on an item and hold down the left mouse button as you move the mouse.
Double-click	Point to an item, rapidly press the mouse button twice, and release it.
Shift+Click	Hold down the Shift key as you click. Shift+Click is used in many Windows programs to select more than one item.

To click on an item, follow these steps:

1. Move the mouse so that the tip of the mouse pointer (usually an arrow) is on the menu name, command, dialog box option, graphics object, or text that you want to select.
2. Quickly press and release the mouse button.

To drag across text or to drag a graphical object, follow these steps:

1. Move the mouse so that the tip of the mouse pointer is on the object or at the beginning of the text. (While on text, the pointer will appear as an I-beam.)
2. Press and hold down the mouse button.
3. While holding down the mouse button, move the mouse. If you are dragging a moveable graphical object, the object will move.

If you are select-
ing text, a high-
lighted area
encloses the text
over which you
move the
pointer.

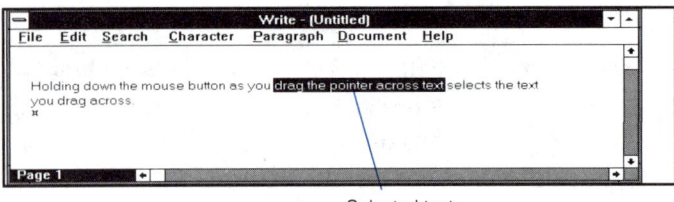

Selected text

4. Release the mouse button.

Using the Keyboard

In addition to typing text and numbers, you can use the keyboard in
Windows programs to choose from menus, select commands, and select
options from dialog boxes.

To choose a menu and select a command in the current Windows program,
follow these steps:

1. Press Alt.

2. Press the underlined letter in the name of the menu you want.

Pressing Alt and
the underlined
letter of a menu
name pulls down
that menu.

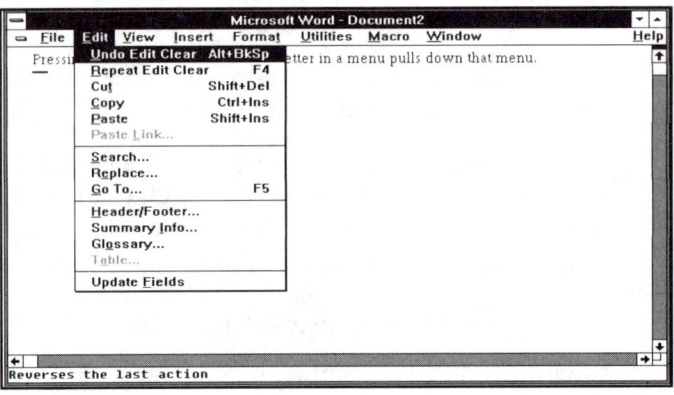

3. Press the underlined letter of the command you want in the menu.

    If you do not want to choose a command from the menu, press Esc.

Shortcut keys can save you steps by bypassing menus, commands, and
actions and immediately producing a result. Shortcut keys usually combine

the Shift, Alt, and Ctrl keys with a function key (F1 to F12) or an alphanumeric key.

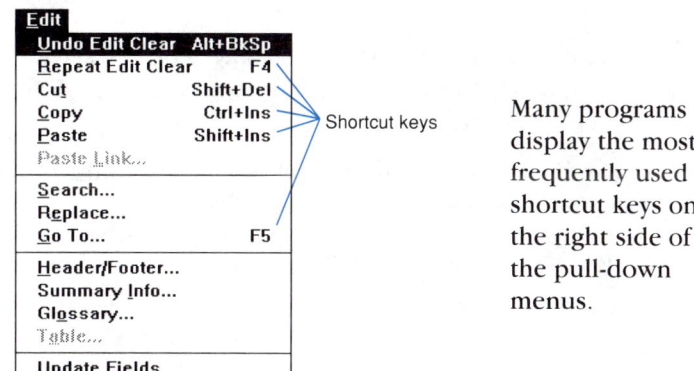

Many programs display the most frequently used shortcut keys on the right side of the pull-down menus.

As you use the keyboard to work with menus and dialog boxes, note how certain keystrokes are indicated in this book:

Key(s)	Action You Take
Alt, *letter*	Press Alt, release it, and then press the underlined letter in a menu name.
Alt+*letter*	Hold down the Alt key as you press the underlined letter in an option name within a dialog box.
letter	Press the underlined letter to execute the command in a menu.

Two other keys have important uses. The Enter key executes the selected command or dialog box. The Esc key backs out of the current menu or dialog box without executing it.

Controlling Menus and Dialog Boxes

Learning how to operate one Windows program puts you well on your way to operating other Windows programs. The menus, commands, and pop-up dialog boxes in all Windows programs operate similarly. And many commands—such as File, Edit, Format, Window, and Help—operate the same way in different programs.

Pop-up dialog boxes appear after you select certain commands. A pop-up dialog box enables you to see every option that is available.

As you begin to use Windows programs, keep in mind one of the most important concepts in Windows programs:

Select, then do!

In all Windows programs, you make changes by first *selecting* text, worksheet cells, or graphical objects, and then *doing* something to them with a command or a shortcut key combination.

As you work with menus and dialog boxes, you should understand how the following terms are used in this book:

Action	Meaning
Choose	Pull down a menu or complete a dialog box. Click on the menu name or press Alt+*letter*.
Select	Indicate which item on-screen will be affected or specify the command you want to execute. Click on the command name or press the underlined letter.
Deselect	Remove the selection from an item on-screen.

Choosing Menus and Commands

Menus display the commands available in the program. Menu names always appear in a menu bar at the top of each program window.

Choosing a menu name, such as **Edit**, displays a list of **Edit** commands.

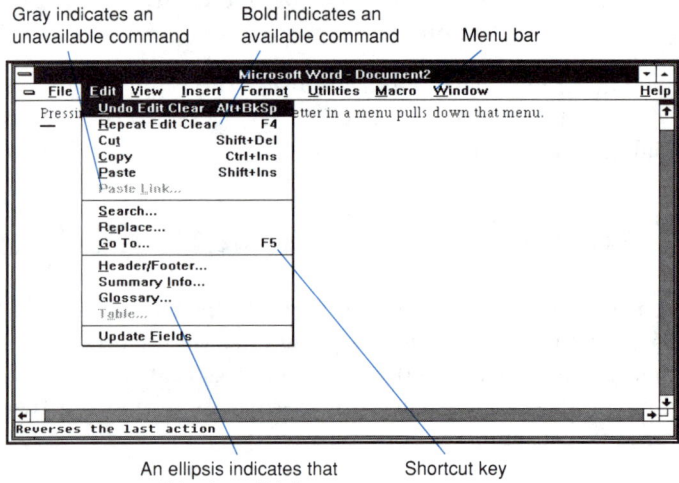

Gray indicates an unavailable command

Bold indicates an available command

Menu bar

An ellipsis indicates that a dialog box will follow

Shortcut key

You choose commands from all Windows programs in the same way. Many programs use similar commands for similar actions—a practice that makes learning multiple Windows programs simpler.

In these menus, bold commands are available for selection, gray commands are unavailable, and an ellipsis (...) following a command means that a dialog box will be displayed. Some pull-down menus display shortcut keys next to the commands.

To choose a menu and then select a command with the mouse, follow these steps:

1. Put the tip of the mouse pointer on the menu name and click on the mouse button.
2. Put the tip of the mouse pointer on the command and click on the mouse button.

To choose a menu and then select a command with the keyboard, follow these steps:

1. Press [Alt] and then release it to activate the menu bar.
2. Type the underlined letter in the menu name you want to choose.
3. Type the underlined letter in the command you want to select.

Note: Back out of menus or dialog boxes by pressing the Esc key. It cancels the current menu, dialog box, or edit action. Many Windows programs have an **Edit Undo** command. Undo undoes the last command you gave. With the mouse, you can back out of a menu by clicking a second time on the menu name. To back out of a dialog box, click on Cancel.

Selecting Options from Dialog Boxes

Some commands need additional information before an operation can be performed. On a pull-down menu, the names of these commands are followed by an ellipsis (...). For example, Format **Number** in Excel requires the numeric or date format you want to use or create. When you select **Number** from the Format menu, a list is displayed from which you can choose existing predefined or custom formats. Also displayed is a text box in which you can type new custom formats.

In the following Word for Windows screen, the File Open dialog box illustrates a text box in which you type a file name. The scrolling list boxes are used for changing directories or selecting file names.

The File Open dialog box in Word for Windows.

Text box

Command buttons

List boxes

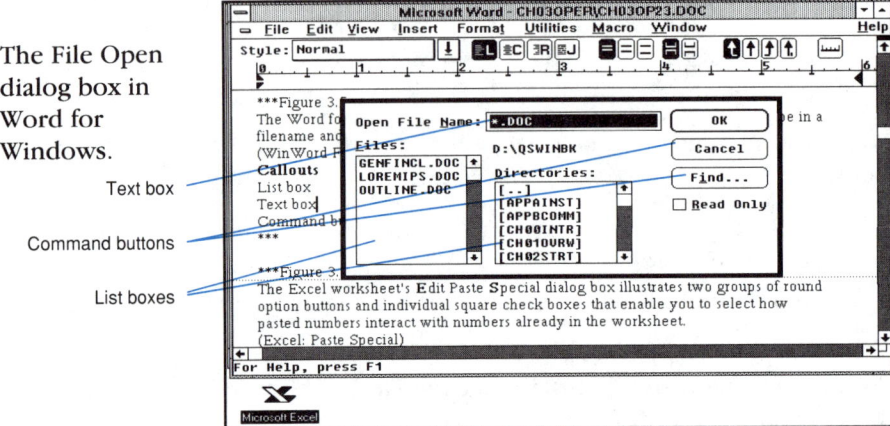

The Excel worksheet's Edit Paste Special dialog box illustrates two groups of option buttons and individual check boxes that enable you to indicate how pasted numbers interact with numbers already in the worksheet.

The Paste Special dialog box in Excel.

Option buttons

Command buttons

Check box

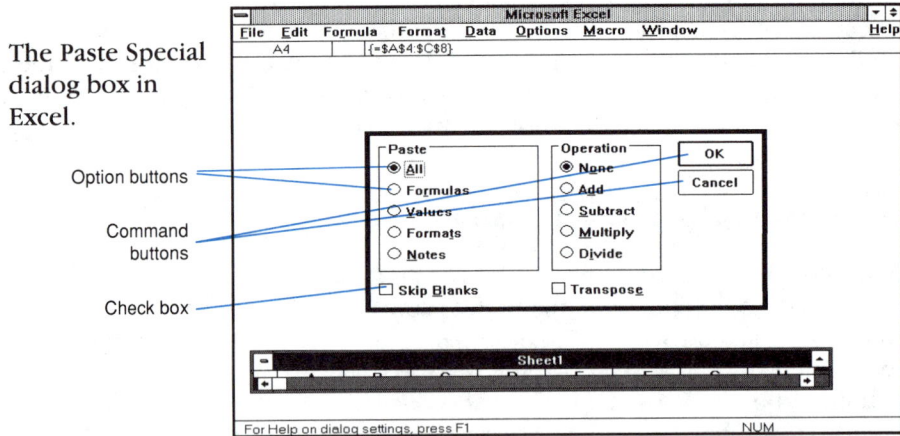

In character-based programs, you have to move through as many as twelve layers of menus to see the available options. Dialog boxes, however, display all possible options for a command. This means that Windows programs give beginners and experts quick access to the full power of the program. No options are hidden.

Dialog boxes contain different items designed to help you enter data or select options for a command. Table 3.1 lists the items in a dialog box and describes their uses.

3

Table 3.1
Items in a Dialog Box

Item	Description
Text box	A data-entry area for text, data, or numbers.
List box	A list of predefined data-entry items or options.
Option button	A round button that specifies an option. You can select only one button from a group; the selected button is filled.
Check box	A square box that specifies an option. An X indicates the selected check box.
Command button	A large rectanglar button that executes or cancels a dialog box.

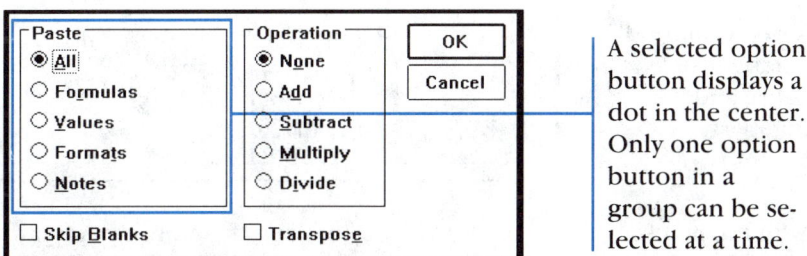

A selected option button displays a dot in the center. Only one option button in a group can be selected at a time.

With the mouse, click on another option button in the same group to select a new option and to deselect the original option.

With the keyboard, press Alt+*letter* (*letter* is the underlined letter for each option button). A dashed line surrounds the active option button. Move the selection to another button in the same group by pressing the left- or right-arrow key.

A selected check box contains an X. More than one check box can be selected at a time.

Empty check boxes mean that those options are deselected.

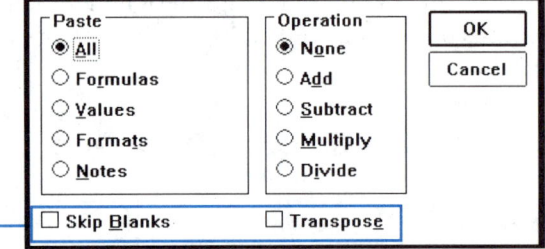

With the mouse, click on a blank check box to select it. Click on the check box a second time to remove the X and deselect the check box.

With the keyboard, press Alt+*letter* to select a check box (*letter* is the underlined letter for the check box). Each press of Alt+*letter* toggles the check box between selected and deselected. If a check box does not contain an underlined letter, press Tab until the check box is enclosed in a dashed line and then press the space bar.

A text box is used for entering and editing text, dates, and numbers.

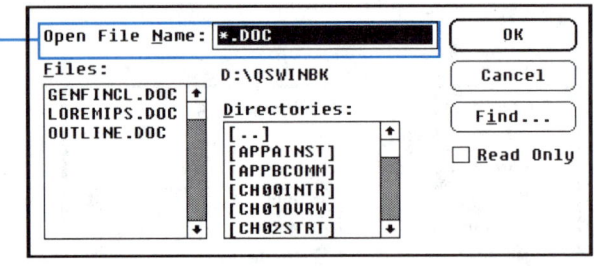

With the mouse, activate the text box by moving the mouse pointer (an I-beam) to the location where you want to type or edit; then click on the mouse button. This positions the flashing insertion point, the point where new text or edited text will appear. Press the left- or right-arrow keys to move the insertion point forward or backward. Press the Del (Delete) key to delete a character on the right of the insertion point, or press the Backspace key to delete a character on the left. Select multiple characters by positioning the mouse just before the first letter you want selected. Click on the mouse button, and while holding it down, drag across the text you want selected.

Then use the editing techniques described in the section "Editing Text" later in this chapter.

With the keyboard, activate the text box by pressing Alt+*letter* (*letter* is the underlined letter in the name of the text box). Type new text or edit the existing entry. Again, use the editing techniques described in the section "Editing Text."

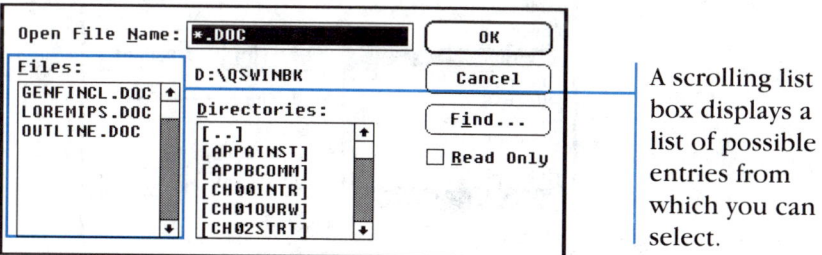

A scrolling list box displays a list of possible entries from which you can select.

With the mouse, scroll through the list by clicking on the up or down arrow at the right side of the scroll bar. Make large jumps through the list by clicking in the gray area of the scroll bar. Drag the white square (the thumb) in the scroll bar to new locations for long moves. Click once on the item you want to select. The selected item in the list is highlighted.

With the keyboard, select the list box by pressing Alt+*letter* (*letter* is the underlined letter in the name of the list box). Once the list box is active, use the up- or down-arrow key or use PgUp or PgDn to move through the list. The selected item in the list is highlighted.

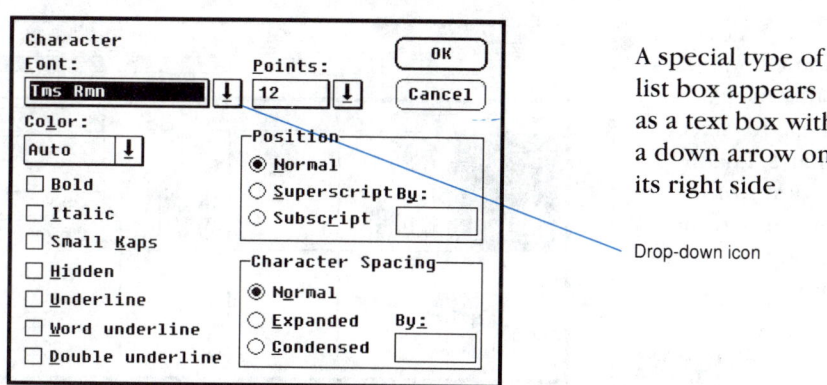

A special type of list box appears as a text box with a down arrow on its right side.

Drop-down icon

A drop-down list box conserves space by not showing the full list until you request it.

With the mouse, you can display the drop-down list box by clicking on the down arrow to the right side of the text box. When the scrolling list appears, select the item you want by clicking on it.

The selected item in the list is high-lighted.

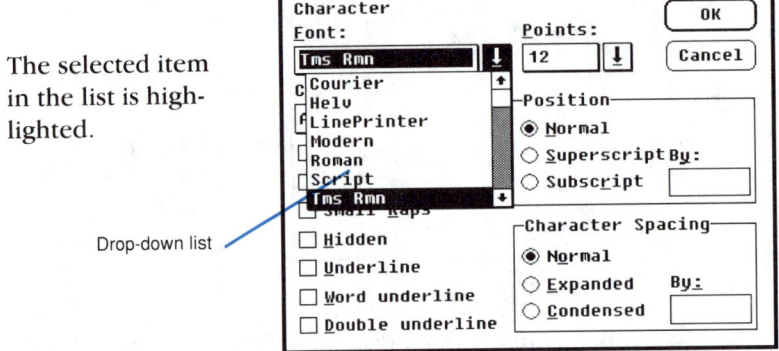

Drop-down list

With the keyboard, select the list box by pressing Alt+*letter* (*letter* is the underlined letter in the name of the list box). Once the list box is active, press Alt and then press the down-arrow key to make the list appear. Use the up- or down-arrow key or use PgUp or PgDn to move through the list. The selected item in the list is highlighted.

Command buttons complete or cancel a dialog box. Choosing OK completes the command; choosing Cancel backs out of the command.

Some command buttons, like these for Excel charts, enable you to *tunnel through* to the dialog box of another command.

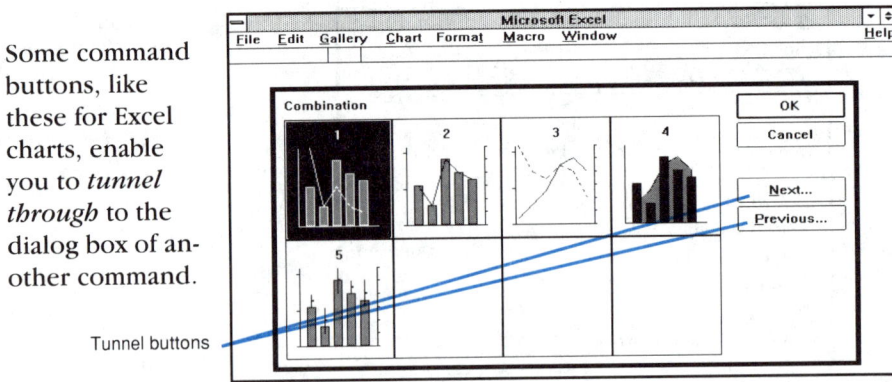

Tunnel buttons

50

With the mouse, choose a command button by clicking on it.

With the keyboard, choose the command button enclosed in a bold rectangle (usually OK) by pressing Enter. Choose the Cancel button by pressing Esc. Choose other buttons by pressing Alt+*letter* (*letter* is the underlined letter for the button).

Note: In some dialog boxes, double-clicking on an option button or a list item selects that option button or item and simultaneously chooses the OK command button.

Operating Menus in Non-Windows Programs

When you are operating a non-Windows (DOS) program, use the normal operating procedures and keys you use in that program. Although programs such as Lotus 1-2-3, WordPerfect, and dBASE operate under Windows, their menus and control keys remain the same. These non-Windows programs do not take on the pull-down menus, dialog boxes, or other features of a program designed for Windows.

Editing Text

With the exception of some shortcut keys, the text-editing techniques described in this section work in all Windows programs, as well as in the text boxes within the dialog boxes displayed by these programs.

Whenever the mouse pointer is over an area of text that can be edited, the pointer appears as an I-beam. This shape indicates that you can edit this text if necessary.

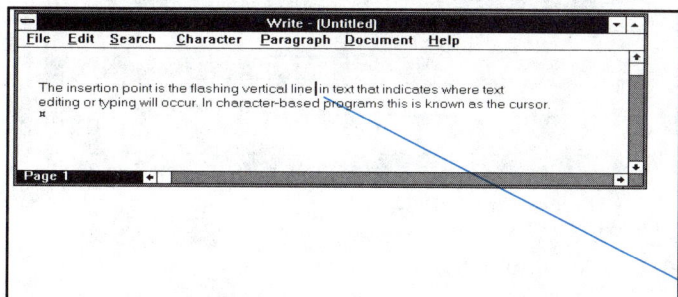

Insertion point

The *insertion point* is the flashing vertical line in text, indicating where text editing or typing will occur.

3

With the mouse, edit single characters in text by following these steps:

1. Move the I-beam between the characters where you want the insertion point.

2. Click on the mouse so that the flashing insertion point appears between the characters.

3. Do one of the following:

    • Press Del to delete a character to the right.

    • Press ↑Backspace to delete a character to the left.

    • Type characters at the insertion point.

With the keyboard, edit single characters in text by following these steps:

1. Press the arrow keys or the page-movement keys (PgUp and PgDn) to move the flashing insertion point next to the character you want to edit.

2. Do one of the following:

    • Press Del to delete a character to the right.

    • Press ↑Backspace to delete a character to the left.

    • Type characters at the insertion point.

With the mouse, edit multiple characters by following these steps:

1. Move the I-beam between the characters where you want the insertion point to appear.

2. Click on the mouse so that the flashing insertion point appears between the characters.

3. Hold down the mouse button and drag the I-beam across the characters you want to edit.

The characters to be edited are highlighted.

Selected text ⎯

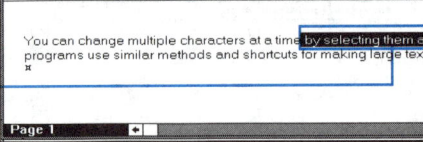

4. Do one of the following:

    • Press Del to delete the selected characters.

    • Press ↑Backspace to delete the selected characters.

    • Type new characters to replace the selected characters.

With the keyboard, edit multiple characters by following these steps:

1. Press the arrow keys or the page-movement keys (PgUp and PgDn) to move the flashing insertion point next to the first character you want to edit.

2. Hold down ⇧Shift and press an arrow key to move the insertion point; the text over which the insertion point passes is selected. Hold down ⇧Shift and Ctrl together to select entire words as you press ← or →.

3. Do one of the following:

   • Press Del to delete the selected characters.

   • Press ⬅Backspace to delete the selected characters.

   • Type new characters to replace the selected characters.

To deselect text with the mouse, click anywhere in the text. To deselect text with the keyboard, press an arrow key, the PgUp key, or the PgDn key.

Some Windows programs include shortcuts for editing text. These shortcuts may work in some parts of the program, such as body copy or a formula bar, but not in other parts, such as a dialog box. Experiment to find the shortcuts that help you. Table 3.2 lists shortcuts you can use for editing in many Windows programs.

Table 3.2
Shortcuts for Editing in Many Windows Programs

Action	*Result*
Double-click	Selects the word clicked on
Click, ⇧Shift+Click	Selects all text between the first click and the Shift+Click
⇧Shift+← or →	Selects multiple adjacent characters
⇧Shift+↓ or ↑	Selects the next or preceding line
⇧Shift+PgUp or PgDn	Selects text from the insertion point to the top or bottom of the page or screen
⇧Shift+Home	Selects text to the beginning of the line
⇧Shift+End	Selects text to the end of the line
Ctrl+⇧Shift+← or →	Selects a word with each left- or right-arrow key pressed

Controlling Window Positions and Sizes

Just as you move papers on your desk, you can move and reorder program windows on your screen. In fact, you can resize windows, expand them to full size, shrink them to small icons to save space, and restore them to original size.

The program window that is topmost is the *active* window. It contains the program in which you are currently working. This section shows you how to make a program window the *active* window.

The following keystrokes are useful in controlling windows:

Alt+Tab	Activates the next program window or icon
Alt, space bar	Selects the program Control menu on the active program
Alt, hyphen	Selects the document Control menu on the active document

Moving a Window

You can move a window to any location on-screen. By moving a program window or document window, you can arrange the work on your screen just as you would on your desk.

To move a window with the mouse, follow these steps:

1. Activate the window by clicking on its title bar or edge.
2. Point to the window's title bar.
3. Hold down the mouse button.
4. Drag the window to its new location by moving the mouse as you continue to hold down the mouse button.
5. Release the mouse button when the window is where you want it.

To move a window with the keyboard, use these steps:

1. Activate the window by pressing Alt + Tab or Alt + Esc until the window is topmost and has a solid title bar.
2. Choose the program Control menu by pressing Alt and then the space bar.

Or choose the document Control menu by pressing [Alt] and then
[-] (hyphen).

3. Select the **M**ove command and press [↵Enter]

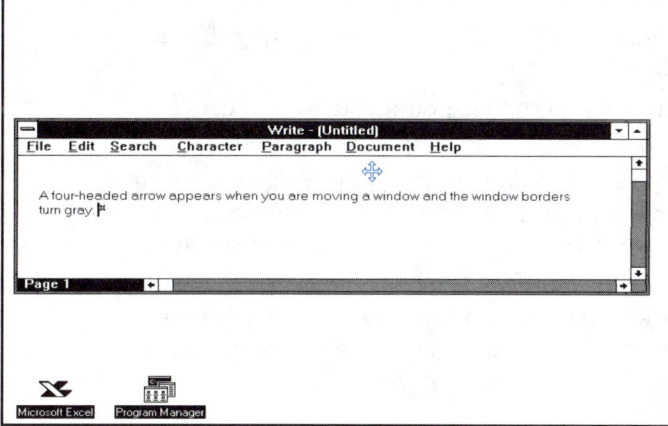

A four-pointed
arrow appears,
and the window
borders turn
gray.

4. Press the arrow keys to move the shadowed borders to where you
   want the window.

5. Press [↵Enter].

Changing the Size of a Window

Changing the size of a window enables you to position and size program and
document windows so that you can see more than one data area. Copying
and pasting data between programs is therefore much easier. To change the
size of a window, you drag one or more window edges to a new position.

With the mouse, change the size of a window by following these steps:

1. Activate the window by clicking on its title bar or edge.

2. Move the pointer to the edge of the window you want to move.
   When the pointer is correctly positioned, it changes into a two-
   pointed arrow.

3. Hold down the mouse button and drag the two-pointed arrow to
   move the edge of the window.

4. Release the mouse button.

With the keyboard, change the size of a window by following these steps:

1. Activate the window by pressing [Alt]+[Tab⇄] or [Alt]+[Esc].

2. Choose the program Control menu by pressing [Alt] and then the space bar.

   Or choose the document Control menu by pressing [Alt] and then [-] (hyphen).

3. Select the Size command. A four-pointed arrow appears in the window.

4. Press the arrow key that points to the window edge you want to move. For example, press [→] to indicate that you want to move the right window edge. A two-pointed arrow appears over the edge you want to move.

5. Press the arrow key that will move the window edge in the direction you want. For instance, if you want to move the right window edge to the left, press [←].

6. Press [⏎Enter].

If you want to return the window edge to its original position before you press Enter, press Esc.

Filling the Screen with a Window

Sometimes, especially when you are working with only one program, you will want the program to fill the entire screen. In programs that contain multiple document windows, such as Excel and Word for Windows, you can make a document fill the entire area within the program window. This feature is useful if you want to see the largest area of a worksheet or letter.

To make a window fill the screen by using the mouse, click on the up-arrow icon at the top right corner of the program or document window.

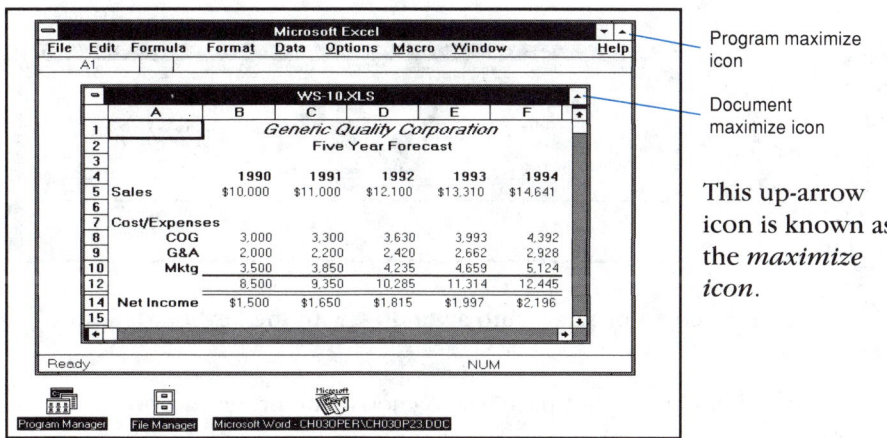

Program maximize icon

Document maximize icon

This up-arrow icon is known as the *maximize icon*.

3

To make a window fill the screen by using the keyboard, follow these steps:

1. Press [Alt] and then the space bar to choose the program Control menu.

   Or press [Alt] and then [-] (hyphen) to choose the document Control menu.

2. Press X to select the Maximize command.

Note: Some Windows programs contain a single document. In these programs, you cannot maximize the document because it already fills the major portion of the program's window.

Restoring a Full-Screen Program or Document into a Window

Often you can see more easily what you want to do, such as cutting or copying text between program windows, if both programs are in windows. In this case, if one of the programs fills the entire screen, you will need to restore it into a window.

To restore a full-screen program into a window with the mouse, click on the two-pointed arrow located at the top right corner of the program window.

Restore icon

This two-pointed arrow is the *restore icon*. It reduces a full-screen Windows program into a window.

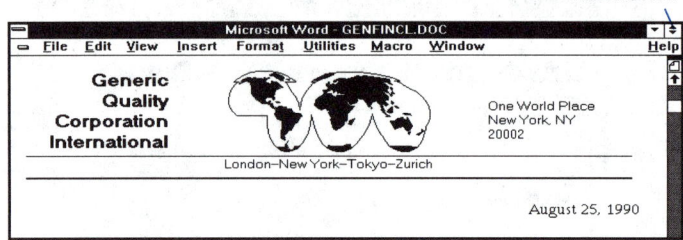

3

To restore a full-screen program into a window with the keyboard, follow these steps:

1. Press Alt and then the space bar to choose the program Control menu.

2. Press R to select the **Restore** command.

In programs that can contain multiple documents, a document can fill the program window or be in its own smaller window. To restore a maximized document into a window with the mouse, you need to use one of two methods. The method you use depends on the program's design.

Document minimize icon

If the program shows a document *minimize icon*, like the two-pointed arrow shown in this Program Manager's document, click on the minimize icon.

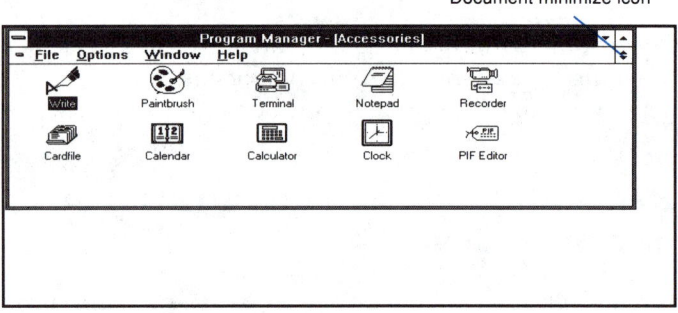

If the program does not show a document minimize icon (a two-pointed arrow), follow these steps:

1. Click on the document Control menu that appears to the left of the **File** menu.

Document Control menu

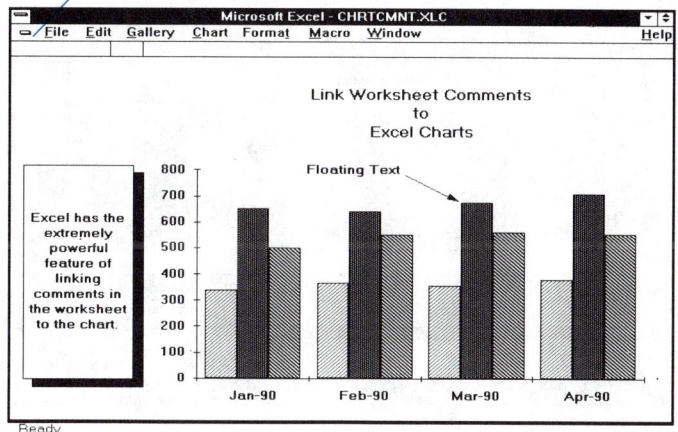

The document Control menu appears as an icon to the left of the **File** menu.

2. Click on the **Restore** command.

Note: The document Control menu may change position. When the document is in a window, its Control menu is at the top left of the document window. When the document is maximized to fill the inside of a program, the document Control menu for some programs appears to the left of the **File** menu.

To restore a document window of either design by using the keyboard, follow these steps:

1. Press Alt and then - (hyphen) to choose the document Control menu.

2. Press R to select the **Restore** command.

Reducing a Window to an Icon

When you need to work with a large number of programs at one time, you may want to reduce some of them to icons. A program icon contains the program and its document; however, they require less space on-screen and can be quickly opened into a window or full screen.

Note: If you are operating Windows in 386-enhanced mode, non-Windows programs can continue to run even when they are icons.

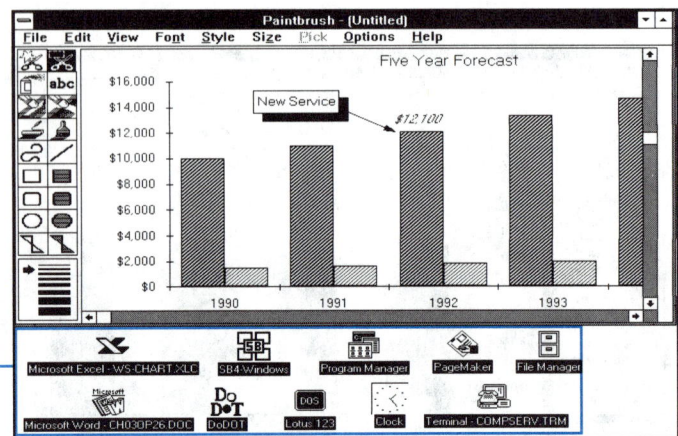

Such programs
as Word for
Windows, Excel,
Terminal,
SuperBase 4,
Lotus 1-2-3, and
Aldus PageMaker
can be arranged
as icons.

With the mouse, shrink a window to an icon by clicking on the down-arrow
icon located on the right side of the program's title bar.

With the keyboard, shrink a window to an icon by first choosing the program
Control menu (press Alt and then the space bar); then press N to select
Minimize.

Note: Most document windows inside a program window cannot be reduced
to icons. Exceptions are the document windows in the File Manager and the
Program Manager.

Restoring an Icon into a Window

You restore an icon into a window by double-clicking on the icon. If you
cannot see the icon, drag the window which is covering the icon so that it is
visible. Or activate the Task List by double-clicking on the desktop's
background and then selecting the program from the Task List window that
appears.

If you want to select an icon but not restore it, press Alt+Esc until the icon is
selected. Once the icon is selected, press Alt and then the space bar to
display the icon's Control menu. Choose any of the Control commands, such
as **R**estore, **M**aximize, or **C**lose.

Note: To quickly restore an icon to its original size with the keyboard, press Alt+Tab until the icon is selected. When you release Alt+Tab, the icon restores itself into a window.

Moving an Icon

You move an icon with the mouse by positioning the pointer on the icon, holding down the mouse button, and dragging the icon to the new location. Release the button when the icon is where you want it moved.

To move an icon with the keyboard, first select the icon by pressing Alt+Esc until it is selected. Next, choose the Control menu by pressing Alt and then the space bar. Press M to select Move. Press the arrow keys to reposition the icon. Finally, press Enter when you are finished moving the icon.

Using the Task List To Arrange Icons and Windows

The Task List is a Windows feature that is always available to help you switch between programs, or arrange windows and icons in predetermined patterns.

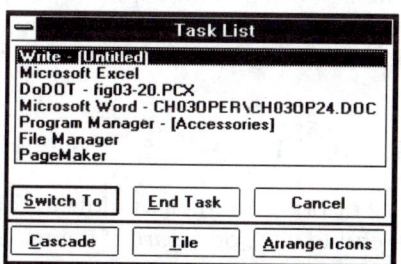

The Task List is displayed when you double-click on the desktop background or when you press Ctrl+Esc.

To arrange windows or icons by using the Task List, follow these steps:

1. Display the Task List by double-clicking on the desktop background or pressing Ctrl + Esc.

2. Choose one of the options listed in table 3.3. Either click on the appropriate button in the Task List dialog box or press Alt +*letter* (*letter* is the underlined letter for the button).

Table 3.3
Options in the Task List Dialog Box

Option	Action
Switch To	Activates the selected program in the Task List.
End Task	Exits the selected program in the Task List.
Cancel	Backs out of the Task List. You can also press Esc.
Cascade	Arranges open windows in an overlapping cascade from top left to bottom right.
Tile	Arranges all open windows to fill the screen with equal-sized windows.
Arrange Icons	Arranges all program icons along the bottom of the screen.

Switching between Programs

When you have many programs running, you need an easy way to switch from one program to another. Remember that the topmost program window with a solid title bar is the active window, the one in which you are working. In most cases, this is also the window on top.

Switching with the Mouse or the Keyboard

With the mouse, you can activate or bring another window to the top by clicking on that window. Be careful to click on a part of the program's window that will not issue a command. You can activate a program icon also by double-clicking on the icon.

With the keyboard, you have two choices of keystrokes to activate another program's window: Alt+Tab and Alt+Esc. Pressing Alt+Tab cycles through program windows quickly; only the title bar of the next program is displayed. When you see the title bar of the program you want, release the Alt and Tab keys. Pressing Alt+Esc cycles through program windows also, but more slowly; each window must be completely redrawn before the next window appears.

Switching with the Task List

If you are using the mouse or the keyboard and must switch among many programs, you may want to use the Task List. The Task List shows you which programs are currently loaded.

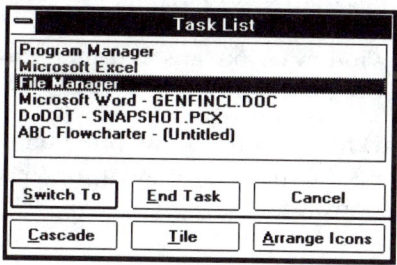

3

You can activate any program you want by choosing it from the Task List.

To activate a program from the Task List with the mouse, follow these steps:

1. Double-click on the desktop background to display the Task List.
2. Double-click on the name of the program you want to activate.

To activate a program from the Task List with the keyboard, follow these steps:

1. Press Ctrl + Esc to display the Task List.
2. Press ↑ or ↓ to select the name of the program you want to activate.
3. Press ↵Enter.

Getting Help

Windows programs have Help information to guide you through new commands and procedures. In some programs, the Help files are quite extensive. They tell you about parts of the screen and the actions of commands, as well as the step-by-step procedures to complete specific tasks.

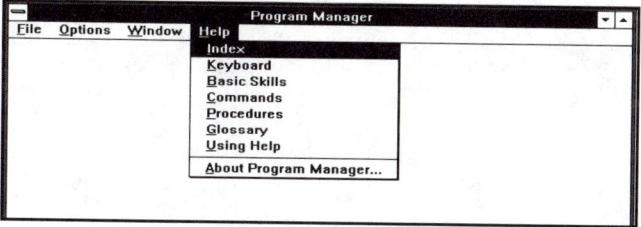

To get help in Windows programs, choose the Help menu by clicking on **Help** or pressing Alt+H.

From the **Help** menu, you can select commands that provide help on using the Help feature itself, the keyboard, and the operating procedures, as well as an index of specific topics.

To get help about how to use Help, choose the **Help** menu and select the **Using Help** command. Or when the Help window is displayed, press Help (F1).

Note: Press Help (F1) in many Windows programs to display immediately the Help topics index for the active program.

Help programs may differ slightly from one Windows program to another, or between older and newer versions, but most Windows programs contain variations of three methods of control:

Method	*Description*
Menus	At the top of the Help window are the menus to control the Help program.
Buttons	Under the menus are buttons for browsing through Help information, jumping forward or backward through previously read topics, or returning to the index.
Hypertext words	In the actual text of a Help screen are underlined words or phrases. Choosing a word or phrase with a solid underline moves you to that topic so that you can learn more about it. Choosing a word or phrase with a dotted underline pops up a window containing a short definition.

Browsing through Help Information

Buttons displaying icons are located under the menu of some Windows Help programs, enabling you to browse through topics or find specific topics quickly.

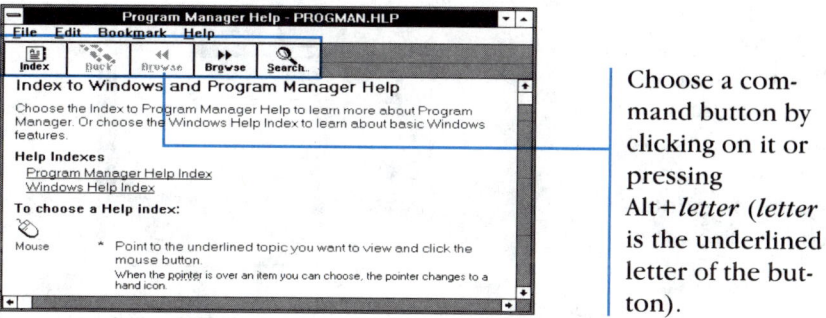

Choose a command button by clicking on it or pressing Alt+*letter* (*letter* is the underlined letter of the button).

Table 3.4 describes the Help buttons displayed in the Program Manager Help screen.

Table 3.4
The Help Buttons

Button	Description
Index	Shows the Help index. (The shortcut key combination is Alt+I.)
Back	Returns to the Help topic displayed previously. You can retrace the topics as far back as the initial Help index. (The shortcut key combination is Alt+B.)
Browse <<	Shows the Help screen that precedes the current topic. If there are no preceding related topics, this button is gray.
Browse >>	Shows the Help screen that follows the current topic. If there are no following related topics, this button is gray.
Search	Displays a dialog box containing a list of key words from which you can choose a topic (see the search procedure in the next section).

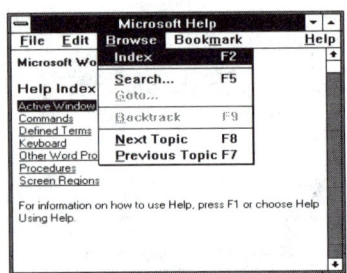

If your Windows
Help program
does not display
buttons under-
neath the menu,
choose **Browse**.

The **Browse** menu offers commands that enable you to search for topics or
browse forward and backward through Help topics.

Getting Help on Specific Topics

Most Windows programs can display context-sensitive help that shows the
next command you choose, the current dialog box, or the current error
message.

Press Shift+F1 to see context-sensitive help. In some Windows programs,
pressing Shift+F1 when a dialog box or error box appears will give you help
about that box. And in some Windows programs, you can press Shift+F1 to
change the mouse pointer into a question mark. If you then click on a
command or on a part of the screen, information is displayed about that
command or that portion of the screen.

Select the **Search** button when you want to search for help on a specific
topic. In the Program Manager, for example, you can search for topics
related to *active window* by following these steps:

1. Click on the **Search** button to display the Search dialog box.

   Or press Alt + S to display the Search dialog box.

2. Click in the **Search** for text box and type the words **active window**.

   Or click on the down arrow in the scroll bar until active window
   appears in the list; then click on that phrase.

   Alternatively, type the words **active window**. Or press Tab⇕ to
   move into the list, and then press ↑ or ↓ to select active
   window.

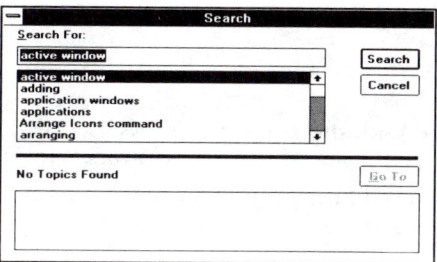

In this Search dialog box, *active window* has been selected as a search topic.

3

3. Click on the Search button at the top right corner of the dialog box. Or press ⏎Enter.

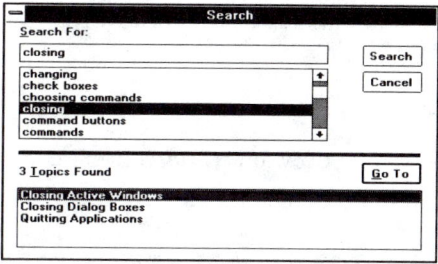

All topics found that are related to the word or phrase you typed appear in the Topics Found list at the bottom of the dialog box.

4. Click on the topic you want to read.

Or press ↑ or ↓ to select the topic you want to read.

5. Click on the **G**o To button to go to the topic.

Or press Alt + G to go to the topic.

Jumping to Another Help Topic

Within the actual Help text are *hypertext* words or phrases that enable you to jump quickly to related information. Two kinds of underlines are used for hypertext words and phrases in Help text:

Underline	*Action You Take*
Solid underline	Click on the underlined word or phrase to jump to that topic. With the keyboard, press Tab or Shift+Tab to select the word or phrase, and then press Enter to jump to the selected topic. Choose the **B**ack button or the **Browse B**acktrack command to return to the previously displayed topic.

Underline	*Action You Take*
Dashed underline	Point to a word or phrase with a dashed underline, and then hold down the mouse button to display the definition. With the keyboard, press Tab or Shift+Tab to select the word or phrase, and then hold down the Enter key to display the definition.

Marking Help Locations for Easy Reference

In some Windows programs, when you find a Help topic that you want to return to again, put a bookmark on it, just as you use a bookmark to mark a location in a book. You can then return to a topic that has your bookmark. You can also use more than one bookmark, labeled with words you type, in a file.

To put a bookmark on a Help topic, follow these steps:

1. Display the Help topic on which you want to put a bookmark.
2. Choose the Bookmark menu and then select the **Define** command.

The Bookmark Define dialog box appears.

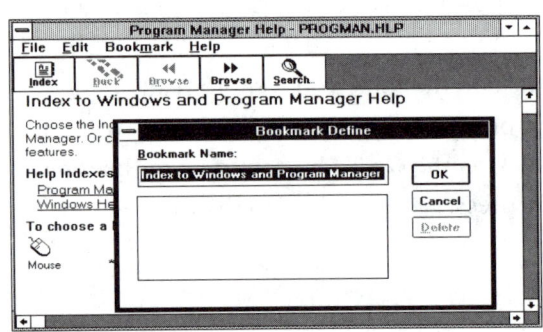

3. Select the **B**ookmark Name text box and type a bookmark name of your choice. Notice that the bookmark which first appears is the title of the current topic.
4. Choose OK or press ↵Enter to attach your bookmark to a topic.

68

To return to a bookmark in a Help file, use these steps:

1. Choose the **Help** command in the Windows program.

2. Choose the **Bookmark** menu by clicking on it or pressing Alt + M .

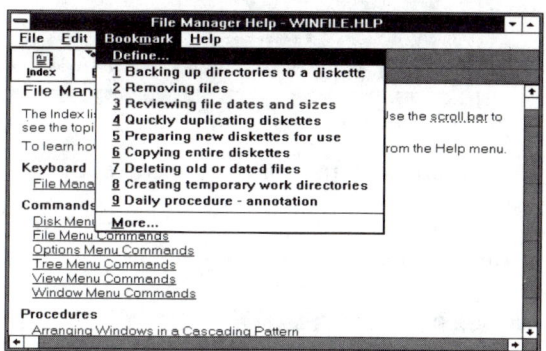

This list of bookmarks shows that more than nine are in the Help program.

3. Click on or type the number of the bookmark you want to go to.

   If more than nine bookmarks are shown, click on **More** at the bottom of the menu or press M . From the Go To list that appears, select the bookmark you want to go to, and then choose OK.

The Help window displays the topic containing your bookmark.

To remove a bookmark, first choose the **Bookmark** menu and then select the **Define** command. Next, click on the bookmark's name in the list or press Tab to move to the list. Press the up- or down-arrow key to select the name. Finally, choose the **Delete** button to delete the bookmark.

Adding Your Own Notes to Help

Besides marking Help topics with bookmarks, in some Windows programs you can attach your own notes to Help topics. Custom notes are helpful in programs such as the File Manager, where, for example, you may want to remind someone how to make hard disk backups with the **File Copy** command. Not all Windows programs have the capability of attaching custom notes to the Help topics. The accessory programs and utilities that come with Windows—such as Write, Paintbrush, and File Manager—include this capability.

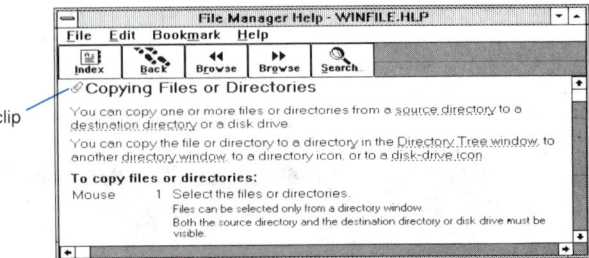

A Help topic with a custom note attached has a paper-clip icon next to the topic's title.

Paper-clip icon

3

To attach your own note, or annotation, to the Help topic currently displayed, follow these steps:

1. Choose the **E**dit menu and select the **A**nnotate command.

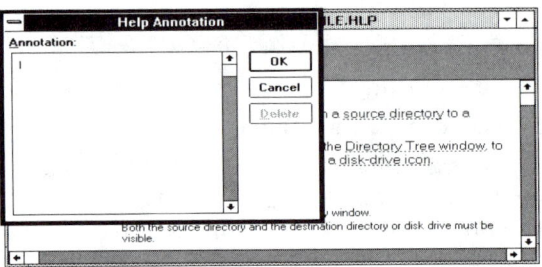

When the Help Annotation window appears, the insertion point will be in the Annotation text box, ready for you to type.

2. Type the text you want attached to the topic. Do *not* press ↵Enter until you are done typing.

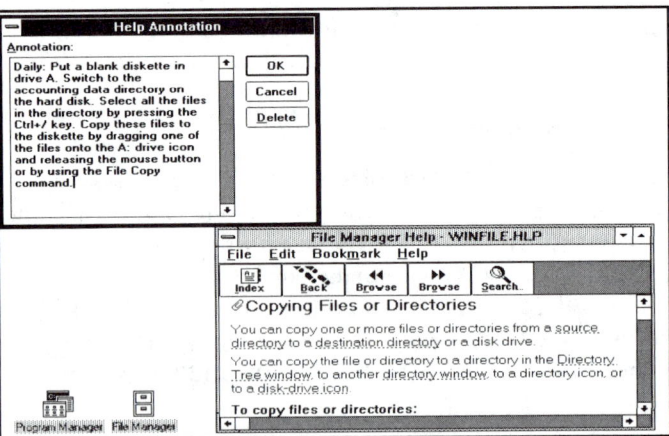

This example shows the Annotation text box after a note has been attached to the help on copying files or directories, found in the File Manager.

3. Choose OK or press ⏎Enter to attach the annotation to this Help topic.

To read a note that has previously been attached, display the topic and click on the paper-clip icon next to the topic's title. Or press Alt and then press E and A to choose the **Edit Annotate** command.

Using Other Help Features

Not all Windows programs contain the same Help features, menus, or buttons. Some additional Help commands are listed in table 3.5.

Table 3.5
Other Help Commands

Command	Action
Edit Copy	Copies the information in the active Help window to another document. You can then switch to the program where the information is to be pasted and choose **Edit Paste**.
File Open	Opens a selected Help file of another program.
File Print Topic	Prints the current Help topic to the default printer.
File Printer Setup	Sets up a selected printer or changes printer settings.
File Exit	Exits the Help program.

Summary

This chapter covered the most important information you need to operate Windows and Windows programs. You learned how to use both the mouse and the keyboard to choose menus, select commands, and select options from dialog boxes. You saw how to switch between programs and how to change the size and position of windows on-screen—all under mouse or keyboard control. Finally, you learned how to get help information about the use of menus and commands.

The following important points were covered in the chapter:

- ■ The mouse pointer's shape tells you what you can do at specific screen locations.
- ■ You select text or graphical items, choose a menu, and then select a command to change what you have selected.
- ■ You choose menus, commands, or dialog box options by pointing to them with the mouse pointer and clicking the mouse button.
- ■ You choose menu or dialog box options by pressing Alt plus the underlined letter in the menu or option name. When a menu is pulled down, you press the underlined letter in the command you want to execute.

Once you learn how to use Windows menus, commands, and dialog boxes in one Windows program, you'll know how to use them in any Windows program. Because it's a good idea to practice what you've learned right away, you may want to open the Games group window and practice Solitaire.

To learn how to start your Windows or non-Windows programs, see Chapter 4, "Grouping Programs and Documents," and Chapter 5, "Managing Files."

Grouping Programs and Documents

4

In this chapter, you learn how to start programs and documents with the Program Manager, as well as how to group programs and documents to fit the way you work. The Program Manager helps you keep programs and their associated documents in groups where you can easily find and start them.

Most people group programs and their data documents together by job type. You may want to group programs and data together into accounting, E-Mail, and report-writing groups. If you have a set of tasks you must do daily, you may want to create a group window that contains the programs, along with their documents, that you use each day. Within a Daily Business group window, for example, you can assign program item icons that represent each program and document you need in your daily work.

The Program Manager is the first program that opens when you start Windows. Within the Program Manager are many group windows or group icons. These either were created automatically when Windows was installed or were added by an operator *after* the installation of the program.

Key Terms in This Chapter

Program Manager   A program that helps you start frequently used
                    programs and documents

Group window   A document window that contains icons used to
                    start programs and documents

Group icon   An icon that represents a group window

Program item icon An icon that is within a group window and starts a
                    program with one of its associated documents

Note: Closing the Program Manager exits Windows. Before Windows quits,
you will be asked whether you want to cancel the close or save unsaved
documents in Windows programs.

Understanding the Program Manager

The Program Manager contains windows and icons that help you quickly find
and run programs and documents you use frequently.

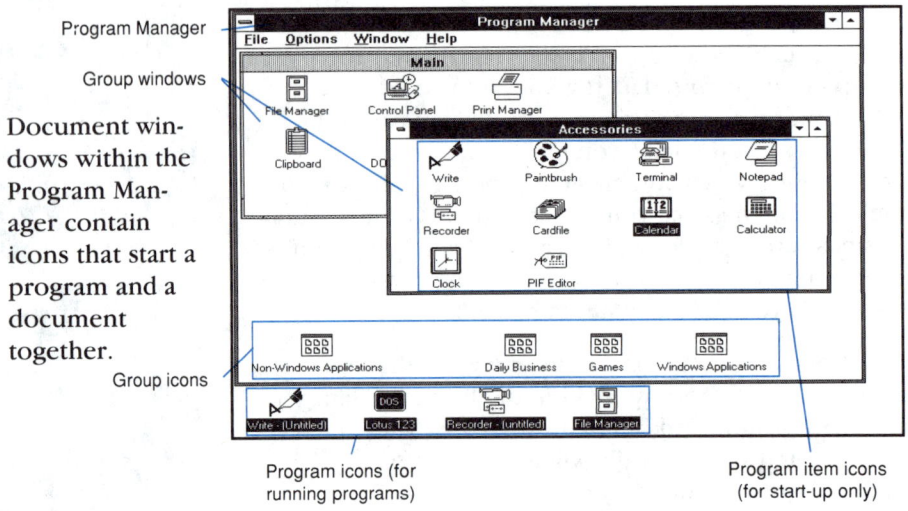

Program Manager

Group windows

Document windows within the Program Manager contain icons that start a program and a document together.

Group icons

Program icons (for running programs)

Program item icons (for start-up only)

Once a program has been started, it runs in its own separate window or appears as an icon at the bottom of the Windows desktop.

Table 4.1 describes the items in the Program Manager window.

Table 4.1
The Program Manager Window

Item	*Description*
Group window	A document window that is within the Program Manager and contains icons used to start programs and documents. Group windows can be created to group together programs that are used at the same time or that contribute to the same job.
Group icon	An icon that represents a group window. Choosing the group icon displays the group window.
Program item icon	An icon that is within a group window and starts a program with one of its associated documents. A program item icon is not the program, but only a start-up icon. Therefore, you can have the same program item icon in more than one group window.
Program icon	An icon that appears on the Windows desktop and represents an actual running program. Program icons are not the same as program item icons, which are used only to start programs.

Windows comes with three sets of group windows that include the free programs which come with Windows. During installation, Windows automatically creates extra group windows to hold the programs you have on your hard disk. At any time, you can create your own custom group windows and program item icons.

The following group windows come with Windows:

Group Window	Description
Main	Includes programs and tools to help you control printing; set up printers, plotters, and modems; customize the desktop; and manage files
Accessories	Includes desktop programs that come with Windows, such as a simple word processor, a drawing program, a calendar, and a calculator
Games	Includes two games, Solitaire and Reversi

4

When you installed Windows, you had the option of letting Windows create a Windows Applications group window and a Non-Windows Applications group window. Windows creates these groups by searching through your hard disk. Windows displays a list of all the programs it finds and asks you to select those that should be placed in the group window for Windows Applications or Non-Windows Applications.

You can create custom group windows, like the Daily Business group, for the programs used together or those used in a specific job.

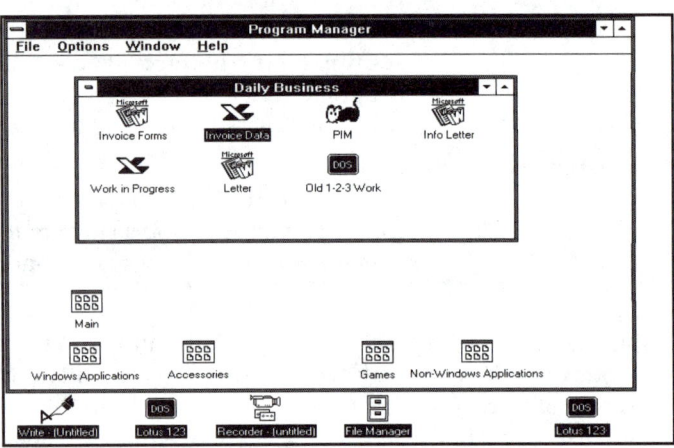

The Daily Business group window contains such programs as Excel, Word for Windows, and PackRat, as well as one document associated with each of them. When you double-click on a program item icon in the group window, the program starts and loads one document associated with that particular program item icon. That is why you see several Word for Windows icons; each contains a different associated document.

Each program item icon represents a specific task. Program item icons in the Daily Business group window have been given names such as PIM (Personal Information Manager), Info Letter, and Work in Progress. When you create your own work groups and program item icons, you can name each one according to the task it performs.

Controlling the Program Manager

The Program Manager is always on-screen in a window or is represented as an icon at the bottom of the screen, giving you quick access to programs and documents. The Program Manager is also the route through which you exit Windows.

4

Opening Group Windows

To start a program with the Program Manager, you must first activate the Program Manager so that it is the topmost window. Once the Program Manager window is active, you can see all the group windows and group icons it contains.

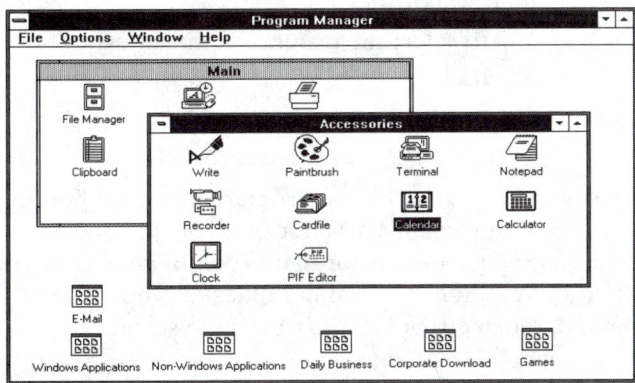

Group icons are usually located at the bottom of the Program Manager window.

If you can see the Program Manager window, you can click on it to bring it to the top. Or, if you can see the Program Manager icon, double-click on it to restore it to a window.

Alternatively, press Alt+Tab until the Program Manager window or icon is selected; then release both keys.

You can activate the Program Manager also by selecting its name from the Task List. To activate the Task List, double-click on the desktop background or press Ctrl+Esc.

Starting Programs from a Group Window

When you open a group window, you will see program item icons. Each icon represents a program and its associated data document. Some program item icons may start a program without loading an associated document.

With the mouse, start a program that is within the active group window by double-clicking on the program item icon.

With the keyboard, select an icon and then start its program by following these steps:

1. Press Ctrl + F6 until the group window or icon you want is selected. (Group windows are document windows within the Program Manager. Ctrl + F6 is used by many Windows programs to switch between document windows.)
2. Press one of the arrow keys to select the program item icon you want.
3. Press ↵Enter to start the program and document represented by this icon.

Note: If you attempt to start a program with the program item icon but the program does not start, or if the program starts but an error message appears, check the program item properties for that program item icon. The name or directory path to the program or document files may be incorrect. Files may have been moved, renamed, or erased. Check the section "Redefining Groups and Program Items" later in this chapter to learn how to correct these problems.

Arranging Group Windows and Icons

You can arrange group windows and icons manually as described in Chapter 3. Or you can use commands in the Program Manager to arrange them.

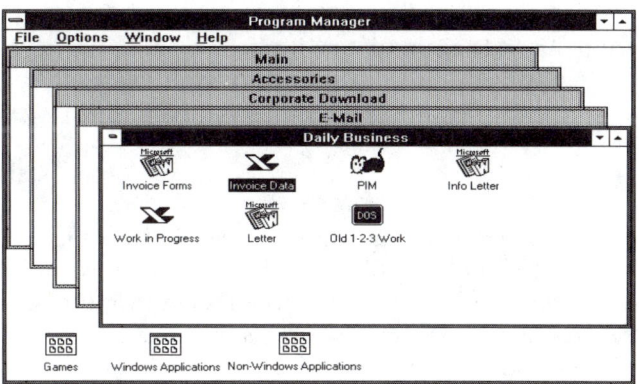

If you want a cascading arrangement of overlapping windows, choose the **Window** menu and select the **Cascade** command.

Cascading windows are useful when you want multiple windows open, but each window contains a large number of program item icons. When you have too many windows to fit in a single cascade, Windows creates a second cascade offset on top of the first.

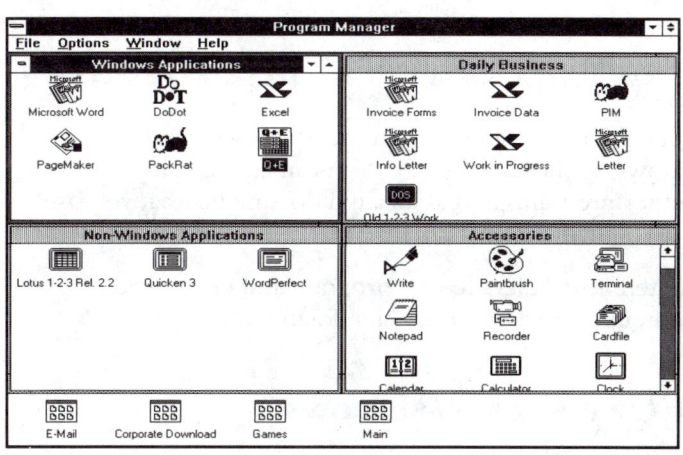

If you want a tiled arrangement so that you can see a portion of all open program windows, choose the **Window** menu and select the **Tile** command.

Tiled windows fill the screen with all open windows. Tiling is useful when you need access to the program item icons from multiple groups, and each group holds only a few program item icons.

To arrange the program item icons within a group window, select the group window by clicking on it or pressing Ctrl+F6 until the window is active. Then choose the **W**indow menu and select the **A**rrange Icons command. If you want Windows to arrange icons automatically whenever you open or resize a window, choose the **O**ptions menu and select the **A**uto Arrange command. A check mark appears alongside the **A**uto Arrange command when it is on. Choose **A**uto Arrange again to turn it off.

4 Automatically Changing the Program Manager to an Icon

The Program Manager window and its group windows are like any other windows. You can use the techniques described in Chapter 3 to move and size the windows or to change them to icons or restore them to windows. An additional feature of the Program Manager, however, is that it can reduce itself to an icon whenever you start a program with a program item icon. This reduction gets the Program Manager quickly out of the way and gives you more room on the desktop.

To reduce the Program Manager to an icon, choose the **O**ptions menu and then select the **M**inimize on Use command. **M**inimize on Use shows a check mark when it is selected. To turn off this command, choose it again.

Customizing Your Own Group Windows

You don't have to keep your programs only in the Windows Applications group and Non-Windows Applications group. You can create your own groups, putting together programs and associated documents that you use for a specific job or at a specific time.

Note: Each program item icon refers to one program and either one associated data document or no associated data document.

Creating Your Own Group Windows

Before creating group windows, imagine the tasks you perform each day. Divide them into related groups, such as writing proposals, managing a project, or contacting clients and sending follow-up letters. Each of these groups of tasks can become a group window. Within each group window, you can add program item icons that start programs and open documents.

To create your own group window, follow these steps:

1. Activate the Program Manager window.

2. Choose the **File** menu and select the **New** command.

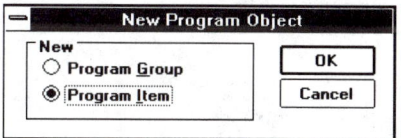

The New Program Object dialog box appears.

4

3. Select the Program **Group** option.

4. Choose OK or press [↵Enter].

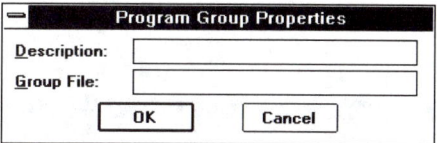

The Program Group Properties dialog box appears.

5. Select the **Description** text box and type the title you want for this group window. Do not make an entry in the **Group** File text box. The Program Manager automatically creates a GRP file extension for the group you are creating.

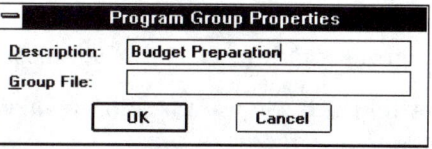

Budget Preparation is the title for the new group window.

6. Choose OK or press [↵Enter].

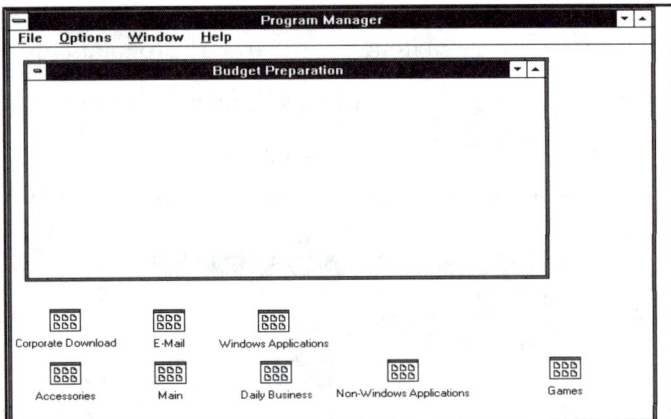

The new group window you create remains open on-screen.

4

If you are going to add program item icons to the window immediately, leave it open. The next section describes how to add the program item icons that start programs.

Adding Program Item Icons to a Group Window

Once you have created a new group window, you will want to add to it the program item icons that start programs and open documents.

Note: Microsoft recommends that you do not include more than 40 program items in a group. A large number of program item icons in a group window defeats the idea of using the Program Manager for quick and easy program start-up.

To add program item icons to a group window, follow these steps:

1. Activate the group window in which you want to add the new program item icons. (Click on the window or press Ctrl + F6 until it is on top.)
2. Choose the **F**ile menu and select the **N**ew command.
3. Select the Program **I**tem option from the New Program Object dialog box that appears.
4. Choose OK or press ↵Enter .

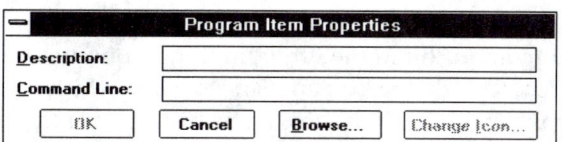

The Program Item
Properties dialog
box appears.

5. From this dialog box, select the **Description** text box and type the
   title for the program item icon.

6. Select the **Command Line** text box and type the path name, file
   name, and extension of the program for this item.

   If you are unsure of the path name or program's file name, choose
   the **Browse** button to display the Browse dialog box.

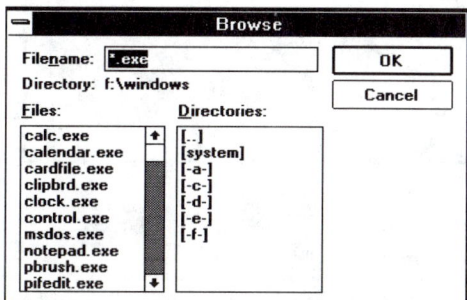

The Browse dia-
log box contains
scrolling list
boxes from which
you can select the
directory and file
name of the pro-
gram you want to
start.

From the **Directories** list, select the directory containing the
program you want. (To go to a higher, or *parent*, directory, choose
[. .] in the **Directories** list.) Select the program's file name from
the **Files** list. Choose OK or press ⏎Enter. The path name and
program name will be inserted in the **Command Line** text box of
the Program Item Properties dialog box.

7. If you want a data document (such as a spreadsheet, letter, or data
   file) to open with the program, type a space after the file name
   followed by the path name and file name of the document.

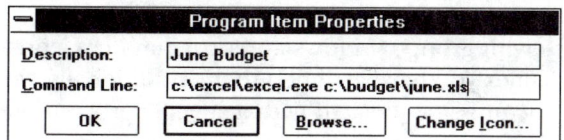

Here the program
and document
are in separate
directories.

8. If you want to select the icon to be used as the program item icon, choose the Change Icon button in the Program Item Properties dialog box. The Select Icon dialog box appears showing which icon will be used. Cycle through the alternative icons by choosing the View Next button. Choose OK or Cancel to return to the Program Item Properties dialog box.

9. Choose OK or press ⏎Enter to display your new program item icon in the group window.

In this example, the June Budget program item icon is displayed with the same icon used by Excel.

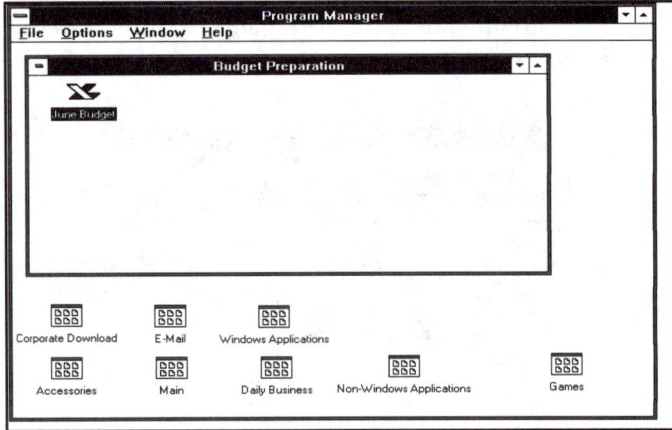

Note: The Browse dialog box initially displays and shows only program files with the extension EXE. To see other types of program files in the Browse dialog box, change the *.EXE in the Filename text box to *.* and press Enter. This will display all files in a directory. Program item icons also can start files that end with COM, BAT, or PIF. You may need to create a PIF file for DOS programs that will not run with the automatic PIF settings. PIF files are explained in Chapter 13, "Running Non-Windows Programs."

Redefining Groups and Program Items

Once you gain experience with group windows and program item icons, you may want to change the names you have assigned them. Additionally, you may want to change the document associated with a specific program item icon.

To change the title of a group window, follow these steps:

1. Activate the group window you want to change.
2. Choose the **F**ile menu and select the **P**roperties command.
3. Select the **D**escription text box and type a new title.
4. Choose OK or press ⏎Enter.

To change the title of a program item icon or to change the program or document started by that icon, follow these steps:

1. Activate the group window containing the program item icon.
2. Select the program item icon.
3. Choose the **F**ile menu and select the **P**roperties command.
4. Change the icon title in the **D**escription text box or change the program file name or document file name in the **C**ommand Line text box.
5. Choose OK or press ⏎Enter.

Deleting a Program Item Icon

As your job changes or as you become more familiar with Windows and group windows, you may want to keep a group but move or delete a program item icon within that group. To delete a program item icon, follow these steps:

1. Activate the group window containing the program item icon.
2. Select the program item icon you want to delete.
3. Choose the **F**ile menu and select the **D**elete command.
4. Choose **Y**es when asked to verify the deletion.

Note: This procedure removes only the icon from the group window. The program and data file remain on disk.

Deleting a Group

If you no longer use any of the program items in a group window or you find the group window unnecessary, you can delete the entire group from the group window. To delete a group, follow these steps:

1. Select the group icon for the group you want to delete. (Do not select an open window.)

85

2. Choose the **File** menu and select the **Delete** command.

3. Choose **Yes** to verify that you want to delete the group.

Note: Deleting the group removes the group window and its program item icons from the Program Manager window. The program files and data files remain on disk.

Moving and Copying Program Item Icons

4

As you become more familiar with Windows or as your needs change, you may want to change group windows and the program item icons within them. That's easy to do once you learn how to copy or move program item icons between group windows.

With the mouse, you can move a program item icon to another group window by dragging the program item icon onto the destination group window and then releasing the program item icon. You can also drag a program item icon onto a group icon, but you have no control over where the program item icon will be positioned within the new window.

With the keyboard, follow these steps to move a program item icon:

1. Activate the group window containing the program item icon.

2. Select the program item icon to be moved by pressing the arrow keys.

3. Choose the **File** menu and select the **Move** command.

The Move Program Item dialog box appears.

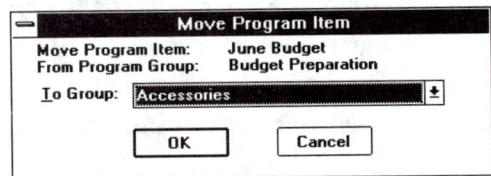

4. Press ⌐Alt⌐+⌐↓⌐ to open the drop-down list box.

5. Press ⌐↑⌐ or ⌐↓⌐ to select the name of the destination group window.

6. Press ⌐↵Enter⌐ to move the program item icon.

With the mouse, copy a program item icon to another group window by following these steps:

1. Arrange the two group windows so that both are visible.

2. Activate the group window containing the program item to be copied.

3. Hold down Ctrl and drag the program item icon to the new group window.

4. Release the mouse button.

With the keyboard, copy a program item icon to another group window by following these steps:

1. Activate the group window containing the program item.

2. Press the arrow keys to select the program item icon to be copied.

3. Choose the File menu and select the Copy command.

4. Press Alt + ↓ to open the drop-down list box.

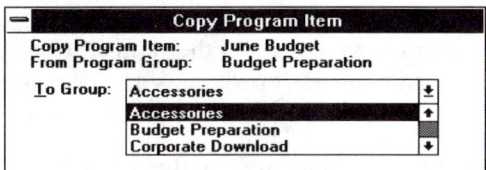

The drop-down list box appears in the Copy Program Item dialog box.

5. Press ↑ or ↓ to select the destination group name from the drop-down list box.

6. Press ↵Enter .

Quitting the Program Manager and Windows

Be careful about quitting the Program Manager. When you close or quit the Program Manager, you will be quitting Windows.

When you are ready to quit Windows, follow these steps:

1. Save the data in your programs by using the File Save As command for each program. You do not need to quit the programs; they will be closed when you quit Windows.

2. Activate the Program Manager.

3. Choose the File menu and select the Exit command.

The Exit Windows dialog box displays immediately before you exit Windows.

87

4. If you want Windows to restart with the same arrangement of group windows in the Program Manager window, select the Save Changes check box from the Exit Windows dialog box.

Summary

In this chapter, you learned that the Program Manager acts as a central coordinator for programs. It eliminates having to search through disks and directories to find and start a program and program document. Instead of searching, you can open the Program Manager and start a program (or a program with a document) by double-clicking on the icon that represents the program. You can create the program item icons that start a program and document. By grouping program item icons together and storing them in a group window, you can easily find and start programs and documents related to a specific task.

Some important points covered in this chapter are the following:

■ Three group windows come with the Program Manager: Accessories, Main, and Games. During Windows installation, you can choose whether the installation program will also create Windows Applications and Non-Windows Applications group windows.

■ You can start a program by opening its group window within the Program Manager and then double-clicking on the program item icon that represents the program.

■ You can add program item icons to an open group window by choosing the File menu, selecting the New command, and selecting the Program Item option. You are then asked for a title for the icon and the location of the program that the icon represents.

■ You can change the names of group icons or program item icons and what they represent by selecting the group icon or program item icon to be changed, choosing the File menu, and selecting the Properties command.

From here, you can move to any of the chapters that describe how to operate Windows or non-Windows programs, or you can move to Chapter 5, "Managing Files." Chapter 5 explains how easily you can manage your disk files when you use the File Manager instead of DOS commands.

4

Managing
Files

The File Manager in Windows acts like an office manager, helping you manage your disk, copy and erase files, and start programs. The File Manager also shows how your files are organized.

You can maintain your files and directories more easily with the File Manager than with DOS commands. For example, with the mouse, you can copy all the files in a directory to a diskette by dragging the directory's icon onto the diskette drive icon and releasing the mouse button.

Note: Use the macro recorder described in Chapter 12, "Creating Macros," to record frequently used File Manager procedures. You can, for instance, record a macro that copies all selected files to a diskette.

5

Key Terms in This Chapter

Memory

The electronic part of your computer where work and calculations are done on programs and data. Memory disappears when power is turned off.

Disk

A hard disk or diskette device that stores programs and data magnetically. Data and programs on disk do not disappear when power is turned off. A hard disk is inside your computer and stores tens of millions of characters. A diskette is a flexible plastic disk that stores approximately a million characters.

Data

The information you create with the help of a computer program. Each type of program has its own unique way of saving data. Data for Windows programs is often referred to as data documents or documents. Data stored on disk is stored in a file.

Program

Instructions that tell the computer how to operate and what to do when you give a command. Programs tell a computer to do word processing at one time and accounting at another time.

Storage

A mechanical part of your computer where data and programs are kept magnetically for long periods while the computer is off. Storage places are also referred to as disk drives, hard disks, or diskettes.

File

A collection of data or program information stored magnetically on a diskette or hard disk. A file is similar to a letter or report within a filing cabinet.

File name

A name by which you can find, open, or manage a file.

Directory

A method of segmenting a disk so that files and programs can be grouped together by type or category. Directories are similar to drawers in a filing cabinet.

Subdirectory

A directory within another directory. Subdirectories are similar to folders within a drawer of a filing cabinet.

Directory Tree	A diagram showing how directories and subdirectories are related.
Focus	A dashed line that indicates which part of a dialog box is active while you are using the keyboard.

Understanding the File Manager

Before you can understand the File Manager, you should understand how computers keep data while they work on it and how they store data for long periods of time. Once you understand the File Manager, managing your disks and the files they contain will be much easier.

5

Understanding Memory, Disks, and Directories

Your computer does all of its calculations and work in electronic *memory*. (Electronic memory is called RAM or random-access memory.) This is where the windows, programs, and data (your work) reside while you work with them. Should the computer loose electrical power, the data, programs, and windows will be lost from memory. Because electronic memory is limited in size and its contents disappear when power is off, the computer needs a way of storing large amounts of data and programs for long periods of time.

Magnetic *storage* is used to store programs and data documents for long periods of time or while the computer is turned off. Magnetic storage takes place on diskettes that are removable and small in volume, and on hard disks that are internal to the computer and large in volume. Diskettes are identified by the letters A: or B:. Hard disks may have identifiers from C: on. When you open a program or data document, the computer puts a copy of the magnetic information into electronic memory. The magnetic program or data document remains on disk while the electronic image of it is used in memory. If the power is lost, the magnetic copy is still available.

When you save your work to disk, a magnetic *file* stores the data in memory onto a diskette or hard disk. Over time, the work you store may amount to hundreds or even thousands of files. It's therefore important to give each file a unique *file name* so that the data can be found again.

To make the job of finding documents easier, you can organize your hard disk into *directories*. If you think of your hard disk as a filing cabinet, directories are like drawers in the cabinet. In a filing cabinet, each drawer holds a different category of document. In a hard disk, each directory also holds a different category of file. The files in a directory can be programs or data documents.

Within a filing cabinet drawer, you put hanging folders to segment the drawer further. Within a hard disk, you segment a directory by putting subdirectories in it. These subdirectories can hold files or other subdirectories. For example, on the C: hard disk, you may have a directory named NEWSLTTR and under it, two subdirectories named CPANEWS and EXCLNEWS. When you create a new edition of your CPA newsletter, you will want to store it with the *path name* identifying where the file is to be located. In this case, the path name should be the following:

> C:\NEWSLTTR\CPANEWS

Using File Manager commands, you can create, name, and delete your own directories and subdirectories. Organizing your hard disk is the same process as organizing a filing cabinet.

Starting the File Manager

The File Manager is easiest to start from the Program Manager. To start the File Manager, you activate the Program Manager and open the Main group window.

The File Manager is located within the Main group window. Appropriately enough, the File Manager icon looks like a filing cabinet.

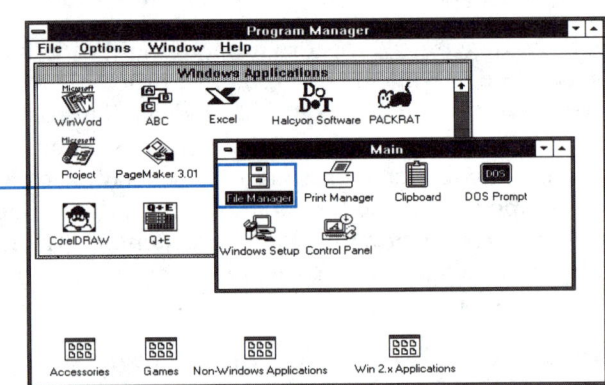

To start the File Manager once the Program Manager is active, activate the Main group window by clicking on it or pressing Ctrl+F6. Open the File

Manager by double-clicking on its icon, or pressing arrow keys until the icon is selected and then pressing Enter.

Understanding the File Manager's Display

The File Manager always contains a *Directory Tree window* and can contain one or more *directory windows*. The Directory Tree window on the left displays the treelike structure that shows how directories and subdirectories are organized on your hard disk.

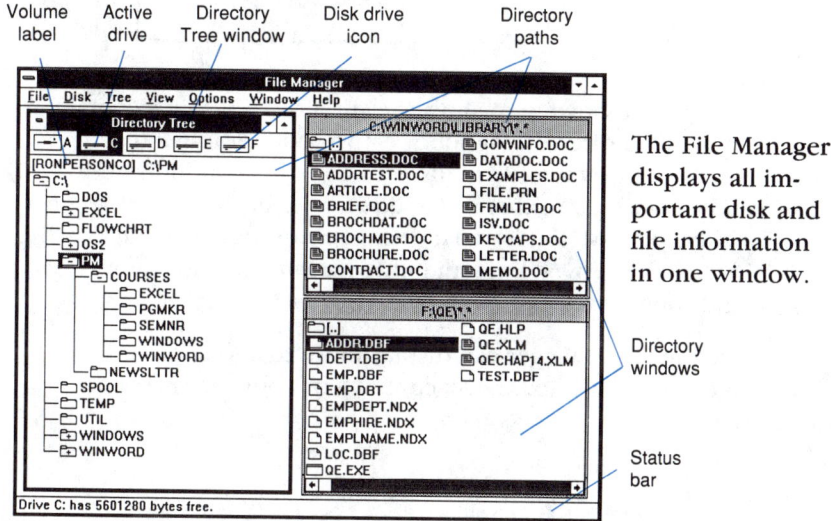

The File Manager displays all important disk and file information in one window.

The directory windows on the right show the files and subdirectories found within selected directories.

A directory window's title shows the path name to the window's contents. At the top of the Directory Tree window are icons representing the available *disk drives*. The active drive is highlighted. Underneath the drives is a bar showing the *volume label* for the disk. (Some disks do not have volume labels.) To the right of the volume label is the *directory path* for the currently selected directory. When the Directory Tree window is active, the *status bar* shows the available storage on the active disk. When a directory window is active, the status bar shows the total size in bytes of selected files. A scroll bar appears on the right of any window when it contains more information than is shown.

The Directory Tree window uses miniature folders as icons to indicate directories or subdirectories.

5

These "folders" can be opened to show the subdirectories they contain. A plus (+) sign within a directory or subdirectory icon indicates that it contains another subdirectory. A minus (−) sign in an icon indicates that the directory can be collapsed so that its subdirectories do not show. When a directory or subdirectory icon is expanded, you can see the subdirectories beneath it. Notice the vertical lines and indentation that show how directories and subdirectories are connected.

Note: Because the File Manager can display more than one directory window, you can easily compare disk contents or copy files between subdirectories.

Selecting and Opening Files and Directories

If you want to affect a file or directory in the File Manager, you must first select that file or directory. Once you select a file, you can display information about it, run it, copy it, move it, or delete it. If you select a directory, you can find out information about the directory contents, copy or move the directory, or open it to see its subdirectories and files.

Selecting a New Disk Drive

Before you can work with files and directories, you must activate the drive containing those files or directories. Disk drives appear as icons under the Directory Tree title bar. The active drive is highlighted.

To activate a new drive with the mouse, just click on the drive icon.

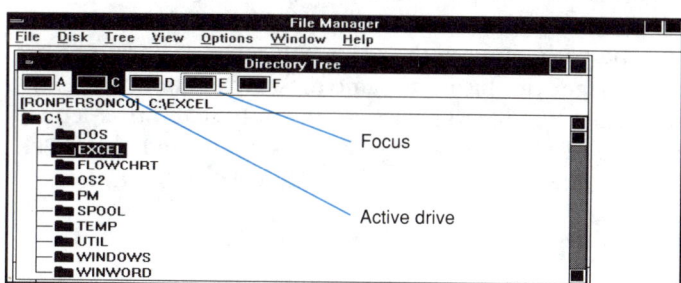

To change to a new drive with the keyboard, you must notice where the *focus*, an enclosing dashed line, is located.

Press the Tab key to move the focus between the row of disk drive icons and the Directory Tree window. The dashed line may be difficult to see if it is on the icon that is highlighted. If the focus is in the drive icon bar, activate a different drive by pressing the left- or right-arrow keys to move the focus to the drive you want active. Then press Enter. If the focus is in the Directory Tree window or in a directory window, activate a different drive by pressing Ctrl+*letter* (*letter* is the letter of the drive you want active).

Connecting to Network Drives

When you connect your computer to a network, you will have additional disk drives available. You can use these additional drives with Windows if you know the path name to the drive and the password. Drives that are on the network show up in the File Manager with a special network disk drive icon.

Note: If you want to use network drives with Windows, you must connect to the network before you start Windows. When you connect to the network and then start Windows, the Windows network commands will be available. If you start Windows without first connecting to the network, the network commands will be gray and therefore unavailable.

95

Note: If you connect a non-Windows program to a network while that program is running in Windows, disconnect from the network before quitting the program.

Once you connect to the network and start Windows, you can connect to the File Manager disk drives that are on the network. You must give the File Manager the path name that describes the location of the drive on the network. Some networks allow you to browse through a list of drives on the network and select the drive to which you want to connect. Other networks require that you know the path name to the drive beforehand. Because no two drives in the File Manager can have the same disk drive letter, you may need to choose a unique drive letter to represent the networked disk icon at the top of the File Manager. Once the network drive is connected to the File Manager, you can treat that drive as you would any disk drive in Windows.

To connect to a network drive manually, follow these steps:

1. Choose the **Disk** menu and select the Connect **Net** Drive command.

The Connect Network Drive dialog box appears.

2. Each disk drive in the File Manager must have its own unique drive letter. Windows automatically enters the next available drive letter into the **Drive Letter** text box. If you want the drive that you are adding to use a different letter, type it in the **Drive Letter** text box or choose a new letter from the **Drive Letter** drop-down list box.

3. Type the network path name in the **Network Path** text box. This name describes where the network disk is located.

   Or choose **Previous** to see a list of path names to which you have previously connected. Select the path name you want from the **Previous Network Connections** list box.

Or choose the **B**rowse button to display a list of available drives on this network. Then choose the drive you want. If the Browse feature is not available on your network, this button is gray.

4. Type your network password into the Password text box.

5. To save the path name so you don't have to retype it, select the **A**dd to Previous List check box. The next time you connect a network drive, you can select the **P**revious button to enter the path name.

6. Choose the **C**onnect button.

In step 3, if you choose the **B**rowse button, a Network Disk Resources dialog box appears. This dialog box appears differently for different types of networks. From this box, you can select the network server you want from the Network **S**ervers list box. Once you have connected to the network server you want, select a share from the **R**esources at list box. When you choose OK, the Connect Network Drive box appears. At that time, choose the **C**onnect button.

Note: Disconnecting from networks while Windows is in 386-enhanced mode may vary. If you connect to a network drive before starting Windows in 386-enhanced mode, you may not be able to disconnect while in Windows. To disconnect, exit Windows.

To disconnect from the network drive, follow these steps:

1. Select a drive other than the network drive from which you want to disconnect.

2. Choose the **D**isk menu and select the Disconnect **N**et Drive command.

3. Select the network drive letter you want to disconnect.

4. Choose OK or press ⏎Enter.

5. To confirm that you want to disconnect, choose OK or press ⏎Enter.

Selecting Directories

The Directory Tree always appears as a window or icon in the File Manager window. This tree shows the hierarchical structure of directories or subdirectories on the active disk.

In this Directory Tree, drive C contains a PM (PageMaker) directory that has within it two subdirectories, COURSES and NEWSLTTR. The COURSES subdirectory contains additional subdirectories.

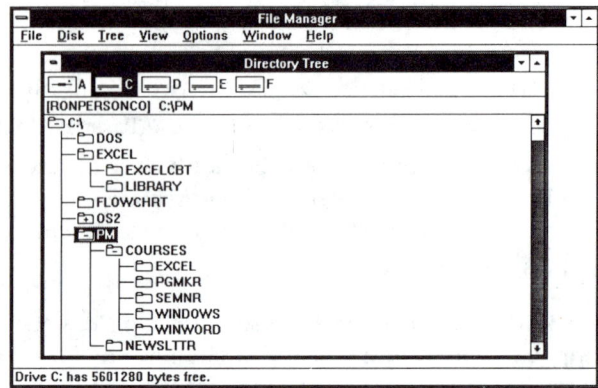

5

Once you activate the disk drive containing your data or program, you must select a directory if you want to display, copy, move, or delete the directory or its contents.

With the mouse, select a directory by clicking on the directory or subdirectory folder (icon). If you cannot see the directory folder, use the vertical scroll bar on the Directory Tree window to scroll the window.

With the keyboard, select a directory from the active drive by pressing one of the following keys or key combinations:

Key(s)	Action
↑ or ↓	Moves the selection to a directory above or below the currently selected directory
→	Selects the first subdirectory below the current directory
←	Selects the directory above the current subdirectory
Ctrl + ↑	Selects the previous directory on the tree at the current indentation level
Ctrl + ↓	Selects the next directory on the tree at the current indentation level
PgUp	Selects the directory one window up
PgDn	Selects the directory one window down
Home	Selects the top directory in the window
End	Selects the last directory in the window
letter	Selects the next directory or subdirectory beginning with that letter

98

Expanding and Collapsing the Directory Structure

Expanding a directory shows you all the *subdirectories* contained within that directory. Collapsing subdirectories hides them within the *directory* in which they are located.

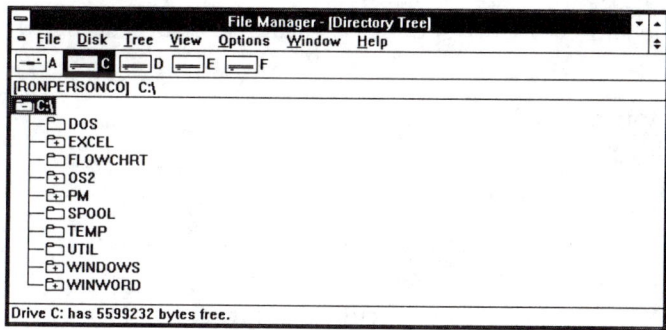

Collapsed directories show only the main directories.

5

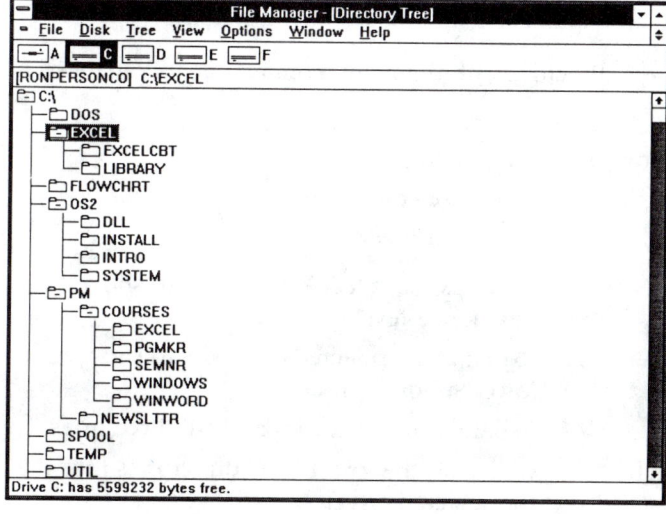

Expanded directories show the subdirectories located within main directories.

To expand or collapse a directory or subdirectory with the mouse, use one of the following actions:

Action	Result
Click on the plus (+) sign in a directory icon	Expands the directory one level
Click on the minus (–) sign in a directory icon	Collapses the directory

To expand or collapse a directory or subdirectory with the keyboard, follow these steps:

1. Select the directory or subdirectory.

2. Press one of the following:

Key(s)	Description
- (hyphen)	Collapses all subdirectories into the selected directory
+ (plus sign)	Expands all subdirectories out from the selected directory for one level
* (asterisk)	Expands all subdirectories in the selected directory
Ctrl + *	Expands all subdirectories on the disk

To expand or collapse a directory with the menu commands, follow these steps:

1. Select the directory or subdirectory.

2. Choose **Tree** and then one of these commands:

Command	Description
Expand One Level	Expands the selected directory to show the next lower-level directory
Expand **Branch**	Expands the selected directory to show all lower subdirectories
Expand **All**	Expands all directories and subdirectories
Collapse Branch	Collapses the lower-level directories into the selected directory

Displaying the Files within a Directory Window

As indicated previously, you can have only one Directory Tree window, showing the overall structure of the disk. But you can have many directory

100

windows, each of which shows the files and subdirectory names contained within a specific directory or subdirectory. You can keep directory windows open even when a different disk or directory is active in the Directory Tree.

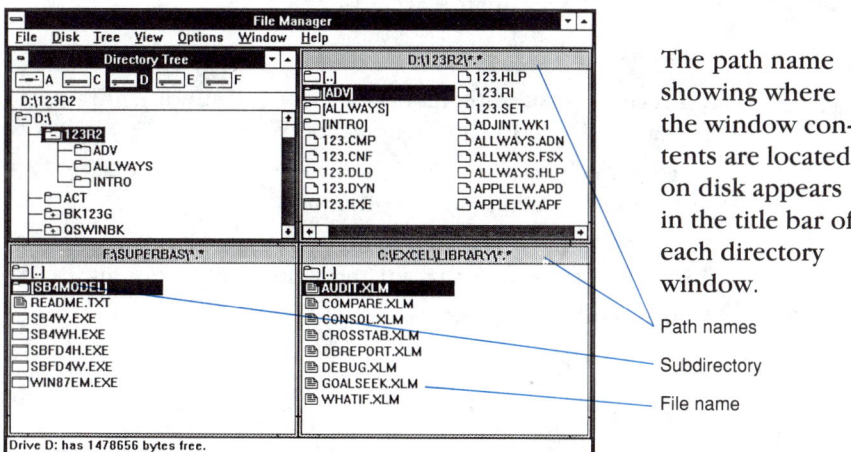

The path name showing where the window contents are located on disk appears in the title bar of each directory window.

Path names

Subdirectory

File name

Note: The Directory Tree window shows how directories and subdirectories are related. A directory window shows the actual contents of a directory or subdirectory. Those contents might be program files, data document files, or additional subdirectories.

With the mouse, display the contents of a directory in the Directory Tree window by double-clicking on the directory name. With the keyboard, display the contents of a directory in the Directory Tree window by selecting the directory name in the Directory Tree and pressing Enter. Or select the directory name, choose the File menu, and select the Open command.

Displaying File Size and Remaining Disk Storage

The status bar at the bottom of the File Manager window displays the storage available on the active disk when the Directory Tree window is active. If a directory window is active, the status bar displays the size or number of selected files. To calculate the total storage of multiple files, select the files and then read the status bar to see the number of bytes used.

Understanding File Icons

Each file within a directory window displays an icon that identifies the file type. Note the following icon shapes:

Icon	Meaning
📁	A directory or subdirectory. Directory and subdirectory names appear enclosed in square brackets.
📁	A program or batch file with the extension EXE, COM, PIF, or BAT. These files may start a program.
📄	A document file associated with a program. Choosing one of these files starts the program and loads the document.
📄	A document file not associated with a program.

Changing or Closing Directory Windows

Because directory windows are document windows, you can use the mouse or document Control menu to resize, move, or close each window. Activate the window you want to change by clicking on it, or choosing the Window command and selecting the name of the directory window.

To close the active directory window, click on the document Control menu at the top left of that window or press Alt, hyphen (-). When the document Control menu appears, select the Close command. If you want to close all directory windows, choose the Window menu and select the Close All Directories command from the File Manager menu.

Selecting Files

Before you can do something to a file—such as copy, rename, or delete it— you must select the file. A number of techniques are available for selecting a single file or multiple files.

To select a single file with the mouse, click on the file. To select multiple adjacent files with the mouse, click on the first file, hold down the Shift key, and click on the last file. All files between these two will be selected also.

5

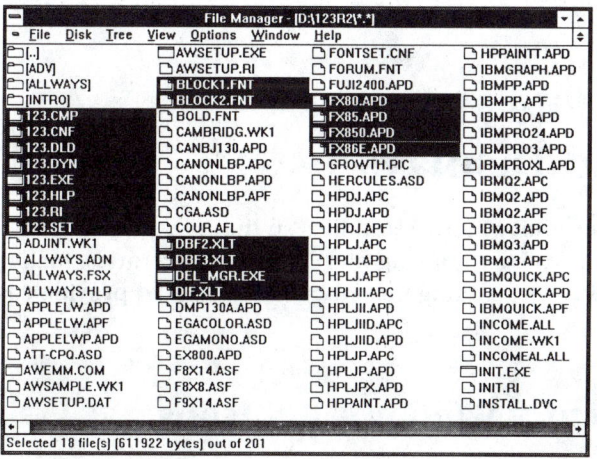

In this example, eight files totaling 452,469 bytes have been selected, as indicated on the status bar.

To select multiple nonadjacent files with the mouse, select the first file and then hold down the Ctrl key as you click on each of the other file names. If you want to retain your selections but deselect one file, use Ctrl+Click on the selected file you no longer want selected.

This window shows that 18 nonadjacent files have been selected.

To select a single file with the keyboard, press the arrow keys to move the selection to the file name you want. To select multiple adjacent files, move the selection to the first file and then hold down the Shift key as you press an arrow key.

103

To select nonadjacent files with the keyboard, select the first file, press Shift+F8, press the appropriate arrow key to move to the next file to be selected, and then press the space bar. Continue moving to files you want to select and pressing the space bar. To deselect a file while retaining other selections, move to the selected file and press the space bar. Press Shift+F8 to return to selecting individual files.

If you want to select all files in the active directory window, choose the File menu and then select the Select All command or press Ctrl+/ (forward slash). To deselect all files, choose the File menu and then select the Unselect All command or press Ctrl+\ (backslash).

5

Restricting the Display to One Directory Window

You may find it confusing to have Windows open a new directory window each time you open a new directory. Soon the screen will be filled with directory windows. If you want only a single directory window open whose contents are replaced, choose the View menu and select the Replace on Open command. When this command is on, a check mark appears next to it on the menu. Choose the command again to turn the feature off.

Controlling File Manager Windows and Displays

You will want to arrange your windows and files so that you can do your work efficiently. Whether you are copying files between directories, making backup copies on diskette, or deleting files, the display should provide easy access to your files.

Arranging Directory Windows and Icons

Directory windows and icons can be arranged in three ways. You can position the windows manually, cascade the windows to show all the window titles and icons, or tile the windows to show each window's contents.

To arrange directory windows in a cascade, choose the Window Cascade command.

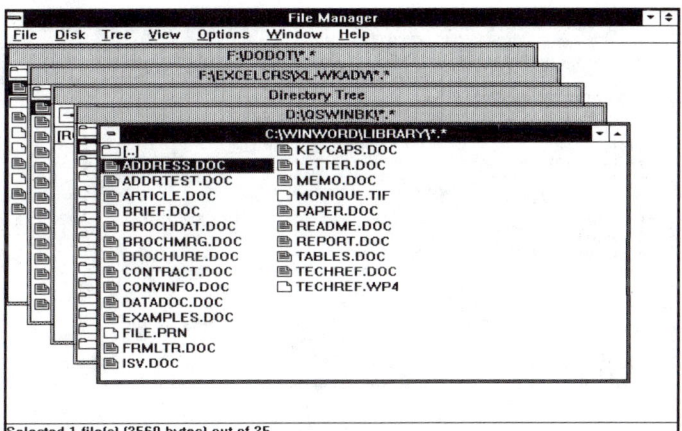

The active window becomes the top window in the cascade.

To arrange directory windows in tiles so that the screen is evenly divided among the windows, choose the Window Tile command.

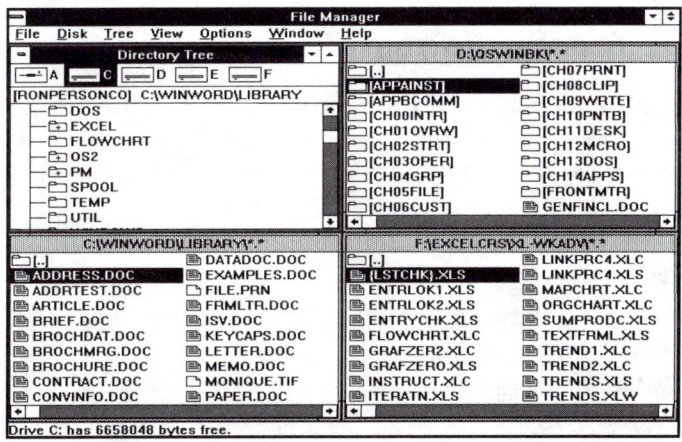

The active window becomes the window at the top left in the File Manager.

To reduce the Directory Tree window or directory windows to icons, click on the minimize icon (the down arrow) to the right of a window's title bar. Or press Alt, hyphen (-) and select the Minimize command.

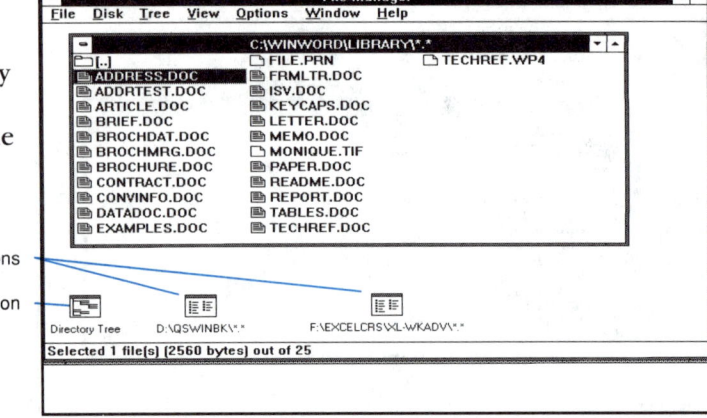

The path name
of each directory
window is dis-
played below the
icon.

Directory window icons

Directory Tree icon

Restore an icon into its window by double-clicking on the icon. Or press
Ctrl+Tab until the icon is selected and then press Enter.

Specifying File-Display Formats

You can specify what file information shows in the directory window. The
two most common displays use **View Name** to show only the file names and
extensions, and **View File Details** to show all file information.

To display file information, follow these steps:

1. Activate the window directory you want reordered.

   Or activate the Directory Tree window if you want all subsequent
   windows reordered.

2. Choose **View** and then one of these options:

Option	Description
Name	Displays only names and directories
File Details	Displays the name, size, date and time last saved, as well as other characteristics about each file

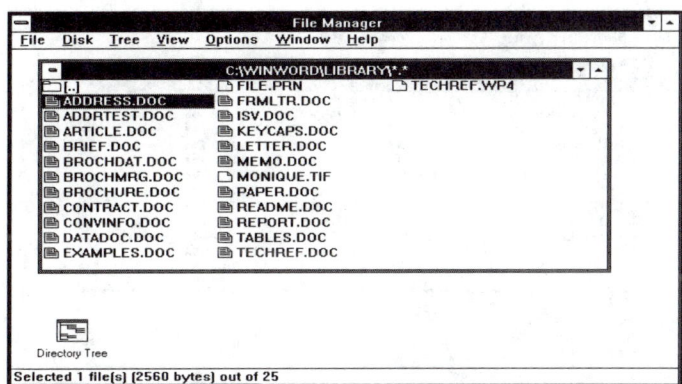

This example shows only file names displayed.

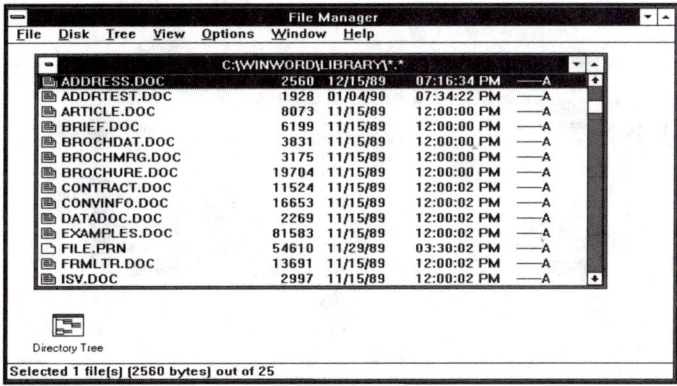

This example shows the name, size, and date and time that each file was last saved.

Note: Some non-Windows programs may not automatically update the information in the File Manager. As a result, you may activate the File Manager and not see a file you have just saved. Update the window manually with the Window Refresh command.

Sorting the Contents of a Window

Finding files or directories in a directory window is easier if you sort the window contents by name, file name extension, file size, or date last saved.

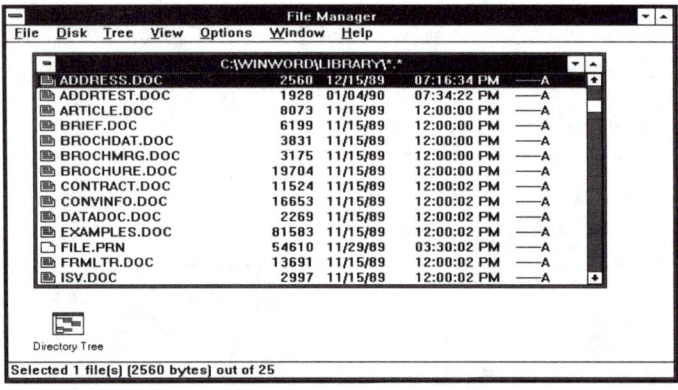

Sorting by name
makes files easier
to find.

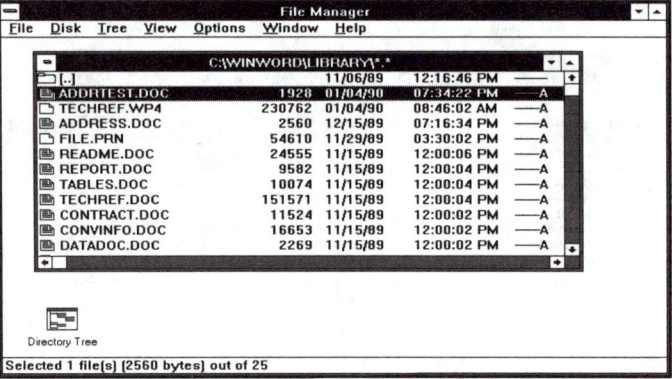

Sorting by date
makes it easier to
find old files that
can be deleted.

To sort a window's contents by name or file type, follow these steps:

1. Activate the directory window you want reordered.

   Or activate the Directory Tree window if you want all subsequent
   windows reordered.

2. Choose **View** and then one of these options:

Option	Description
By Name	Sorts the display alphabetically by file name
By **T**ype	Sorts the display alphabetically by file extension and then by name

To sort a window's contents by any file characteristic, follow these steps:

1. Activate the directory window you want reordered.

2. Choose the View menu and select the Sort command.

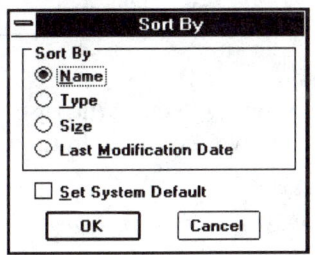

When you choose View Sort, the Sort By dialog box appears.

3. From the Sort By dialog box, select one of the following options:

Option	Description
Name	Sorts alphabetically by file name.
Type	Sorts alphabetically by file extension.
Size	Sorts by file size from largest to smallest.
Last Modification Date	Sorts by last date saved (most recent first).
Set System Default	Applies the sorting options to all directory windows you open. Otherwise, the options apply only to the active window.

4. Choose OK or press ↵Enter.

Displaying Warning Messages

During some File Manager operations, a warning message appears asking you if you really want to do what you have requested. For example, if you select a directory and then choose File Delete, before the file is deleted, you may be asked to confirm that you want it deleted. In some cases, too many confirmation messages are annoying; in other cases, they can save you from disaster. In the File Manager, you have a choice of whether to turn off selected confirmation messages.

You turn off warning messages by first choosing the Options menu and then selecting the Confirmation command.

From the Confir-
mation dialog box
that appears, you
can then deselect
the type of warn-
ing message you
want turned off.

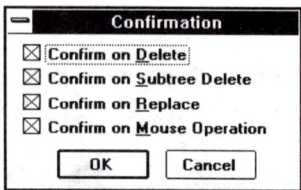

You can turn a confirmation back on by reselecting the option so that the
check box contains an X. Note the following options in the Confirmation
dialog box:

Option	Action Confirmed by Message
Confirm on **Delete**	Each file being erased
Confirm on **Subtree** Delete	Each directory being erased
Confirm on **Replace**	One file being copied over another
Confirm on **Mouse** Operation	Any mouse action that involves moving or copying

Managing Files and Directories

This section shows how easily you can erase unwanted files, copy files to other
disks, or move files between directories. You learn also how to make your own
directories so that you can organize your disk to fit your work and data.

Understanding File Names and Wild Cards

File names and directory names have rules you must follow if you want to
find your data again. If you do not name a file or directory correctly, you may
not be able to find it later, or the name may not be accepted.

File names and directory names have three parts:

The file name or directory name can contain one to eight characters. The separator is a period. The file extension can have from zero to three characters. In most cases, Windows programs add their own file extensions to the file names you type. Therefore, you don't need to add a file extension when you are asked for the file name of a data document. If you do not type a file extension, do not type a period.

File names and directory names can use all the alphabetical and numeric characters, as well as some symbols. However, some symbols cannot be used. Instead of memorizing a list of usable symbols, just remember the hyphen (-), underscore (_), and exclamation point (!). Use the hyphen or underscore instead of a blank space in a name. Use the exclamation point as the first character in a name when you want the name to "float" to the top of lists of files in Windows programs. (The exclamation point comes before letters in alphabetized lists.) Using an exclamation point can save you time in finding file names you use frequently.

Note: Never use a space in a file name or directory name. Include a period only if a file extension is used.

Searching for Files or Directories

Losing a file is frustrating and wastes time, but with the File Manager, you can search disks or directories for file names similar to the one you have misplaced.

To search for a file by its full name or part of its name, follow these steps:

1. Select the disk drive you want to search.

2. Select the directory if you want to search a single directory.

3. Choose the Search command from the File menu.

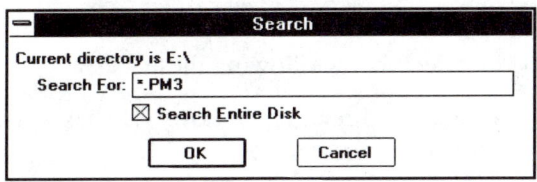

The Search dialog box appears.

4. In the Search For text box, type either the file name or a pattern that contains DOS wild cards (? and *).

111

5. Select the Search **E**ntire Disk check box if you want to search all directories on the current disk.

6. Choose OK or press ↵Enter.

A Search Results window displays all files (and their paths) that match the pattern of the file name for which you are looking.

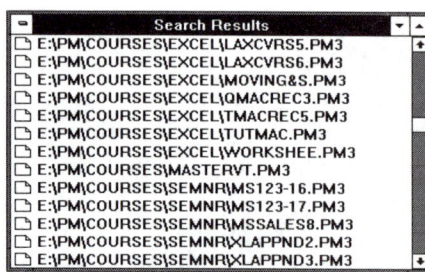

5

If you see the file or program you want, you can start the document or program by double-clicking on it with the mouse, or selecting it and pressing Enter.

When you use DOS wild cards in a name pattern, remember that the * wild card finds any group of characters in the same or following positions. The ? wild card finds any single character in the same position as the ?. For example, use the pattern E*.XLS to search for all file names beginning with E and having the three-letter file extension of XLS. And use the name pattern BDGT???.* to search for file names that start with BDGT and are followed by exactly three characters. Any file extension will match the *.

Copying Files or Directories

Copying files is an important part of keeping your data documents organized and secure. The hard disk on which you store your files is a mechanical device and has one of the highest failure rates among computer components. However, should your hard disk fail, the cost of replacing the disk is insignificant compared to the cost of redoing your documents. Prevent this loss by making copies and storing them in a safe place.

With the mouse, copy a file or directory by following these steps:

1. Make the source and destination directory windows visible so that you can see the file or directory you want to copy.

2. Activate the directory window containing the file or directory to be copied. If you are copying an entire directory, you can activate either the directory window or the Directory Tree window.

3. Select the file or directory to be copied. You can select more than one file or directory by using the techniques described earlier in this chapter.

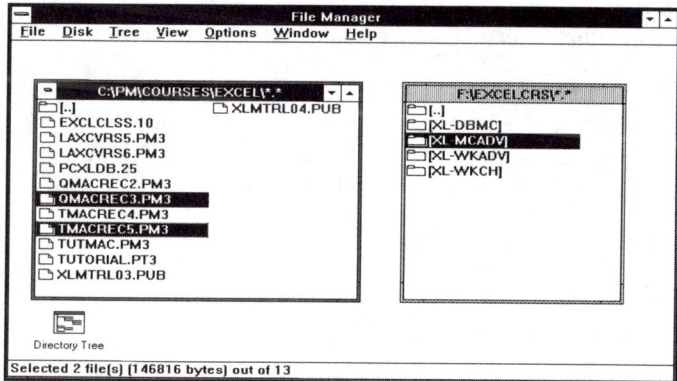

This example shows that several files have been selected.

4. Drag the file or directory to the directory window where you want the copy to go. If the destination is on the same disk, hold down Ctrl as you drag the file.

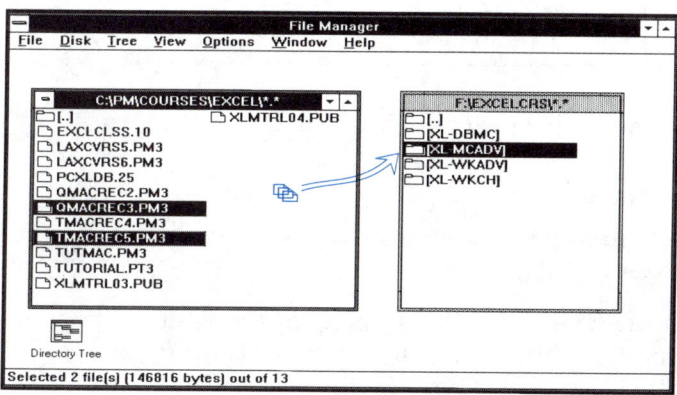

The selected files are being dragged to the destination window.

5. When the icon that you are dragging is over the destination, release the mouse button and Ctrl. If you want to drop the file (or files) into a subdirectory in the destination window, release the file over that subdirectory icon (folder).

6. You may be asked to confirm the copy if the destination has a file with the same name.

Note: Copy all the files from a directory by selecting all of them before you drag them to the new destination. Select all the files by clicking on the first file and then using Shift+Click on the last file.

When copying with the mouse, you can release the icon of the copied file on top of another directory window, on top of a directory icon in the Directory Tree, on top of a directory icon at the bottom of the File Manager window, or on top of a disk drive icon at the top of the File Manager.

With the keyboard, copy a file or directory by following these steps:

1. Activate the window containing the file or directory.

2. Select the file or directory you want to copy.

3. Choose the **File** menu and select the **Copy** command.

The Copy dialog box appears with the selected file(s) in the **From** text box.

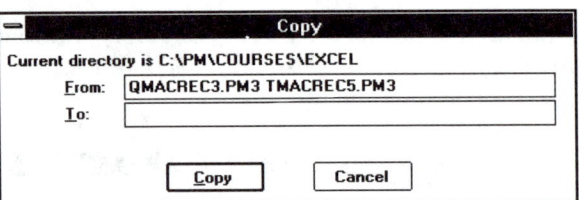

4. In the **To** text box, type the path name (drive and directory) indicating where you want the copy to go.

5. Choose the **Copy** button.

6. You may be asked to confirm the copy if the destination has a file with the same name.

Note: You can select all files in a directory by pressing Ctrl+/. If you want to copy files selectively, you can also include the DOS wild cards (* and ?) in the **From** text box of the Copy dialog box.

Moving Files or Directories

You can move files just as easily as you copy them. Moving a file puts it in a new location and removes the original file from the old location. Moving files or directories to a new directory or disk is useful in reorganizing your disk. Moving a directory moves that directory's files and subdirectories.

With the mouse, move a file or directory by following these steps:

1. Make the directory windows of both the original and the destination locations visible.

2. Select the file or directory you want to move.

3. Drag the file or directory icon to the destination if the destination is on the same disk. If the destination is on a different disk, hold down the Alt key as you drag the file or directory icon.

4. Release the mouse button and Alt key when the file or directory icon that you are dragging is over the destination.

5. You may be asked to confirm the copy if the destination has a file with the same name.

With the keyboard, move a file or directory by following these steps:

1. Make the directory windows of both the original and the destination locations visible.

2. Select the file or directory you want to move.

3. Choose the **File** menu and select the **Move** command.

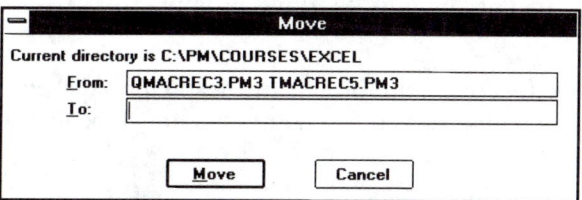

The Move dialog box appears with the selected file(s) in the From text box.

4. In the **To** text box, type the destination path name. This is the drive and directory where you want the file or directory to go.

5. Choose the **Move** button.

Copying Diskettes

Make duplicate copies of diskettes whenever you need a copy for off-site storage or you need to transport information. The File Manager will copy diskettes even if you have a single disk drive on your computer. To duplicate a diskette, follow these steps:

1. Protect your original diskette by putting a write-protect tab over the notch on 5 1/4-inch diskettes or by sliding the protect notch open on 3 1/2-inch diskettes.

2. Insert the original diskette into disk drive A.

3. Insert the diskette to receive the copy into disk drive B. If you do not have a second disk drive, you will still be able to make a duplicate; just skip this step.

4. Select the disk drive icon marked A by clicking on it or pressing `Ctrl` + `A` .

5. Choose the **Disk** menu and select the **Copy Diskette** command.

6. A message warns you that all data on the destination diskette will be destroyed. Choose the **Copy** button to continue.

7. Select the drive letter for the destination drive—in this case, B—and choose OK or press `↵Enter` . (You can skip this step if you have a single disk drive.)

8. Choose the **Copy** button to complete the copy.

9. If you have only a single disk drive, you will be asked to switch the source and destination diskettes in and out of your single drive. Don't confuse these two diskettes as Windows prompts you to exchange them.

Note: The **D**isk Copy Diskette command formats the destination diskette if it is not formatted. If the destination diskette contains data, it will be lost.

Creating New Directories

Creating new directories or subdirectories on your disk is like adding additional drawers or folders to a filing cabinet. Once you build directories and subdirectories, you can put files in them with the **File Move** and **File Copy** commands.

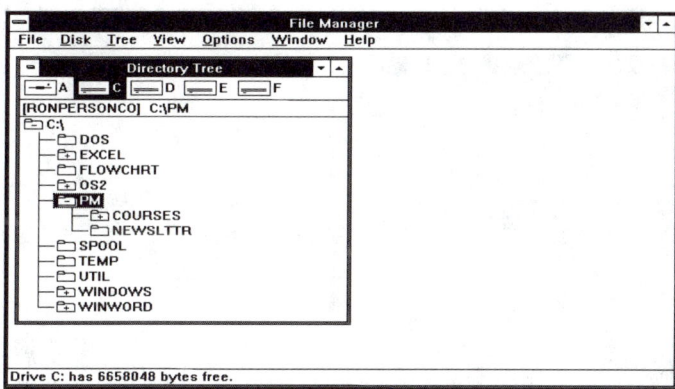

Adding a directory to a disk gives you a location in which you can store files belonging to a new category.

5

To make a new directory, follow these steps:

1. Activate the Directory Tree window or the directory window in which you want the new directory.

2. Select the directory or subdirectory name under which you want a new subdirectory.

3. Choose the File menu and select the Create Directory command.

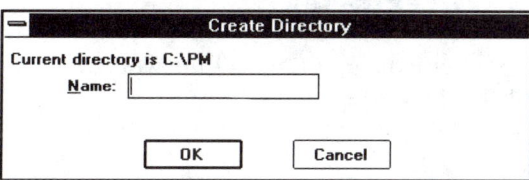

The Create Directory dialog box appears.

4. In the Name text box, type the name of the new directory.

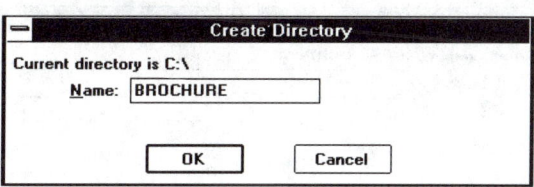

Directory names follow the same rules as file names. Here the name of the new directory is BROCHURE.

5. Choose OK or press ↵Enter.

117

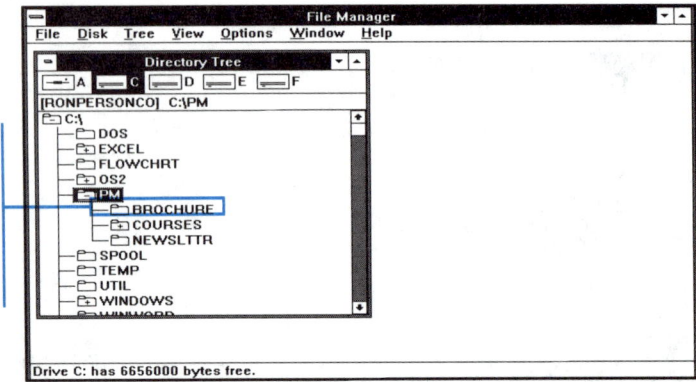

The directory name BROCHURE has been added to the Directory Tree window.

Adding new subdirectories is like putting hanging folders or manila folders into a filing cabinet drawer. The drawer must exist before a hanging folder can be inserted, and the hanging folder must be in the drawer before you can put a manila folder into the hanging folder. With directories and subdirectories, the preceding level of directory or subdirectory must exist before you can add more levels.

Renaming Files or Directories

Unless you do everything perfectly the first time, a time will come when you'll want to rename a file or directory.

To rename a file, follow these steps:

1. Select the file from a directory window.

2. Choose the File menu and select the Rename command.

The Rename dialog box appears.

3. In the To text box, type the new file name.

4. Choose the Rename button or press ⏎Enter.

118

To rename a directory, follow these steps:

1. Select the directory from the Directory Tree window or a directory window.

2. Choose the **File** menu and select the Re**n**ame command.

3. In the **T**o text box, type the directory name that will replace the name selected in step 1. (Do not type the entire path name.)

4. Choose the **R**ename button or press ⏎Enter .

Deleting Files or Directories

Delete files or directories when you need to remove old work from your disk. Deleting files makes more storage available on a disk. You may want to save backup copies of some files to diskette before deleting them from your hard disk. Having backup copies enables you to copy deleted files from the backup diskette to your hard disk at a later time.

Unless you have prepared your hard disk with special software, you cannot recover files or directories once they are deleted. Be sure that you have selected only the files or directories you want deleted.

A convenient but potentially dangerous feature of the File Manager is that deleting a directory or subdirectory name deletes all the files underneath it. If you want to be asked to confirm each file or each directory before it is deleted, choose the **O**ptions menu and select the **C**onfirmation command. Make sure that the Confirm on **D**elete and Confirm on **S**ubtree Delete check boxes are selected.

To delete files or directories, follow these steps:

1. Activate the directory window containing the files.

   Or activate the Directory Tree window if you want to delete one or more directories and their entire contents.

2. Select the files or directories you want to delete.

3. Choose the **File** menu and select the **D**elete command, or press Del .

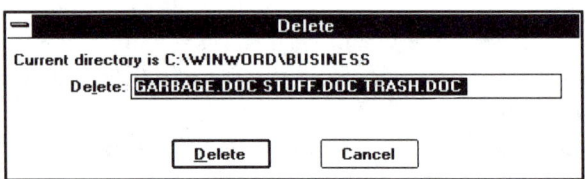

The Delete dialog box appears.

4. Choose the **Delete** button.

5. If you are asked to confirm deletions, choose **Yes** when appropriate.

If you have many files to delete, you can use the DOS wild cards (* and ?) to specify the files you want to delete. In the preceding steps, skip step 2 and when the Delete dialog box appears, type in the Delete text box a DOS wild-card pattern that identifies the file names you want deleted.

For example, you type *.* to specify every file in the current directory.

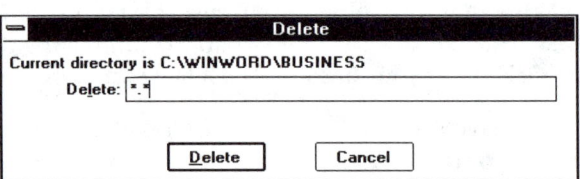

Formatting Diskettes

Most new boxes of diskettes are unusable until you format them. Formatting prepares diskettes for use on a specific type of computer and operating system. Formatting is like preparing a new blank book by writing in page numbers and making a blank table of contents.

Note: If a diskette has data on it, formatting will completely erase all existing data.

To format a diskette, follow these steps:

1. Put the diskette into the disk drive.

2. Activate one of your hard disk drives.

   If you have more than one disk drive, select the letter of the disk drive containing the diskette.

3. Choose the **Disk** menu and select the **Format Diskette** command.

4. A message warns you that formatting erases the contents of the disk.

120

5. Choose the **F**ormat button.

6. If you are using a 1.2M 5 1/4-inch or 1.44M 3 1/2-inch high-capacity diskette, select the **H**igh Capacity check box.

7. Select **M**ake System Disk if you want to use the diskette to start your computer. Do not use this option unless it is needed because it takes up 40K or more of disk space.

8. Choose OK or press `↵Enter`.

9. When the diskette is formatted, you will be given a chance to format additional diskettes.

You may want to format an entire box of diskettes at one time and put a paper label on each diskette when it is formatted. Then you'll know that open boxes contain formatted diskettes and that a diskette with a label has been formatted.

5

Starting Programs and Documents

Starting your programs from the Program Manager, as described in Chapter 4, is usually more convenient than starting them from the File Manager. If, however, you have a program you use infrequently, you may not want to add it to the Program Manager. In that case, you can start the program from the File Manager.

Starting a Program

With the mouse, you can easily start a program from the File Manager by opening the directory window containing the program's file and double-clicking on the program's file name.

With the keyboard, you can start a program almost as easily. Just open the directory window containing the program's file, select the file, and press Enter. Or select the file, choose the **F**ile menu, and select the **O**pen command.

You can identify file names of programs because the names end with the extensions EXE or COM. Some programs are also started by files that end with the extensions BAT or PIF. These are described more fully in Chapter 13, "Running Non-Windows Programs."

Choosing a document file can also start a program, if the extension on the document's file name has been associated with the program. This association between a document file and a program tells Windows which documents and programs belong together.

To start a document file and a program together, choose the document file just as you would choose a program file. Double-click on the file name, or select it and press Enter. Windows will start the program first and then open the document file. This technique works only when the document file and program have been associated, as the next section explains.

To start a program with a document or with special arguments that modify how the program runs, choose the File menu and select the **R**un command. In the Command Line text box, type the directory path and full program name. Press the space bar once and then type the name of any special arguments required to start the program. Choose OK or press Enter.

Starting Programs with Associated Documents

Windows can start a program when you choose one of the program's documents. When Windows programs are installed, Windows is informed of which programs to start when specific documents are chosen. This relation between documents and their programs is called *association*. You can also associate Windows and non-Windows documents after programs have been installed.

Association is accomplished when you tell Windows which document file extensions belong to a specific program. When you choose a document file, Windows examines the file extension and starts the associated program.

Following are some programs and their common document file extensions:

Microsoft Excel	XLS, XLC, XLM
Word for Windows	DOC, DOT
Aldus PageMaker	PM3
Lotus 1-2-3	WKS, WK1

Some programs, such as WordPerfect, do not use a standard file extension for document files. However, if you consistently add your own file extension for WordPerfect documents, you can associate your document files with WordPerfect.

5

122

To associate a document file with a specific program, follow these steps:

1. Activate the directory window containing the type of document file you want associated.

2. Select a file name with the file extension you want associated.

3. Choose the **F**ile menu and select the **A**ssociate command.

4. When the Associate dialog box appears, type the program's file name in the text box. If the program is in a different directory from the one containing the document file, include the disk drive and the full directory path name.

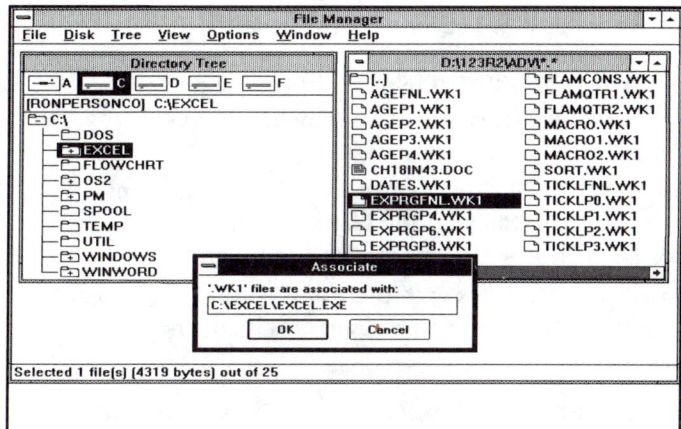

Some Windows programs automatically translate or convert data documents from other programs. Here, Lotus 1-2-3 files are being associated with the Excel program located in C:\EXCEL.

From this point on, double-clicking or choosing a Lotus 1-2-3 spreadsheet starts Excel, converts the sheet into an Excel worksheet and chart, and loads them into Excel. (You should not have to do this process for Windows programs. Correctly installed Windows programs automatically associate with their usual documents.)

5. Choose OK or press ⏎Enter

Note: Some non-Windows programs may not start directly from an associated document file or if they do start, they may not run in the best Windows configuration. In these cases, refer to Chapter 13, "Running Non-Windows Programs," for information on creating a PIF file that tells Windows how best to run the non-Windows program. If you have to create a PIF file, in step 4 of the preceding procedure, use the PIF file name (instead of the program file name) to start the program.

Summary

The File Manager can help you sleep better at night. Having backup copies of your important document files stored in a location separate from your computer has a very calming effect.

The File Manager is also an excellent tool for organizing your hard disk. Use the File Manager to keep directories and files organized just as you would organize a filing system. And don't let old and unused files overwhelm you. They waste space, slow down performance, and are hard to get rid of when you don't remember what they contain.

The following important points were covered in this chapter:

- Only one Directory Tree window appears in the File Manager.
- You can open multiple directory windows to help you in copying, moving, or comparing directory contents.
- Using the mouse with the File Manager makes file management easy. Just click or use Ctrl+Click on the files you want to copy, move, or delete. Then choose the appropriate command.
- You can associate document files with programs so that choosing a document automatically starts the program and loads the document.

If you haven't learned about the Program Manager yet, return to Chapter 4, "Grouping Programs and Documents," and learn how the Program Manager can save you time in starting programs and documents you use frequently.

If you'd like to learn how to customize Windows to use the desktop background and colors you want, to add new printers, and to change mouse speed, move to the next chapter, "Customizing Your Work Area."

If you want to begin using Windows with the Windows and non-Windows programs you have used in the past, turn to Chapter 13, "Running Non-Windows Programs," and to Chapter 14, "Integrating Programs."

Customizing Your Work Area

With the Control Panel, you can customize Windows in many ways to suit your needs. For example, you can add printers, change window colors or background colors, and add patterns and pictures to the desktop.

Key Terms in This Chapter

Color scheme	A predefined set of colors for Windows backgrounds, title bars, edges, and other elements
Wallpaper	The bit-map (BMP) drawing used as a backdrop behind windows on the desktop
Printer driver	The software that enables Windows to use special features in your printer
Printer port	A physical connection point (LPT1, LPT2, LPT1.OS2, or LPT2.OS2) where most printers are connected
Communication port	A physical connection point (COM1 or COM2) where modems and some printers are connected

Operating the Control Panel

The Control Panel is a program item icon within the Main group window of the Program Manager. The tools contained in the Control Panel enable you to customize many features in Windows.

To open the Control Panel, you first open the Program Manager and then activate the Main group window.

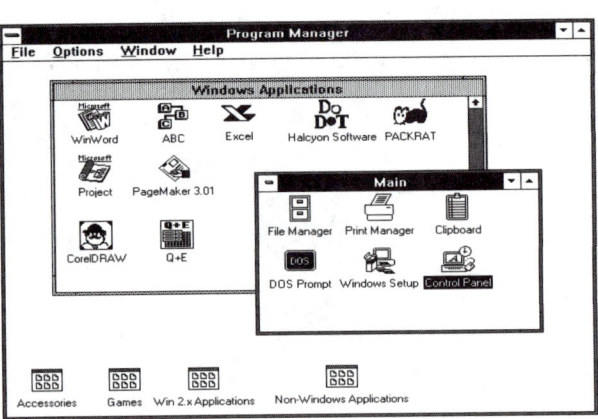

126

You then double-click on the Control Panel icon, or select it with the arrow keys and press Enter.

Each icon within the Control Panel window represents a different Windows feature you can customize.

A Network icon and a 386 Enhanced icon are displayed only when you are connected to a network or are running in 386-enhanced mode.

Table 6.1 lists the Control Panel's tools and describes how they are used.

Table 6.1
Tools in the Control Panel

Tool	Description
Color	Changes the colors in the desktop and parts of windows.
Fonts	Adds or removes printer or screen fonts.
Ports	Defines and connects your printer or communication ports.
Mouse	Adjusts mouse speed and left or right button control.
Desktop	Changes the patterns or pictures used as the desktop background.
Network	Controls how you connect with your network. (This icon is visible only if you are correctly connected to a network.)
Printers	Adds or removes printers.
International	Changes displays for different languages, dates, times, and currencies.

127

Table 6.1—(continued)

Tool	*Description*
Keyboard	Changes the keyboard's rate of repeating.
Date/Time	Resets the computer's date and time.
Sound	Turns the warning beep on or off.
386 Enhanced	Indicates how programs share the power when Windows is in 386-enhanced mode. (This icon appears only when you are running in 386-enhanced mode.)

You start one of these customizing tools by double-clicking on its icon, or by pressing the arrow keys to select the icon and then pressing Enter.

This chapter discusses all the tools listed in table 6.1 except Fonts and 386 Enhanced. The Fonts tool is an advanced topic covered in the Que book *Using Microsoft Windows 3*, 2nd Edition. The 386 Enhanced tool is discussed in Chapter 13, "Running Non-Windows Programs."

Customizing Windows with Color

You can customize the color schemes that define colors for window elements. The colors you use can make working with Windows programs more enjoyable than working with monochrome non-Windows programs.

Using Existing Color Schemes

Windows comes with a list of predefined color schemes. You can use them or create your own. To select from one of the predefined color schemes, follow these steps:

1. Choose the Color icon from the Control Panel.

128

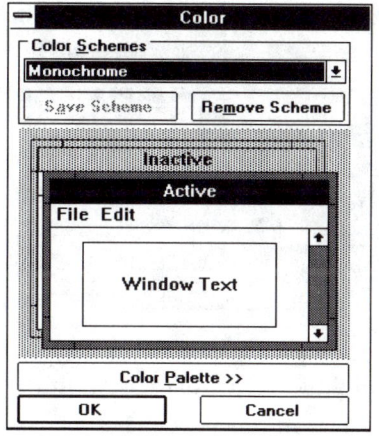

The Color dialog
box appears.

2. Click on the down arrow at the right side of the Color **S**chemes drop-down list box.

3. Select a named color scheme from the list. The demonstration window shows how windows will appear with these colors.

4. Select a different color scheme or choose OK.

Creating New Color Schemes

You can apply your own colors to different parts of windows. To choose colors, follow these steps:

1. Open the Control Panel and choose the Color icon.

2. Select the Color **S**chemes list and then select the color scheme that most closely matches the colors you want.

3. Choose the Color **P**alette >> button.

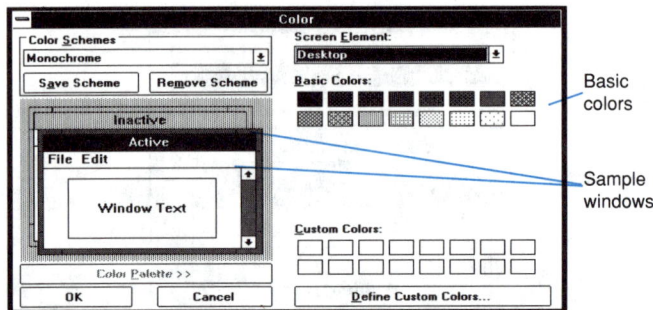

The right side of the Color dialog box expands to show the palette of **Basic Colors**.

4. Click on the part of the sample window that you want to change.

   Or select from the Screen Element drop-down list the part of the window that you want to change.

5. Click on the color you want from the **Basic Colors** palette.

   Or press Tab to move to the **Basic Colors** palette, press the appropriate arrow key to move to the color you want, and then press the space bar to select the color.

   The sample window changes to the new color you selected.

6. Repeat steps 4 and 5 until the sample windows show the colors you want in your programs.

   Or if you want to save the color scheme, choose the **Save Scheme** button and type a name that will appear in the Color **Schemes** box.

   Or choose Cancel if you do not want to use the colors.

Note: Windows programs use, as standards, a solid title bar for an active window and a shaded title bar for an inactive program.

If you do not save your custom color scheme, you will not be able to return to that color scheme should you change schemes later.

To remove a color scheme, select it from the Color Schemes drop-down list box, choose the Re**m**ove Scheme button, and then choose the **Yes** button for confirmation.

Blending Your Own Colors

If you are feeling artistic, you can create your own palette of colors to use instead of the basic colors offered. You can put up to 16 custom-blended colors into the **Custom Colors** palette. Once they are there, you can use them to color window elements as you would use the **Basic Colors** palette.

To blend your own colors, follow these steps:

1. Open the Control Panel and choose the Color icon.
2. Choose the Color **Palette** >> button to expand the Color dialog box.
3. Choose the **Define Custom Colors** button.

    The Custom Color Selector window is displayed on top of the Color dialog box.

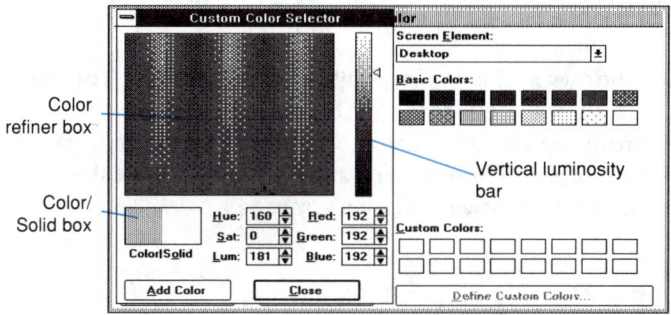

Color refiner box

Color/ Solid box

Vertical luminosity bar

You can blend your own colors in this window and add them to the Custom Colors palette in the Color dialog box.

4. To select the **Custom Colors** box that you want to hold your custom color, click on that **Custom Colors** box.

    Or press Alt + C, use the arrow keys to move to the box to hold your custom color, and then press the space bar.

5. Choose the color you want from the Custom Color Selector window by clicking the pointer on that color in the Color Refiner box. Adjust the luminosity (brightness) by dragging the arrowhead up or down along the side of the vertical luminosity bar.

    Or select a **Red**, **Green**, or **Blue** box and adjust its value by typing a new number. Select a **Hue**, **Saturation**, or **Luminosity** and adjust its value by typing a new number. The Color/**Solid** box shows how the color will appear in a large area.

6. If you want a solid color, select **S**olid by double-clicking on the solid side of the Color/**S**olid box or by pressing Alt + O.

7. Choose the **A**dd Color button to add the color to the box you selected in the **C**ustom Colors palette.

8. Return to step 4 if you want to add more colors to the palette.

   Or choose the **C**lose button to close the Custom Color Selector window.

Use the **C**ustom Colors palette to select new colors for window elements in the same way that you choose them with the **B**asic Colors palette.

Customizing the Desktop

In addition to changing the colors used in windows, you can change the pattern or picture used in the desktop behind windows.

The desktop behind windows and icons can have a color, selected from the Color dialog box; a pattern, selected from the Desktop dialog box; or a picture, selected also from the Desktop dialog box. A picture that covers the desktop is known as *wallpaper*. (Even when wallpaper is on the desktop, the desktop color and pattern affect how icon titles appear.)

Customizing the Background Pattern

In this section, you learn how to put a pattern over the color you choose for the desktop. Windows comes with predefined patterns you can select, or you can create your own. The color of the pattern is the same as the color for window text, which you define in the Color dialog box.

To choose an existing desktop pattern, follow these steps:

1. Choose the Desktop icon from the Control Panel.

132

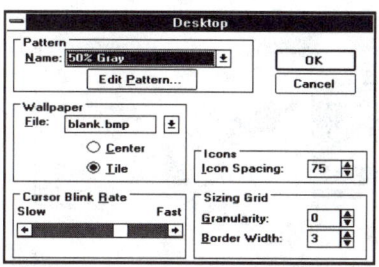

The Desktop dialog box appears.

2. Select the Pattern **Name** drop-down list and then select a pattern from the list.

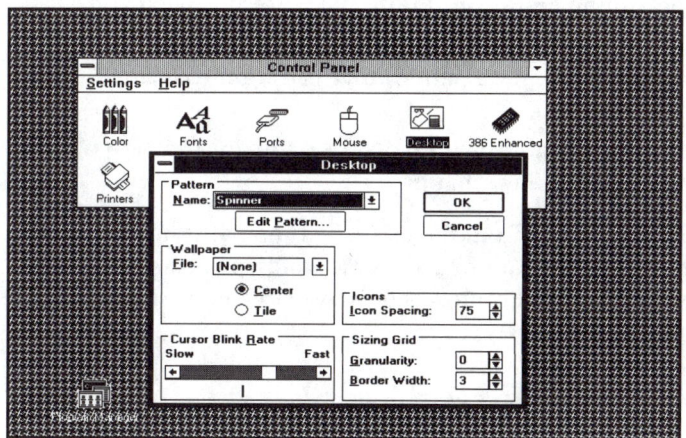

Many predefined background patterns are available, such as the Spinner pattern shown here.

3. Choose OK to add the pattern to the desktop.

You must use a mouse to edit or create new patterns. To edit an existing pattern or create a new pattern, follow these steps:

1. Choose the Desktop icon.
2. Choose the Edit **P**attern button.

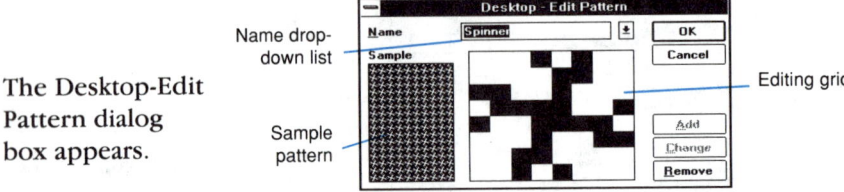

Name drop-down list

The Desktop-Edit Pattern dialog box appears.

Sample pattern

Editing grid

3. Select the **Name** drop-down list box and then select a name from the list or type a new name.

4. Click in the editing grid where you want to reverse a dot in the pattern. Watch the Sample area to see the overall effect.

5. Continue to click in the editing grid until the pattern is what you want.

6. If you started with a predefined pattern that you want to change, choose the **Change** button.

   Or if you created a new pattern and typed its name in step 3, choose the **Add** button to save that pattern.

To remove an unwanted pattern from the list, select the pattern from the list and choose the **Remove** button. Confirm the deletion by choosing the **Yes** button that appears. The **Remove** button is only available immediately after you select a new pattern name.

Displaying Graphics as a Desktop Background

You can customize the desktop so that it is a picture or graphic. For the desktop wallpaper, you can use the drawings that come with Windows, create your own drawings with Windows Paintbrush, or scan photographs with a scanner.

Wallpaper uses files stored in bit-map format, with a BMP extension. To be used as wallpaper, these files must be stored in the Windows directory. You can edit existing BMP files or create new ones with Windows Paintbrush. Save in the Windows directory the BMP file that you want to use as a wallpaper.

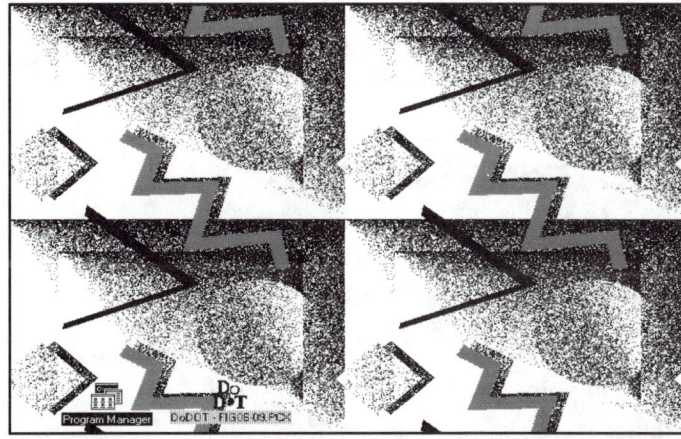

The PARTY.BMP file produces a festive desktop background.

The CHESS.BMP file offers another desktop background.

Note: Using wallpaper for a desktop background takes up memory. If your computer is low on memory, do not use a wallpaper desktop.

To display an existing BMP file as the desktop background, follow these steps:

1. Choose the Desktop icon from the Control Panel.

2. Select the Wallpaper **F**ile drop-down list box and then select a BMP file from the list.

3. Select **C**enter to center the image in the desktop, or **T**ile to fill the desktop with the image. **T**ile uses multiple images if necessary.

4. Choose OK.

If you are running in standard or 386-enhanced mode, you will see the new desktop background immediately. If you are in real mode, you must restart Windows to see the new desktop background.

Adjusting the Insertion Point's Blink Rate

If the insertion point blinks at a rate that annoys you, you can change it by choosing the Desktop icon and selecting the Cursor Blink **R**ate box. Drag the box in the scroll bar or press the right- or left-arrow keys to adjust the rate. Watch the sample insertion point for the blink rate you prefer.

Resetting the Date/Time

Choose the Date/Time icon from the Control Panel to reset the date or time in your computer.

When you choose the Date/Time icon, the Date & Time dialog box appears.

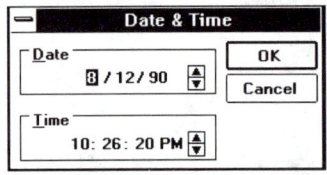

Select either the **D**ate or the **T**ime option. Click on the up or down arrows to scroll rapidly to the date or time you want. Or with the keyboard, tab to the date or time box and then type the new number. Choose OK or press Enter to reset the date and time.

Changing Keyboard Speed

You can change the rate that repeat characters are typed by choosing the Keyboard icon from the Control Panel.

6

136

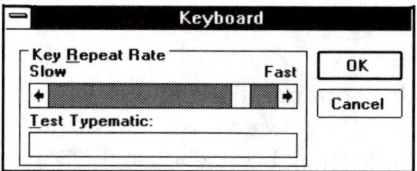

When you choose the Keyboard icon, the Keyboard dialog box appears.

Select the Key **Repeat** Rate scroll bar and click on the left or right arrows or press the left- or right-arrow keys to change the repeat rate. Test the repeat rate by selecting the **Test Typematic** box and holding down a letter key.

Changing the Mouse

To switch the mouse buttons or to speed up mouse reaction times, choose the Mouse icon to display the Mouse dialog box. To change the speed with which the pointer moves, select the **M**ouse Tracking Speed option. Then click on the left or right arrows or press the left- or right-arrow keys to change the pointer's speed.

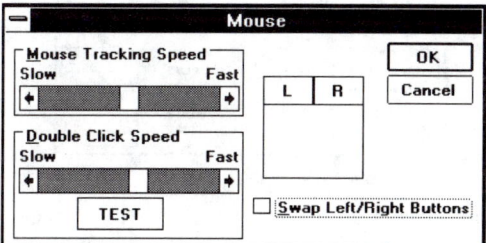

If you are left-handed, you may want to select the Swap Left/Right Buttons check box to switch the mouse buttons.

Press the left and right buttons and watch the test L and R to see the buttons' reactions.

If you want faster or slower double-click response rate, select the **Double** Click Speed scroll bar. Click on the left or right arrows or press the left- or right-arrow keys to change the response. Double-click in the TEST box to test the new rate.

137

Turning Sound On or Off

When you are tired of announcing your mistakes with a beep, or when you need to hide the fact that you're playing a game, you can turn off the computer's beep. To turn off the warning beep, choose the Sound icon, select or deselect the **Warning Beep** check box, and choose OK. This action disables all beeping for all applications used in Windows.

Customizing International Settings

Most Windows programs can switch between different international character sets, time and date displays, and numeric formatting. Use the International icon in the Control Panel to choose these settings.

The International
dialog box
changes date,
time, currency,
and numeric for-
mats for different
languages and
countries.

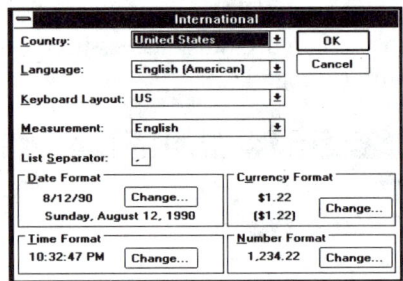

Make sure that you select the correct language as well as the correct country.

To set up Windows for one of the predefined country formats, languages, and measurement systems, follow these steps:

1. Choose the International icon from the Control Panel.

2. Select the **Country** drop-down list box and select a country from the list.

3. Select the **Language** drop-down list box and select the language you use. This selection can affect sorting in a program.

4. Select the **Keyboard Layout** drop-down list box and select the international keyboard style your keyboard uses. This selection enables you to use keyboard characters specific to your language.

6

5. Select the **Measurement** drop-down list box and select either English or Metric.

6. Select the List **S**eparator text box and type the character you want for separating lists. This selection is useful in programs such as Excel in which you might want to separate a list of arguments used in math functions.

7. Choose OK or press ↵Enter.

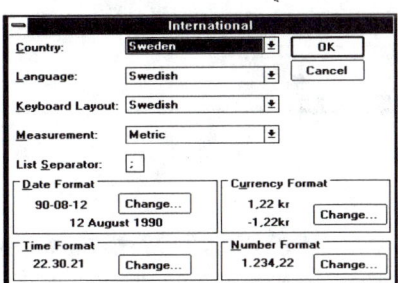

Watch the sample formats change in the Date, Time, Currency, and Number Format boxes.

6

If the number, currency, date, and time formats do not change to reflect what you want when you select a Country setting, you can change these formats manually to formats you define. This procedure is described in the Que book *Using Microsoft Windows 3*, 2nd Edition.

Adding and Setting Up Printers

With the Control Panel, you can add printers that were not installed initially with Windows. To do this, you may need your original Windows installation diskettes or the diskette from your printer's manufacturer that contains the Windows printer driver for your printer. (A printer driver tells Windows how to control your printer and use the printer's features.)

To install a new printer, follow the procedures in the next sections in the order in which the procedures appear.

Installing a New Printer

To install a new printer, follow these steps:

1. Choose the Printers icon.

The Printers dia-
log box appears.

2. Choose the **Add Printer >>** button.

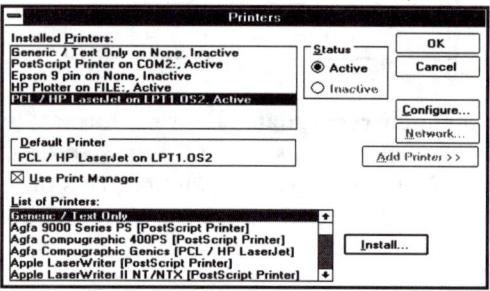

The bottom of
the Printers dia-
log box expands
to show you a list
of printer drivers
that came with
your Windows
installation
diskettes.

The printers listed in the **List of Printers** list box are those that all Windows programs work with.

3. Select the printer you want to install from the **List of Printers** box. If you do not see your printer listed, select an earlier model from the manufacturer's same family of printers. If you have a diskette from your printer's manufacturer containing the Windows driver for your printer, select `Unlisted Printer` at the bottom of the list.

4. Choose the **Install** button.

5. If you are installing a new driver that you have not used before or if you are updating an existing driver, Windows prompts you to insert into drive A the diskette containing the printer driver. This diskette is either one of your initial installation diskettes or a manufacturer's diskette with a new printer driver. If the printer driver files are located on another disk or directory, change the path name and choose OK.

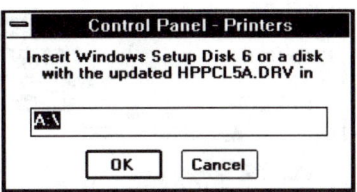

The Control
Panel-Printers
dialog box asks
for the location
of new printer
drivers.

6. If Windows needs additional screen fonts to use with this printer,
   you will be prompted to insert the diskette containing the fonts.
   Choose OK or press ⏎Enter after inserting the diskette(s).

7. Windows adds the printer driver to the Installed Printers list. The
   driver will be connected to None port, and the Status will be
   inactive.

8. Move to the following sections and continue the installation and
   configuration.

Note: If you don't have a printer driver for your printer, call Microsoft or the
printer's manufacturer to see whether one has been written. Or use a printer
driver for an earlier model of the same printer. Another alternative is to
select the Generic/Text Only printer from the List of Printers list box. This
selection enables most printers to print but will not use any enhanced
features, such as graphics, fonts, styles, or sizes.

Connecting and Setting Up the Printer

When your printer shows in the Installed Printers list, you need to connect
the printer to a printer port (physical connection). Once you have told
Windows which port the printer is connected to, you can set up the printer
for special features, such as font cartridges, paper size, bins, and printing
orientation.

To configure the printer for a port, follow these steps:

1. Choose the Printers icon if the Printers dialog box is not already
   open.

2. From the Installed Printers list box, select the printer you want to
   configure.

3. Choose the Configure button.

141

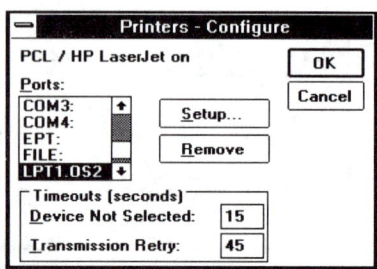

The Printers-
Configure dialog
box appears.

4. Select from the **Ports** list box the hardware port (the connection for the printer cable) to which the current printer is connected. (Most printers are connected to LPT1. If you are not sure, experiment with other ports or call your dealer or PC administrator.)

   Note: If your printer is on LPT1 or LPT2 but the printer does not work when you select either port from the **Ports** list, select instead LPT1.OS2 or LPT2.OS2 from the **Ports** list.

5. Select Timeout settings as defined by your printer manual or the README.TXT file for your printer. Read the file with Notepad. If there is no information for your printer, leave these settings as they are.

   Now that you have connected the printer, set it up for the special features available for that printer.

6. Choose the **S**etup button to display the printer-setup dialog box.

   Note: You can change the printer setup at a later time while you are in a Windows program by using the program's **File P**rinter Setup command.

Because each
printer has differ-
ent capabilities,
each printer-setup
dialog box is dif-
ferent. Here is the
setup dialog box
for the HP
LaserJet family of
printers.

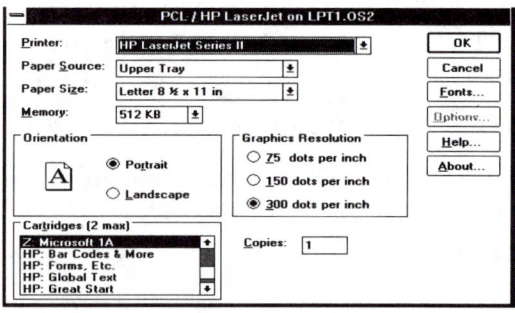

Be sure to select your printer model or a compatible model from the **P**rinter drop-down list. For laser printers, selecting the memory and font cartridges available is also important.

Pages printed vertically have a portrait orientation; pages printed sideways have a landscape orientation. Graphics resolution defines how finely graphics will print; a higher dots-per-inch setting is slower but better.

Note: If your printer will accept two font cartridges, you can select both at one time from the **C**artridges list by clicking on one cartridge, and then scrolling to the second one and holding down ⇧Shift as you click on the second cartridge.

7. Select the options you use most frequently for your printer; then choose OK. You will return to the Printers dialog box.

8. If you want to leave the printer inactive, choose OK. If you want to use the printer when you return to Windows, follow the next procedure.

6

Selecting the Active and Default Printer

Windows can have multiple printers connected to the same port, but only one printer can be active at a time. To make a printer active or inactive, follow these steps:

1. Choose the Printers icon if the Printers dialog box is not displayed.

2. From the Installed **P**rinters list, select the printer you want to activate.

3. Select **S**tatus and then select the Active or Inactive option.

4. Choose OK.

Note: Two printers cannot be active and connected to the same port at the same time. When you configure the second printer on the port, it will be inactive. Use the **S**tatus box to change the second printer's status to Active. The other printer on this same port will automatically change to Inactive.

At this point, you can start your Windows programs and print to the newly installed printer. Before using the program or printing with it, use the program's **F**ile **P**rinter Setup dialog box to confirm that the new printer is active and set up correctly.

143

The default printer is the printer that Windows assumes you normally use. To select the default printer, display the Printers dialog box and double-click on the printer in the Installed Printers list, or select the printer and press Alt+D. The printer must be active when you make it the default.

Connecting to and Disconnecting from a Network Printer

If you are connected to a network printer, you can print from Windows to that printer. To connect to a network printer, follow these steps:

1. Choose the Printers icon if the Printers dialog box is not already displayed.
2. Choose the Network button. This button is gray if you are not connected to a network printer.
3. Choose the printer port from the Port drop-down list box in the Printers-Network Connections dialog box.
4. In the Path text box, type the path to the printer or choose the Browse button to look for printers. Select a printer from the Resources box and then choose OK.
5. Type a password if requested.
6. Choose Connect to link with the network printer.

Some networks do not allow browsing; in that case, the Browse button is gray.

To disconnect from the network printer, follow this same procedure, selecting the printer from the Printers-Network Connections dialog box and choosing the Disconnect button.

Removing a Printer

Removing a printer saves only a small amount of disk space, but unclutters the printer selection and setup dialog boxes. To remove a printer, choose the Printers icon from the Control Panel. When the Printers dialog box appears, select the printer from the Installed Printers list and choose the Configure button. Choose the Remove button from the Printers-Configure dialog box that appears. You are then asked to confirm that you want to remove the printer driver.

6

Note: Some printer drivers are used by more than one printer from the same family. For example, all the Hewlett-Packard LaserJets use the same driver, and all the PostScript printers use the same driver. Deleting the driver for one printer in the family may remove the driver used by a printer from the same family. Some families of printers include printers from more than one manufacturer.

Turning Print Manager On or Off

If you do not want to use the Print Manager, you can print only one document at a time, yet printing may be faster. The Print Manager is usually turned off for printing to a network printer. To turn off the Print Manager, choose the Printers icon from the Control Panel and deselect the Use Print Manager check box.

Setting Up Communication Ports and Printer Ports

6

Serial ports are hardware connections (in a computer) to which you connect a few types of printers and all modems. If you do not have a serial printer or a modem, you do not need to set up these ports.

To set up a serial port, follow these steps:

1. Choose the Ports icon from the Control Panel.

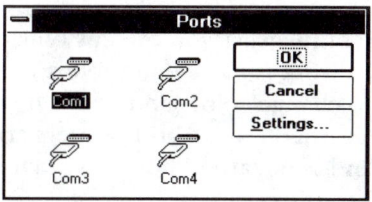

Windows 3 can have up to four communication ports for modems or serial printers.

2. Select the COM port that you want to set up.
3. Choose the **Settings** button.

145

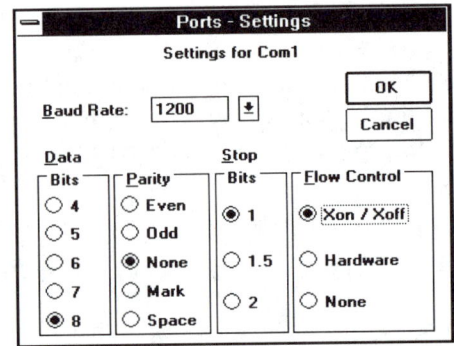

The Ports-
Settings dialog
box appears.

4. Select the COM settings you need for your modem (telephone connection) or serial printer. See your modem or printer manual or contact your modem or printer manufacturer or dealer for these settings:

Setting	Description
Baud Rate	Determines the speed at which information is sent
Data Bits	Determines the amount of information sent
Parity	Determines the type of error checking
Stop Bits	Determines how data packets are marked
Flow Control	Determines how the computer and the device signal each other

Summary

This chapter showed you some of the ways you can customize Windows and Windows programs so that your work is more enjoyable and more productive. You learned how to change colors and desktop backgrounds to personalize your screens. You learned how to add printers and set them up for best use of their features. And you learned how to switch mouse buttons and adjust mouse or keyboard sensitivity.

Some important points covered in this chapter are these:

■ You can customize the appearance of Windows and some operating characteristics to fit your style of work.

6

■ You customize the color, pattern, or graphics background of your windows with the Color and Desktop tools from the Control Panel.

■ You adjust your mouse and keyboard operation with the Mouse and Keyboard tools from the Control Panel.

■ The Printers tool enables you to install, configure, and set up new printers. Printers or modems connected to a COM port need to have the port configured with the Ports tool. You can change printer setup within Windows programs through the use of the Printer Setup command on the File menu.

You are now ready to learn about some of the free programs included with Windows. These programs are described in Chapters 7 through 12. If you work with non-Windows programs, you will want to read Chapter 13's description of how to customize Windows to handle your non-Windows programs better.

6

Controlling
the Printer

7

Windows programs share more than a common graphical interface. They share printing resources also. Windows' Print Manager manages printing for all Windows programs, transferring information and instructions to your printer while you continue working.

In this chapter, you learn how to determine which print jobs are waiting in the printing queue and how to pause, remove, or change the order of print jobs.

Note: The Print Manager works only with programs designed for Windows. If you are running non-Windows (DOS) programs within Windows, they cannot use the Print Manager. A non-Windows program prints just as though it were not in Windows. Non-Windows programs cannot share the common printer drivers used by Windows programs. You therefore must complete the printer installation and setup required for each non-Windows program.

Key Terms in This Chapter

Queue   A list of print jobs waiting to be printed.

Print spooler A software program that stores print jobs on a *spool*
                 (the hard disk) so that they can be printed in order at a
                 later time or while other programs continue to work.
                 The Print Manager is a print spooler.

Understanding How Windows Manages Printing

When you issue a print command for a Windows program to print, the Print
Manager springs into action, doing two things. First, the Print Manager sends
your file to a buffer, or *queue*, where files to be printed are lined up (or
queued) for printing. Second, the files are routed, in the order received, to
your printer.

If your program
is in a window so
that you can see
program icons at
the bottom of the
screen, you will
see the Print
Manager icon.

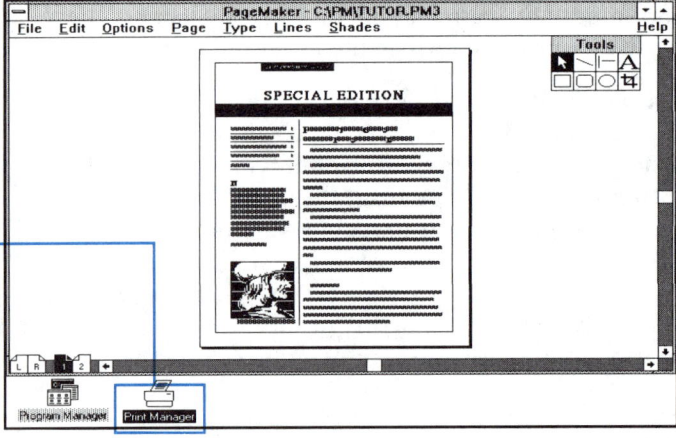

There is an important reason for Windows to give the Print Manager control
over your printing, instead of letting your program control printing (as
happens with non-Windows programs). You can continue working in your

Windows program while the Print Manager handles your print job from the program you're using or from another Windows program.

Controlling Print Jobs

The Print Manager is located in the Main group window of the Program Manager. When you print from a Windows program, the Print Manager automatically starts, appearing as an icon at the bottom of the desktop. If you are not printing, you can start the Print Manager from the Main group as you would any program in a group window.

If you want to restore the Print Manager icon into a window so that you can view or control your print jobs, just double-click on the icon. Or press Alt+Tab until the icon is selected and then release both keys.

Viewing the Order of Print Jobs

The Print Manager window shows the status of your print queue. You can see which printer or printers are active, which is printing, which file is being printed, what other files are in queue for printing, and optionally, the file's size and the time and date you sent the file to the printer.

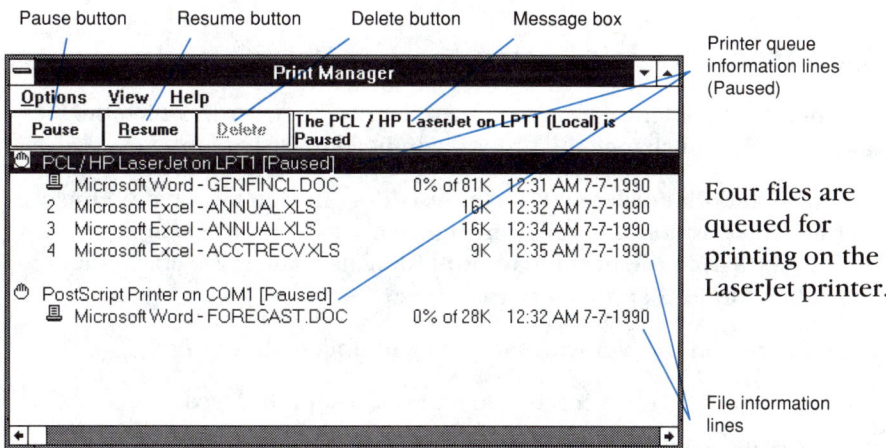

Pause button   Resume button   Delete button   Message box

Printer queue information lines (Paused)

Four files are queued for printing on the LaserJet printer.

File information lines

7

Table 7.1 describes the items in the Print Manager window.

Table 7.1
The Print Manager Window

Item	Description
Pause button	Temporarily stops a printer from printing.
Resume button	Restarts printing after pausing.
Delete button	Removes a file from the print queue.
Message box	Provides information about the print job.
Printer queue information lines	Tell you the printer name, printer port, and printer status. (If you have more than one printer connected to your computer, you'll have a printer queue information line for each printer.)
File information lines	Show you the file's position in the queue, the title of the print job, and, optionally, the file size (as well as the percent of the file that has already printed), and the time and date you sent the file to the printer. When a print job is complete, its file information line disappears.

Changing the Print Order

The number at the left of each file line tells you the order in which the files will print. You can change the order if you need to rush a job.

To change the print order with the mouse, drag the file information line up or down to reposition it in the Print Manager window. For example, to move file 4 up so that it's the next file to print, drag its printer line above the printer line for file 2 and then release.

To change the print order with the keyboard, follow these steps:

1. Press ↑ or ↓ to select the file line you want reordered.
2. Press and hold down Ctrl.
3. Press ↑ or ↓ to move the file to its new position in the queue.
4. Release Ctrl and the arrow key.

152

Pausing or Resuming Printing

You may want to pause the Print Manager temporarily to fix a printer problem or to give more computer power to a program you are operating. When the printer is paused, the word Paused appears in brackets at the end of the printer queue information line.

To pause printing, follow these steps:

1. Select the printer queue information line for the printer you want to pause. (Do not select the file information line.)
2. Choose the **P**ause button or press [Alt]+[P].

To resume printing after you have paused, follow these steps:

1. Select the printer queue information line that was paused. (Again, do not select the file information line.)
2. Choose the **R**esume button or press [Alt]+[R].

Deleting a Print Job

If you want to cancel a specific print job, you can delete a file information line from the print queue. If you want to cancel all printing, exit the Print Manager.

To delete a print job from the print queue, follow these steps:

1. Select the file information line of the job you want to delete.
2. Choose the **D**elete button or press [Alt]+[D].

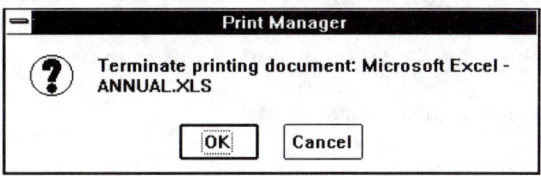

A Print Manager dialog box appears, asking you to confirm the deletion.

3. Choose OK or press [↵Enter] to confirm that you want the print job deleted. Or choose Cancel or press [Esc] to cancel the deletion request.

153

To cancel all printing, follow these steps:

1. Choose the **O**ptions menu and select the E**x**it command.

Another Print Manager dialog box appears, asking for confirmation.

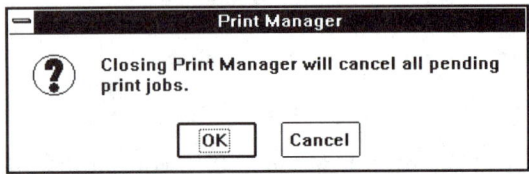

2. Choose the OK button or press ⏎Enter to confirm that you want to exit Print Manager and cancel all print jobs. Or choose Cancel or press Esc to cancel the request.

Note: If you delete a file that is currently being printed, especially if the file contains graphics, you may need to reset your printer to clear its print buffer. You can reset the printer by turning it off and then back on (or by selecting the reset option, if your printer has one). Laser printers often need to be reset after you delete a print job.

Changing Printer or Program Performance

When the Print Manager prints while programs are running, your computer must divide the amount of processing power it has between the Print Manager and the programs. You can choose which has greater priority—and therefore gets a greater share of computer power. If you give the Print Manager *high* priority, jobs print faster, but your programs may slow down. If you give the Print Manager *low* priority, jobs print slower, but your programs operate faster. If you give the Print Manager *medium* priority (which is Windows' automatic choice), your computer shares its computing power equally between the Print Manager and other programs.

To change the printer priority, follow these steps:

1. Choose the **O**ptions menu.
2. Select one of the following options:

Option	*Description*
Low Priority	Prints slower but increases program speed
Medium Priority	Splits computer power evenly
High Priority	Prints faster but decreases program speed

154

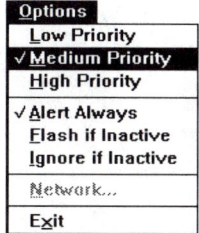

A check mark appears to the left of the printer priority option you select from the **Options** menu.

The selection remains in effect—for all printing—until you change it again.

Note: Holding all your print jobs and doing them at one time, after you've finished working, enables your computer to devote all its power to the program you are using. If you want to do all your printing at one time (while you're not continuing to work), open the Print Manager from the Main group. Select and pause your printer and then issue all the **File Print** commands. When you are ready to print, check to make sure that the printer has enough paper, activate the Print Manager, select your printer, and choose the **Resume** button.

Displaying Print Manager Alert Messages

Occasionally, the printer needs your attention. For example, the printer may run out of paper. You can control whether the Print Manager *always* alerts you, whether the Print Manager icon *flashes* to alert you, or whether the Print Manager icon does nothing when your printer needs attention.

To specify how the Print Manager handles alert messages, follow these steps:

1. Choose the **Options** menu.
2. Select one of the following options:

Option	Description
Alert Always	Always alerts you with a message box
Flash if Inactive	Beeps and flashes when the Print Manager is inactive
Ignore if Inactive	Ignores the printer program if the Print Manager is inactive

7

155

If you choose the **Flash if Inactive** option, the Print Manager icon flashes when there is a problem. To see what the problem is, restore the Print Manager icon into a window.

Note: If you choose the **Ignore if Inactive** option, you may miss an important message.

Displaying File Size and Print Time and Date

You have the option of displaying each file's size, as well as the time and date you sent the file to the printer. To display this information, follow these steps:

1. Choose the **View** command.
2. Select one of the following options:

Option	Description
Time/Date Sent	Displays the time and date
Print File Size	Displays the size of the file

The selected file information line shows that zero percent of an 81K file has been printed, as well as the time and date of printing.

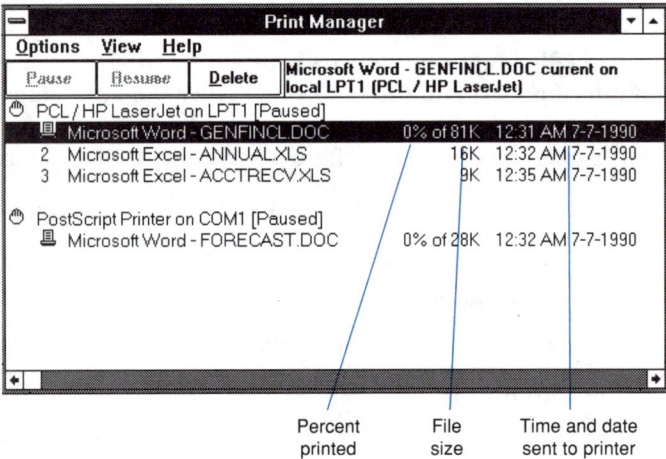

Percent printed   File size   Time and date sent to printer

The percent of the file printed shows to the left of the file size, letting you know how close a print job is to being complete.

7

Closing the Print Manager Window

Usually when you print, the Print Manager appears as an icon at the bottom of the screen. When all print jobs are finished, the Print Manager shuts itself down. However, if the Print Manager is in a window, you must exit the Print Manager manually to close it when it is finished printing.

Note: If you exit the Print Manager while print jobs remain, they will be canceled. To reduce the Print Manager window to an icon—and not lose print jobs—minimize the window by clicking on the down arrow at the top right of the window. Or press Alt, space bar to display the program Control menu, and then select the Minimize command. When the window is minimized to an icon, the Print Manager will shut itself down automatically when printing is completed.

To exit the Print Manager so that it disappears from the screen, choose the **O**ptions menu and select the E**x**it command.

Printing on a Network

7

If you share a printer with other people on a local area network, printing is a little different from the previous procedures. You will have additional Print Manager options, such as viewing the print queue for the entire network and updating the network queue status. You also have the option of bypassing the Print Manager altogether, which is sometimes a faster way to print on a network.

Viewing Network Print Jobs

When you print to a network printer, the Print Manager lists the files you have sent to the printer. But by choosing the **S**elected Net Queue command, you can see all the files that everyone on the network has sent to the same printer. Seeing this list will help give you an idea of how long it will be before the printer gets to your job.

To view a network print queue, follow these steps:

1. Print your file and open the Print Manager window.
2. Select the printer queue information line.

157

3. Choose the **View** menu and select the **Selected Net Queue** command. The Print Manager displays a list of all files queued for the printer.

4. Select **Close** to close the dialog box.

Viewing Other Printer Queues on a Network

If you have access to a number of printers on a network, you can view queues for any of the printers before deciding which one to use. To view network queues for printers you are not connected to, follow these steps:

1. Open the Print Manager window.

2. Choose the **View** menu and select the **Other Net Queue** command. The Other Net Queue dialog box appears.

3. In the **Network Queue** box, type the network path name for the network queue you want to view.

4. Choose the **View** button.

5. Type the name of another queue or choose the **Close** button.

Note: Before you can print to any printer on the network, you must be connected to the printer. Chapter 6, "Customizing Your Work Area," describes how to use the Control Panel to connect to a network printer.

Updating Network Queue Status

The Print Manager, by default, tracks and periodically updates the status of a network queue. If you prefer, you can turn off network queue updating so that you can update the status manually.

To turn off the automatic network status updating, follow these steps:

1. Open the Print Manager window.

2. Choose the **Options** menu and select the **Network** command.

3. Deselect the Update Network Display check box so that no check appears inside it.

4. Choose OK or press ⏎Enter.

To update the network queue status manually, choose the **View** menu and select the Update Net Queues command.

158

Printing Directly to a Network

In most cases, printing is faster when you bypass the Print Manager and print files on a network directly. Printing on the network is therefore the Print Manager's default choice. Because networks differ, however, experiment with printing times on your own network to find out whether printing directly to the network printer is faster than using the Print Manager.

To print directly to a network printer, follow these steps:

1. Open the Print Manager window.
2. Choose the **O**ptions menu and select the **N**etwork command.
3. Select the **P**rint Net Jobs Direct check box.
4. Choose OK or press `⏎Enter` .

When you are printing directly to network printers or network print spoolers, no Print Manager icon appears at the bottom of the Windows desktop.

Handling Printing Problems

7

Sometimes things go wrong when you try to print. If they do, read through the following checklist. The solution to a printing problem may be much simpler than you expect. Many printer difficulties arise from installation and setup errors. Usually, these can be corrected by reconnecting the printer with the Printers program in the Control Panel, described in Chapter 6, "Customizing Your Work Area."

The printer prints with fonts and sizes different from those shown on-screen.

In some Windows programs, you can use fonts and character sizes on-screen that are not available with the printer you select. You therefore can create a document for printing on someone else's printer. But in most cases you will want to ensure that the fonts and sizes you use on-screen match those your printer can print. To set this up, check your program's documentation for a printer fonts option. In Excel, for example, choose the Forma**t** menu and select the **F**onts command. When the Fonts dialog box appears, choose the Fonts >> button and select the **P**rinter Fonts check box. In Word for Windows, choose the **V**iew menu, select the P**r**eferences command, and then select the **D**isplay as Printed check box. Make sure that you have the correct printer selected when you are creating the document.

The printer prints garbled characters, or you get a "printer not available" error.

Check that the printer is plugged in and turned on. Check also that all cables are securely connected.

Nothing happens when you try to print.

Check the File Printer Setup command to make sure that you have the correct printer selected. If the printer does not appear on the list, you need to install that printer's driver so that Windows will know how to work with it. Use the Printers program in the Control Panel, described in Chapter 6, to install the printer driver for your printer.

Summary

In this chapter, you learned how the Print Manager manages printers and print jobs while you continue working in other Windows programs. With the Print Manager, you can control the order in which jobs print, pause a printer, and delete specific print jobs. You can even determine how much computer power to devote to printing and to the programs that are running.

As long as you operate with the Print Manager on, you can use it to control printing from Windows programs. This chapter covered the following important points:

- You view the order of print jobs by choosing the Print Manager icon at the bottom of the desktop. The order in which documents print is shown by the number on the left of the lists.

- You pause or resume printing from a specific printer by selecting the printer queue information line for the printer you want to pause or resume, and then clicking on the Pause or Resume button (or pressing Alt+P or Alt+R).

- You delete a print job by selecting the file information line for the job you want to delete, and then clicking on the Delete button (or pressing Alt+D).

Now that you are familiar with the Print Manager, you should become familiar with your own Windows programs or the free programs that came with Windows, such as Windows Write or Windows Paintbrush. Experiment with printing multiple documents from various programs and see how the Print Manager can make your work easier.

Using the Clipboard To Copy and Paste

A special advantage you have with Windows is that you can run multiple programs and copy information easily between them. New opportunities are therefore available to you. For example, you can copy budgets out of a spreadsheet, switch to your word processor, and paste the budgets into a report. Or you can copy an outline from a word processor and paste the outline into a slide-show presentation program. No longer do you need to waste time or introduce errors by retyping.

An important part of the copy-and-paste process is the Clipboard. Like an artist's clipboard, the Clipboard is a Windows program that holds copied information so that it can be pasted.

Key Terms in This Chapter

Copy   An operation that stores in the Clipboard a duplicate of selected text or graphics from a program until the information can be pasted elsewhere.

Paste   An operation that inserts the information in the Clipboard into the active program at the current insertion point or cursor.

Cut   An operation that removes selected text or graphics from a program and stores the text or graphics in the Clipboard until the information can be pasted elsewhere.

Clipboard   An area of memory reserved to hold text or graphics that you cut or copy.

Copying and Pasting in Windows Programs

8

Nearly all Windows programs contain the commands Cut, Copy, and Paste on the Edit menu. These commands enable you to cut or copy information you have selected in one Windows program and to paste the information into another program.

Because copying information between programs is fairly new, you may not think of many ways to use the feature at first. But as you work more with multiple programs, you will find that copying and pasting between programs saves you time, eliminates typing errors, and gives you the chance to use programs together as though they were part of a single program.

Copying and Pasting Text

You can copy text from a Windows program and paste the text into any Windows or non-Windows program that will accept your keystrokes. To copy and paste text between Windows programs, follow these steps:

1. Select the text you want to copy.

2. Choose the **Edit** menu and select the **C**opy command.

3. Activate the other program by clicking on its window, or pressing Ctrl + Esc and selecting the program from the Task List.

4. Position the insertion point where you want the text to appear.

5. Choose the **Edit** menu and select the **P**aste command.

Copying and Pasting Graphics or Screen Images

Copying and pasting graphics between Windows programs uses a nearly identical process to copying and pasting text. To copy and paste graphics or screen images between Windows programs, follow these steps:

1. Select the graphics you want to copy. If you want to capture an image of the screen, skip to step 2.

8

Scissors and Pick tools   Selected graphical area

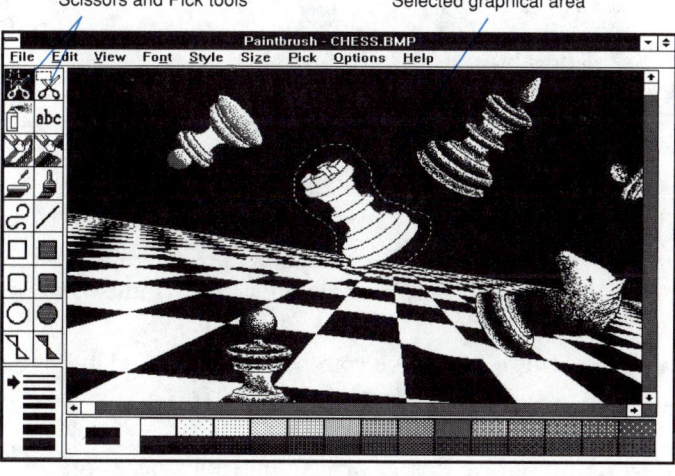

Graphics can be selected in different ways. Some programs, such as Windows Paintbrush, use a *lasso* or *scissors* to draw around the area being copied.

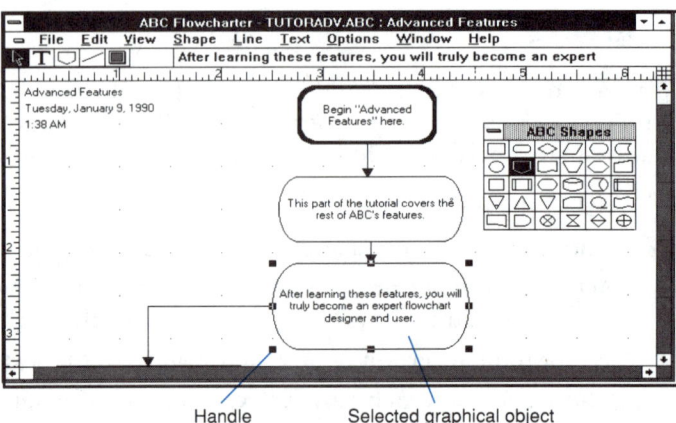

Other programs, such as ABC Flowcharter from Roykore, Inc., display *handles* to indicate that a graphical *object* has been se-lected.

Handle   Selected graphical object

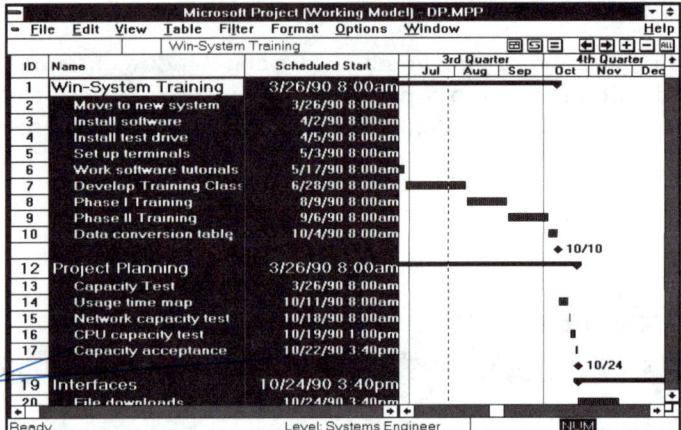

Some programs, such as Microsoft Project, display selected text in inverse video.

Selected text

8

2. Choose the **E**dit menu and select the **C**opy command.

   Or capture the entire screen as a graphics image by pressing the `PrtSc` key. Press `Alt` + `PrtSc` to capture only the active window as a graphics image. (You will not see a change on-screen.)

3. Switch to the program where the image is to be pasted by clicking on its window, or by pressing `Ctrl` + `Esc` and selecting the program from the Task List.

4. Position the insertion point or graphics placement tool where you want the text or graphics to appear.

5. Choose the **E**dit menu and select the **P**aste command.

164

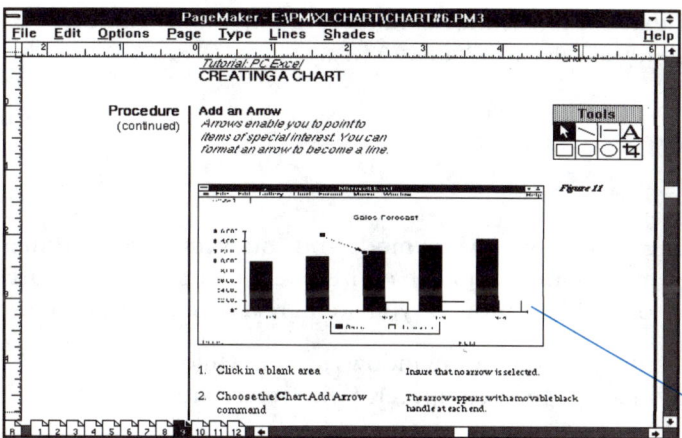

Pasting a screen image of a program such as Excel into PageMaker or Word for Windows is an excellent way of creating training materials or documentation.

Pasted image of window

Note: If the Print Screen key does not work on your keyboard, you may have an older keyboard. Try Alt+Print Screen or Shift+Print Screen as alternatives. (On some computers, the Print Screen key may be named PrtScrn or PrtSc and may be co-located with another key.)

The screen images you capture by pressing Print Screen or Alt+Print Screen have the same resolution as your display. CGA displays have the lowest resolution, EGA displays have higher resolution, and VGA displays have the highest resolution.

Note: You may find that after you copy a graphics image from one program, the **Paste** command in the other program is gray on the **Edit** menu. The two programs use different methods of drawing graphics, and you cannot copy and paste between them. Check the documentation in the first program for alternative methods of copying, such as holding down the Shift key while you choose the **Edit** menu. You may then see alternative copying commands.

Copying and Pasting in Non-Windows Programs

Non-Windows programs can use the copy-and-paste capability provided by Windows, but they have some limitations. For example, you cannot paste graphics into a non-Windows program. And if you are running Windows in real or standard mode, you can capture only an entire screenful of text, not a selected portion of text. For more information on running non-Windows programs under Windows, refer to Chapter 13.

Copying When Windows Is in Real or Standard Mode

If Windows is running in standard or real mode and you want to copy from a non-Windows program, you must copy the entire screenful of text. If you are using an 8088, 8086, or 80286 computer, you are in real or standard mode.

To copy the entire contents of the non-Windows screen while in any Windows mode and on any type of computer, follow these steps:

1. Scroll or position the screen to show what you want to copy.
2. Press PrtSc.

Note: If the Print Screen key does not work on your keyboard, you may have an older keyboard. Try Alt+Print Screen or Shift+Print Screen as alternatives. (On some computers, the Print Screen key may be named PrtScrn or PrtSc and may be co-located with another key.)

If the non-Windows program is in text mode, you will copy the text on the screen. If the program is in graphics mode, you will copy an image of the screen. Although you cannot edit the text on a screen image after it is pasted, the image can be pasted as a graphic into such programs as Word for Windows, Windows Write, and PageMaker. Screen images are extremely useful for training and documentation.

Copying in 386-Enhanced Mode

In 386-enhanced mode, you can run non-Windows programs in windows even though they are not Windows programs. Running such programs in windows enables you to see multiple programs and copy selected text from the screen. Or you can copy the entire graphics screen.

With the mouse, copy selected text from a non-Windows program by following these steps:

1. If the non-Windows program is running full screen, put the program in a window by pressing Alt + ↵Enter. (Press Alt + ↵Enter a second time to restore the non-Windows program to full screen. The mouse will not work for copying text if the program is full screen.)

166

2. Select the text you want to copy by pointing to a corner of the area you want selected, and then holding down the mouse button and dragging across the area.

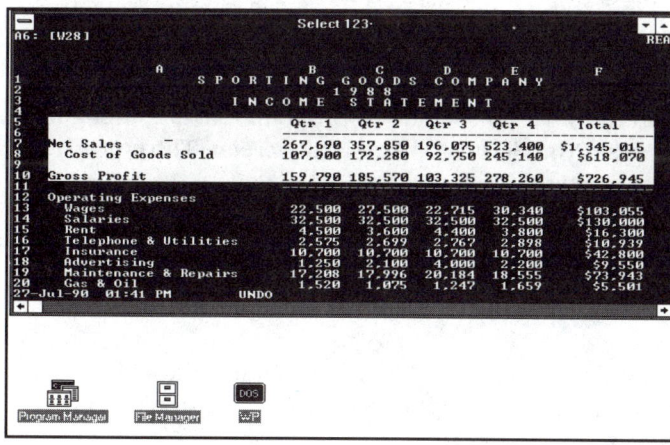

Selected text in a non-Windows program appears in inverse video.

3. Click on the Control menu icon at the top left of the window and choose the **Edit** command.

4. Select the **Copy** command from the **Edit** menu.

5. Follow the appropriate set of instructions for pasting, as described in the next sections of this chapter.

Note: While you are selecting text or graphics with the mouse, the title bar of the program changes to show the word Select. You cannot paste or use the program while you are selecting. Press Esc to return to program control.

With the keyboard, copy selected text from a non-Windows program by following these steps:

1. If the non-Windows program is running full screen, put the program in a window by pressing Alt + ↵Enter (Press Alt + ↵Enter a second time to restore the non-Windows program to full screen.)

2. Press Alt space bar to open the Control Panel.

3. Choose the **Edit** command.

4. Select the **Mark** command. Notice the rectangular cursor that appears at the top left corner of the screen.

8

167

5. Press the arrow keys to move the cursor to the top left corner of the area you want to copy.

6. Press and hold down ⧉Shift and then press the arrow keys to select the text to be copied.

7. Press Alt, space bar to open the Control Panel; then choose **Edit** and select **C**opy.

To copy a graphics screen from a non-Windows program that is running in 386-enhanced mode, press Print Screen or Alt+Print Screen. The entire screen is copied to the Clipboard.

Pasting from a Non-Windows Program into a Windows Program

You can paste text or graphics from non-Windows programs into Windows programs. Only Windows programs designed to work with graphics will receive graphics, however.

To paste text or graphics from a non-Windows program into a Windows program, follow these steps:

1. Activate the receiving program by clicking on its window, or by pressing Ctrl + Esc and choosing the program from the Task List.

2. Position the insertion point or graphics placement tool. The program must be ready to receive the text or graphics you are about to paste.

3. Choose the **E**dit menu and select the **P**aste command.

4. Edit out unnecessary text that may have been included in the copy.

Pasting Text into a Non-Windows Program

You can paste only unformatted text into non-Windows programs. Two methods are used to paste, depending on whether the non-Windows program you are pasting into is full screen or in a window.

To paste text into a non-Windows program that is full screen, follow these steps:

1. Activate the receiving program.

8

2. Position the program's cursor where you want the pasted text to appear.

3. Press <kbd>Alt</kbd>+<kbd>Esc</kbd> to return to Windows and minimize the non-Windows program to an icon.

4. Open the Control menu on the non-Windows program's icon by clicking on the icon, or by pressing <kbd>Alt</kbd>+<kbd>Esc</kbd> until the icon is selected and then pressing <kbd>Alt</kbd>, space bar.

5. If you are running in real or standard mode, choose the **P**aste command.

   If you are running in 386-enhanced mode, select the **E**dit menu and then choose **P**aste.

6. Edit out unnecessary text that may have been included in the copy.

As soon as you choose **P**aste, the program icon expands and fills the screen. You will see the text typed in just as though you were typing it.

To paste text into a non-Windows program that is running in a window, follow these steps:

1. Position the program's cursor where you want the pasted text to appear.

2. Open the Control menu by clicking on it or pressing <kbd>Alt</kbd>, space bar.

3. Choose the **E**dit menu and select the **P**aste command.

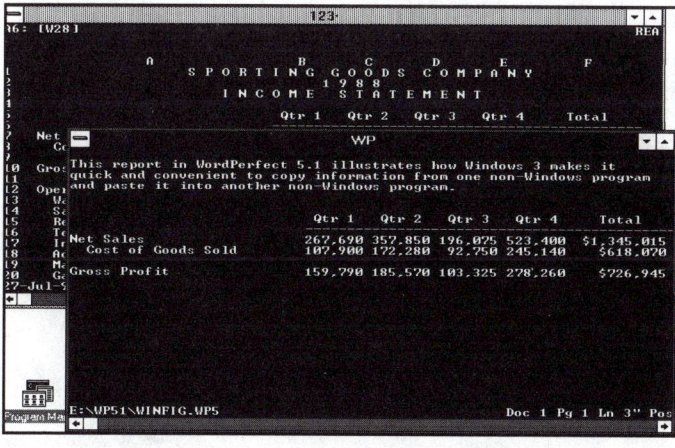

Even though WordPerfect and Lotus 1-2-3 are non-Windows programs, you can copy numbers from 1-2-3 and paste them into WordPerfect.

Using the Clipboard To View and Save Cut or Copied Data

When you cut or copy information, Windows stores it in a special part of memory called the Clipboard. The information stays in the Clipboard until it is cleared or until new information is cut or copied. Therefore, you can repeatedly paste the same item until the Clipboard is cleared or changed.

With the Clipboard program, found in the Main group window, you can view the Clipboard contents, clear the Clipboard, and save and retrieve Clipboard contents. This last feature is convenient because you can make a library of different clippings for repeated use, or a set of clippings for sending to someone through diskette or E-Mail.

Viewing Clipboard Contents

To see the contents of the Clipboard, choose the Clipboard icon from the Main group in the Program Manager.

You can see the current clipping in the Clipboard's window. Use the scroll bars to move the window's contents if you need to see more. The contents may look out of alignment, but they will be OK when pasted.

Saving and Retrieving Clipboard Contents

You can save and retrieve Clipboard contents for later use or for use on a different computer. You can also create libraries of files on disk that contain clippings you use frequently.

To save the contents of the Clipboard to a file, follow these steps:

1. Choose the **File** menu and select the Save **As** command.
2. Choose a new directory from the **Directories** list if needed.
3. Type a file name in the Filename text box. The Clipboard saves the file with the extension CLP.
4. Choose OK or press ⏎Enter

8

170

To retrieve the Clipboard contents that have been saved as a file, follow these steps:

1. Save or paste the current Clipboard contents—a retrieved clipping replaces the current Clipboard contents.
2. Choose the **File** menu and select the **O**pen command.
3. Select the directory from the **Directories** list box and press `⏎Enter`.
4. Select the file from the **File** list box or type the file name into the Filename text box.
5. Choose OK or press `⏎Enter`.

Clearing the Clipboard To Regain Available Memory

Large clippings may take up a great deal of memory. To delete the Clipboard contents and regain memory, display the Clipboard window, choose the **E**dit menu, and select the **D**elete command.

Summary

This chapter described one of the more important features of Windows: copying and pasting data between programs. When you use Windows programs only, you'll find that you can use programs together as though they were a single program. Even if you use non-Windows programs, you will be able to reduce the amount of retyping you do as well as the number of typing errors you introduce into the transferred data.

The following important points were covered in this chapter:

■ Windows programs accept pasted text or graphics. Non-Windows programs accept only pasted text.

■ To transfer text or graphics to another program, select what you want to transfer, choose Copy from the **E**dit menu, switch to the other program, and choose **P**aste from the **E**dit menu.

8

■ The Clipboard program, found in the Main group of the Program Manager, enables you to view, save, retrieve, or delete the contents of the Clipboard.

Now that you are familiar with how to copy and paste between programs, you should turn to Chapter 13 to learn how to run non-Windows programs. If you work with more than one Windows program, or if you want to see how Windows programs are designed to work together, turn to Chapter 14. It shows how you can tie Windows programs together so that they pass data between themselves automatically.

8 .

Using Windows Write

Windows Write is a word processing program that's simple to use but powerful enough to help you get a lot of work done quickly. The two main benefits to using any word processing program are that you can edit your work on the computer screen and save your work as a file for use later. But Windows Write goes much further than that.

With Write, you can enhance typed text by making it bold, italic, a larger size, or a different font (type style). You can add automatic headers and footers to your pages, including automatic page numbers. You can control the line spacing and change how the text is aligned with the margins of the pages—whether text is centered, aligned to the left or right, or justified (with both margins even). You can move text from one place in a document to another, and you can search for specific words (and even replace them). You can do all these tasks efficiently, using the Windows Write pull-down menus and dialog boxes. And you don't have to memorize commands.

Typing text in a new document

Saving, opening, and printing a document

Moving around in a document

Searching a document and editing text

Enhancing the text by changing fonts

Changing alignment, spacing, and indents

Changing margins and tabs

Adding headers, footers, and page breaks

Adding pictures or graphics

Key Terms in This Chapter

Word processor	A program that enables you to work with words to create such documents as memos, letters, and reports.
Document	The text you create in a word processing program.
File	A magnetic copy of your document after you name it and save it on the computer.
Margins	The space between the working area on your page and the edges of the paper.
Select	To highlight text so that you can make some change to it.
Format	To make some change to the appearance of selected text, such as making it bold or aligning it at the center of the page.
Cut and paste	The process of moving text from one area of a document to another area or to another document.
Clipboard	The temporary file that stores text you have cut or copied. (Because the Clipboard is shared by all Windows programs, you can cut or copy, and then paste between programs.)

9

Learning Windows Write has another advantage. When you become proficient with it, you can easily make the switch to a word processing program that has even more power, such as Word for Windows. Many of the commands and shortcuts you learn to use in Write are similar (or the same) in Word for Windows, and you can use all your Write files in Word for Windows.

Starting Windows Write

To start Write, you must have already started Windows. (Refer to Chapter 2, "Getting Started," if you need help starting Windows.) When you first start Windows, a window called the Program Manager appears on-screen. The Program Manager contains the following program groups: Main, Accessories, and Games. (Because you can create your own program groups, you may see additional groups on your screen.) The program groups may appear as icons (pictures) or as open windows.

You can open a program group icon, such as Accessories, into a window by double-clicking on the icon. When the program group is open as a window, you can see the programs it contains. Windows Write is a Windows accessory program located in the Accessories program group.

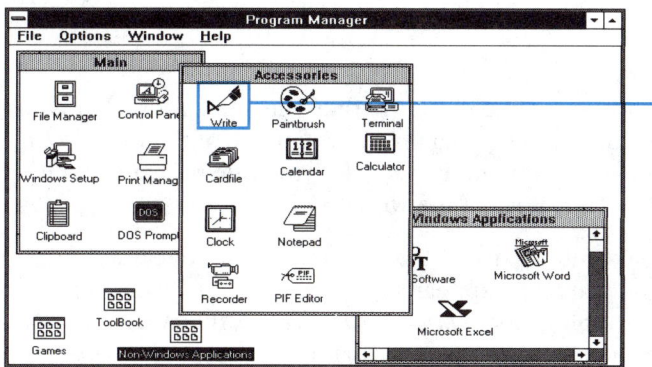

When the Accessories window is open, Write appears as an icon with its name, Write, below the icon.

9

To start the Write program, double-click on its icon. Or, if you are using the keyboard, use the arrow keys to select the icon, and then press Enter to activate the program. This procedure is the same for starting any Windows program.

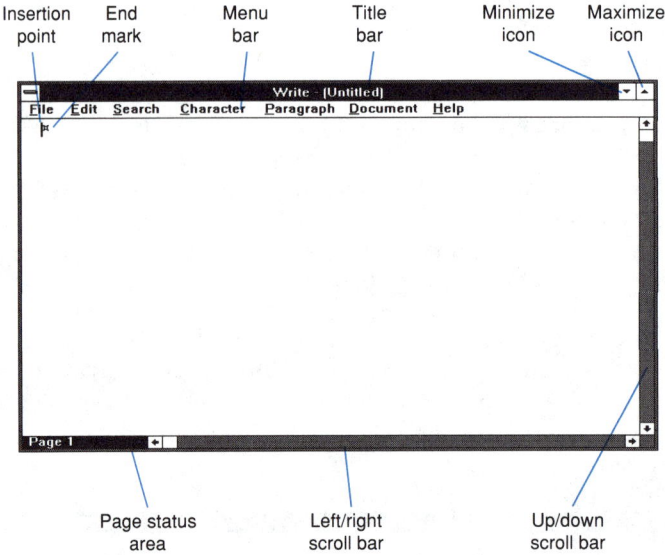

Insertion point · End mark · Menu bar · Title bar · Minimize icon · Maximize icon

Page status area · Left/right scroll bar · Up/down scroll bar

When you first open Write, a new window appears containing a blank Write document.

Some parts of the window are like those in other windows. A title bar across the top tells you the name of the program and the name of the document (untitled until you name it). A menu bar is below the title bar, and scroll bars are on the right and bottom sides of the window.

Besides these familiar window parts, Write has some unique features: an *insertion point* where characters appear as you type, an *end mark* that shows the end of your typing, and a *page status area* at the bottom left of the window. Also on the screen is a *pointer* that moves around as you move the mouse. The pointer may appear as an arrow (over a menu name or scroll bar) or as an I-beam (in the typing area of the screen).

Typing Text in a New Document

When you start Write, you open a new Write document. You are then ready to start typing. Like all word processing programs, Write offers wordwrap, a feature that enables you to type to the right margin—and just keep typing. The text you are typing automatically wraps to the next line. When you get to the end of a paragraph, just press Enter. (Press Enter twice to leave a blank line between paragraphs.)

9

Note: Be sure that you don't press Enter until you reach the end of a paragraph.

As you're typing, you will notice that each character you type appears at the blinking insertion point, pushing the insertion point one character to the right.

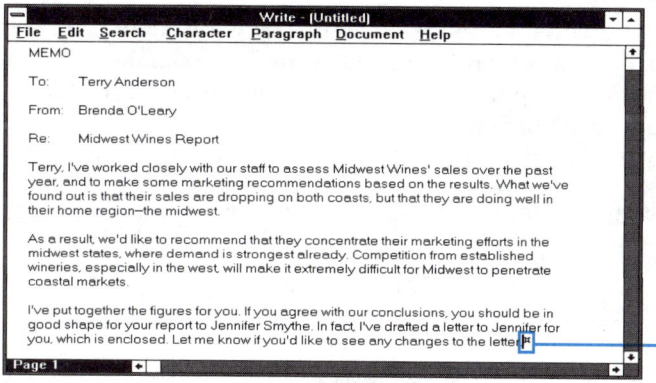

Notice that the end mark stays ahead of the insertion point.

If your computer screen is not wide enough to show the full document width, the typing area may be wider than the screen. In that case, the screen will scroll left and right as you type, attempting to show you each word typed. If you find the scrolling annoying, move to the section "Changing Margins and Tabs" to set your margins wider (so that the typing area is narrower).

If you make a mistake as you type, you can erase it by pressing the Backspace key. Backspace erases the character to the left of the insertion point. You'll learn many other ways to edit text in later sections of this chapter.

Saving and Opening a Document

Until you save a document, it's like a song on the radio. If the radio goes off, you lose the song. A saved file, however, is like a song on a CD. Even if the electricity goes off, the song is still there because it was recorded on the CD. Therefore, to make sure that you can get your document back, save it every 15 minutes or so. Saving the document "records" it on disk. A good rule of thumb is to save your work as often as you can't afford to lose it! Once a document has been saved, you can open it again at a later time to edit or print it.

Saving a Document

Until you save the document, it has no name; it is called "Untitled." The first time you save the document, you give it a name. From then on, the document has a name, which appears in the title bar at the top of the Write window. Your file name can contain up to eight letters or numbers; Write automatically assigns the three-letter extension WRI to each file name.

When you save a document, you save it as a computer file.

You use the File menu, therefore, to choose the command to save your file.

To save and name the file, follow these steps:

1. Choose the **File** menu and select the Save **As** command. The File Save As dialog box appears.

2. In the Filename text box, type the file name for the document.

In this example, the file name MEMO has been typed in the Filename text box.

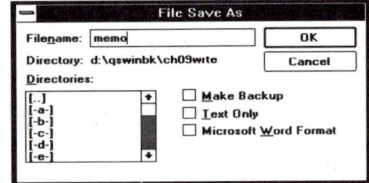

3. From the **Directories** list box, select a directory if you want to save the file in a directory other than the current one (which is shown below the Filename text box).

4. Choose OK.

178

You may notice three additional check boxes in the File Save As dialog box. Select **M**ake Backup to make an automatic backup (an extra copy) of the file. Select **T**ext Only to save the file in text (ASCII) format. Or select Microsoft Word Format if you want to save your Write file to be used in Microsoft Word.

Now that the document has a file name, you have two options the next time you want to save the file. If you want to keep only one copy of the file on disk, you can choose the **F**ile menu and select the **S**ave command (instead of Save As). The **S**ave command saves the new version of the file on top of the previous version, thus replacing it. The second option is to select the Save **A**s command and give the file a new name. By creating a new file, you preserve the previous version of the file.

Opening a Saved Document

Often you will want to edit a document you created earlier. You must first use the **O**pen command to retrieve the document you saved earlier.

Notice that when you open an existing file, you close the one you're currently working on. If you have made changes to the current document since you last saved, Write asks whether you want to save your changes. Choose **Y**es, **N**o, or Cancel.

To retrieve an existing file, follow these steps:

1. Choose the **F**ile menu and select the **O**pen command.

9

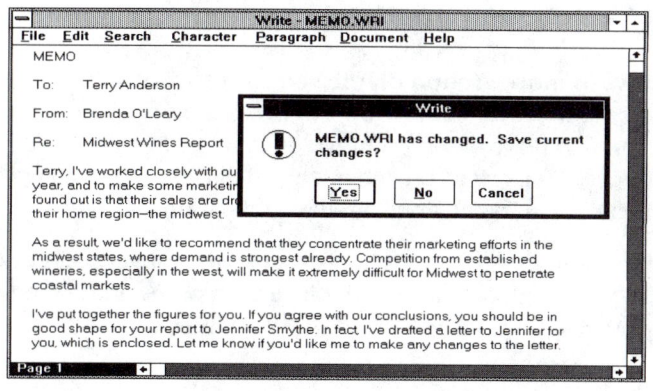

Write gives you a chance to save your current document before opening another document.

When you select
the **Open** com-
mand, the File
Open dialog box
appears.

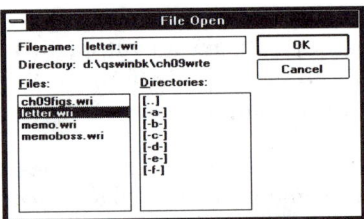

2. From the **Directories** list box, select the directory containing the file
   you want to open.

3. From the **Files** list box, select the file you want to open. Its name
   appears in the File**n**ame text box.

4. Choose OK.

Moving Around in a Document

Because one of the biggest advantages of a word processor is its capability to
edit text, you need to know how to move around on the screen to locate the
text you want to edit. You can move around in many ways, including using
the arrow keys, using the mouse, and using special keys (such as PgUp and
PgDn). You are not restricted to one method; people who use a mouse often
use keyboard shortcuts as well.

You can move the insertion point anywhere within the document's text. You
cannot, however, move the insertion point beyond the end mark.

Moving Around with the Keyboard

One of the simplest ways to move around on the screen is to move the
insertion point by pressing the arrow keys. You can press the up-arrow key
to move up one line, the down-arrow key to move down one line, or the left-
or right-arrow key to move left or right one character. By holding down any
of the arrow keys, you can move many lines or characters at once.

If you want to move the insertion point a little faster, use the movement keys
on the numeric keypad. The PgUp key moves the insertion point one screen
up, and the PgDn key moves the insertion point one screen down. The

9

Home key moves the insertion point to the beginning of the line, and the End key moves the insertion point to the end of the line.

Using the Control (Ctrl) key in combination with other keys extends their movement. For example, if you hold down Ctrl while you press the left- or right-arrow key, the insertion point moves one word at a time. Ctrl+Home or Ctrl+End moves the insertion point to the beginning or end of the document. Ctrl+PgUp or Ctrl+PgDn moves the insertion point to the top or bottom of the current window.

You can use one final key, the number 5 on the numeric keypad, to move the insertion point. (If your numeric keypad is on, turn it off by pressing the Num Lock key.) Press 5+left arrow or 5+right arrow to move left or right by one sentence. Press 5+up arrow or 5+down arrow to move to the previous or next paragraph. Press 5+PgUp or 5+PgDn to go to the previous or next page. Alternatively, you can select the **G**o To Page command from the **S**earch menu, type the number of the page you want to go to, and press Enter.

Table 9.1 summarizes the keystrokes you can use to move the insertion point.

Table 9.1
Keystrokes for Moving the Insertion Point

Movement	Keystroke(s)
Single character	← or →
Single line	↑ or ↓
Next or previous word	Ctrl + ← or Ctrl + →
Beginning of the line	Home
End of the line	End
Next or previous sentence	5 + ← or 5 + → (Use the 5 on the numeric keypad. Turn off the keypad first by pressing Num Lock.)
Next or previous paragraph	5 + ↑ or 5 + ↓ (Use the 5 on the numeric keypad. Turn off the keypad first by pressing Num Lock.)
Top or bottom of the window	Ctrl + PgUp or Ctrl + PgDn

9

Table 9.1—(continued)

Movement	Keystroke(s)
Continuous movement	Hold any of the keys or key combinations listed in this table
One screen	`PgUp` or `PgDn`
Beginning of document	`Ctrl` + `Home`
End of document	`Ctrl` + `End`
Next or previous page	`5` + `PgUp` or `5` + `PgDn`
	(Use the `5` on the numeric keypad. Turn off the keypad first by pressing Num Lock.)

Moving Around with the Mouse

As you move the mouse, a pointer moves correspondingly on the screen. The pointer generally has two different shapes. It becomes an I-beam in the typing area of the screen, and an arrow near a menu, a scroll bar, or the left margin. (The pointer has a third shape—a double-headed arrow—when you move the pointer over a window border.)

The I-beam serves a special function: that of moving the insertion point to a new location on the screen. Suppose, for example, that you have just finished typing a letter three paragraphs long, and you want to edit a word in the first paragraph. Use the mouse to move the I-beam to the right of the word, and then click the mouse button. The insertion point moves to the I-beam's position.

You can use the mouse also to scroll the screen. Suppose that your letter is instead two pages long, and you want to move from the second page back to the first page. Use the mouse to point to the right scroll bar, and click on the up arrow at the top of the scroll bar. You'll scroll upward, toward the beginning of the document. To move down, you can point to the down arrow and click. To move left or right, you can click on the left or right arrow

9

182

at either end of the bottom scroll bar. (If you click on the scroll arrows and hold them down, you'll scroll continuously.)

Scrolling isn't quite the same as moving. When you scroll, you display a different part of the document, but the insertion point remains where it was. You will often use the scroll bars together with the I-beam, first scrolling to display the text where you want to move and then clicking the I-beam to move the insertion point there.

Editing a Document

With Write, you can edit, or revise, your documents easily. Editing includes such changes as correcting spelling errors, rewording sentences, and reorganizing paragraphs.

Inserting and Deleting Characters

The simplest way to edit text is to delete and insert characters. Start by moving the insertion point where you want to delete or insert text. Then press the Backspace key to erase the character to the left of the insertion point (if you hold down Backspace, you'll erase a string of characters). Or type the new text; it will be inserted to the left of the insertion point, and the text to the right will move farther right to make room for the new text.

9

Selecting Text

More complicated editing requires that you begin by selecting the text you want to edit. *To select* simply means to highlight text, identifying it as the text to be acted on when you press a key or choose an editing command. If you want to erase an entire paragraph from a letter, first select the paragraph, and then press the Backspace key or the Del (Delete) key.

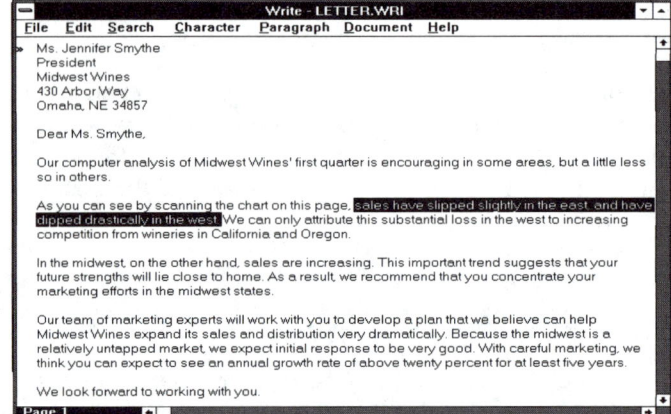

Selected text is highlighted, ready to be edited.

You can select text in several ways, using the keyboard or the mouse.

To select text with the keyboard, follow these steps:

1. Move the insertion point where you want to begin selecting text.

2. Press and hold down ⇧Shift.

3. Press any arrow key to move the insertion point across the text you want to select. (The text will be selected because you are holding down ⇧Shift.)

4. Release both keys.

You aren't limited to using just the arrow keys to select text. You can use the Shift key in combination with any of the other keys that move the insertion point. For example, to select one word at a time, hold down the Shift and Ctrl keys while you then press the left- or right-arrow key.

One way to select text with the mouse is to follow these steps:

1. Move the I-beam to one side of the text you want to select.

2. Hold down the left mouse button.

3. Drag the I-beam over the text you want to select (you can drag in any direction).

4. Release the mouse button.

9

184

If you need to select more than a screenful of text, continue holding down the mouse button while you drag the I-beam until it touches the edge of the screen. The screen will scroll automatically.

Several shortcuts are available for selecting text with the mouse. You can, for example, double-click on a word to select it. Or you can move the I-beam into the left margin of the document, until the I-beam becomes an arrow that points toward the text. The area to the left of the left margin is called the *selection bar*; you can use it to select large areas of text. Table 9.2 shows a number of techniques for selecting text with the mouse.

Table 9.2
Techniques for Selecting Text with the Mouse

Selection	*Technique*
One word	Double-click on the word
Several words	Double-click on the first word and drag to the end of the last word
Any amount of text	Drag from the beginning to the end of the text
Text between two distant points	Move the insertion point to the beginning point, click, move to the second point, press and hold down the Shift key, and click on the second point
One line	Click in the selection bar (white space) to the left of the line
Several lines	Click and drag up or down in the selection bar
Paragraph	Double-click in the selection bar to the left of the paragraph
Entire document	Press Ctrl and click in the selection bar

Deselecting Text

When you finish editing the selected text, you may want to deselect it. With the keyboard, press any arrow key to deselect text. With the mouse, click the I-beam anywhere on the text to deselect the current selection.

Replacing Text

One way to replace text is to delete it and type new text. Another way can save you a step. Simply select the text you want to replace, and then type the new text. The new text replaces the old.

Undoing an Edit

Because no one is perfect and people sometimes change their minds, many programs—including Write—come equipped with an "Oops" key. More accurately, it's called the Undo command, and it undoes your most recent edit. For example, if you delete a paragraph and then realize that you deleted the wrong one, you can undo the deletion. You can even undo an undo.

To undo an edit, follow these steps:

1. Choose the **Edit** menu.

2. Select the **Undo** command.

The "undo" command may appear as Undo, Undo Typing, or Undo Editing, depending on your last action.

Copying and Moving Text

One of Windows' most important features, the Clipboard, is shared by Write. The Clipboard is a temporary holding file that stores text you have selected and then cut or copied with the **Cut** or **Copy** command in the **Edit** menu. To retrieve text from the Clipboard, you then use the **Paste** command from the **Edit** menu. You can use these commands to move text (by first cutting and then pasting it) or to duplicate text (by first copying and then pasting it).

To copy text, follow these steps:

1. Select the text you want to copy.

9

186

2. Choose the **Edit** menu and select the **Copy** command.

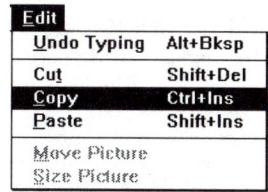

The **Copy** command's shortcut key combination is Ctrl + Ins.

A copy of the selected text is stored in the Clipboard.

3. Move the insertion point to where you want to put the text you've copied.

4. Choose the **Edit** menu and select the **Paste** command.

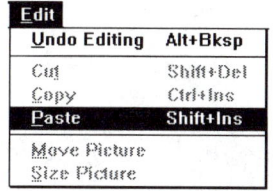

The **Paste** command's shortcut key combination is ⇧Shift + Ins.

Text stays in the Clipboard until you replace it with different text or turn off your computer. You can paste the contents of the Clipboard as many times as you want, duplicating the original text indefinitely.

To move text, follow these steps:

1. Select the text you want to move.

2. Choose the **Edit** menu and select the **Cut** command.

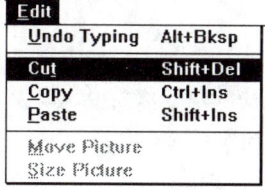

The **Cut** command's shortcut key combination is ⇧Shift + Del.

9

187

The text is moved into the Clipboard (and removed from the document).

3. Move the insertion point to where you want to move the text.

4. Choose the **Edit** menu and select the **Paste** command.

Searching a Document and Changing Text

In a long document, finding a single word may be difficult. And if your document contains many occurrences of a word or phrase that you must change, making the changes one by one can be tedious. Write can help you with both tasks through the **Find** and **Change** commands in the **Search** menu.

Finding Text

When you ask Write to find text, the program searches through the document from the insertion point forward, selecting the first occurrence of the text.

To find text, follow these steps:

1. Choose the **Search** menu and select the **Find** command.

The **Find** command is selected from the **Search** menu.

When you choose **Find**, the Find dialog box appears.

2. In the **Find What** box, type the text you want to find.

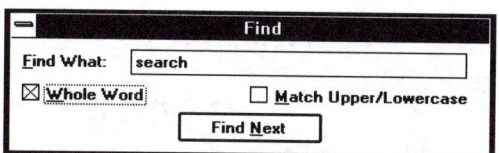

In this example, Write will look for only occurrences of the complete word *search*.

3. Choose Find Next. Write finds and selects the text.

4. Press Esc to close the Find dialog box.

   Or choose Find Next again to find the next occurrence of the text.

The Find dialog box contains two check boxes: **Whole Word** and **Match Upper/Lowercase**. Select **Whole Word** to find your text only if it is a whole word—for example, *put* but not *computer*. Select **Match Upper/ /Lowercase** if you want to find exact upper- or lowercase matches of your text— for example, *Computer* but not *computer*.

To search again for the same text, choose the **Search** menu and select the **Repeat Last Find** command.

Changing Text

The Change command is handy when you need to change text. This command will help you find every occurrence of the text you want to change. By using the **Change** command, you can be sure that you won't miss any occurrences. Like **Find**, **Change** searches for and changes text from the insertion point forward in the document.

To change text, follow these steps:

1. Choose the **Search** menu and select the **Change** command.

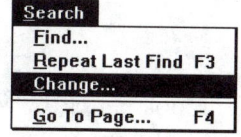

The Change command is selected from the **Search** menu.

9

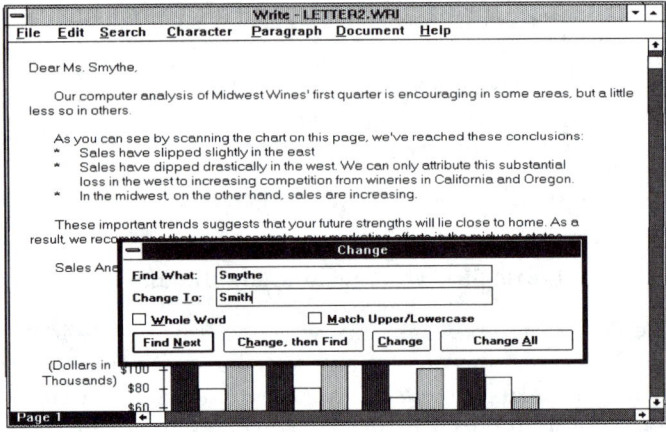

When you select the **Change** command, the Change dialog box appears.

2. Type the text you want to change in the **Find What** box.

3. Type the replacement text in the Change **To** box.

4. Choose Find **Next**. Write selects the next occurrence of the text you typed in the **Find What** box.

5. Choose the "Change, then Find" button to change the selected text and find the next occurrence of the text you want to change.

   Or choose **Change** to change the selected text.

   Or choose Change **All** to change all occurrences of the text.

6. Press `Esc` to close the Change dialog box.

The Change dialog box contains two check boxes: **Whole Word** and **Match Upper/Lowercase**. Select **Whole Word** to find and change your text only if it is a whole word. Select **Match Upper//Lowercase** if you want to find exact upper- or lowercase matches of your text.

Enhancing the Text

Enhanced text not only makes a document look better, by adding variety to your pages, but also helps make the document more organized and thus more readable, by adding emphasis to important words or headings. Write includes many tools for enhancing characters, including bold and italic, different font styles, and different font sizes. All text-enhancement commands are located in the **Character** menu.

9

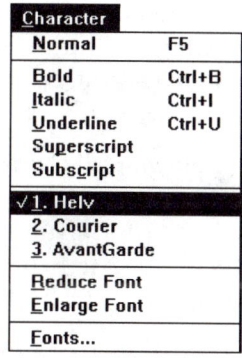

The currently selected text-enhancement command appears with a check mark to its left in the Character menu.

To enhance text, you must first select it. If you don't remember how to select text, refer to the section "Editing a Document," earlier in this chapter.

Keep in mind that your printer plays a part in text enhancement. If you make a headline bold in Write but your printer can't print bold text, your text won't be printed in bold.

Emphasizing Characters

Bold text stands out and is excellent for adding emphasis to headlines, subheadings, or other important text. Italic text adds more subtle emphasis and is also useful for identifying titles and names within a document. Underlining is less useful (it's more of a holdover from the days of the typewriter) but may be appropriate for headings in tables or for dividing sections of text. Superscript and subscript characters are raised or lowered from the rest of the text and are used for footnotes or scientific notations.

To emphasize characters, follow these steps:

1. Select the text you want to emphasize.
2. Choose the Character menu.
3. Select the emphasis command you want to apply to the selected text:
   Bold
   Italic
   Underline
   Superscript
   Subscript

9

You can apply several styles of emphasis to the same text. For instance, you can make text both bold and italic by selecting the text, selecting the **Bold** command, leaving the text selected, and then choosing the **Character** menu again and selecting the **Italic** command.

To return text to its normal appearance, removing all character emphasis, follow these steps:

1. Select the text you want to return to normal.

2. Choose the **Character** menu and select the **Normal** command.

Changing the Font and Size

A font is a type style. The type style of a newspaper is different from that of a stop sign—each is printed with a different font. Write enables you to change your text to any font your printer can print. Font sizes are measured in points, with 72 points per inch. Newspaper text may be 9 or 10 points in size, and headlines may be 18 to 36 points (72 if they are really important). A stop sign, of course, is printed in a much larger font size.

The **Character** menu provides two ways to change fonts. One is to use the **Fonts** command to display the Fonts dialog box, in which you can change not only the font but also the font size. The fonts and sizes that appear in the Fonts dialog box depend on the printer and the fonts that are currently selected. The other way you can change fonts is to select one of the three fonts listed in the **Character** menu. These three fonts may change from time to time; they are simply the three fonts you have selected most recently.

The **Character** menu also provides two ways to change font sizes. One is to select the **Fonts** command to display the Fonts dialog box, and the other is to use either the **Reduce Font** command or the **Enlarge Font** command.

To change fonts and font sizes, follow these steps:

1. Select the text you want to change.

2. Choose the **Character** menu and select the **Fonts** command.

9

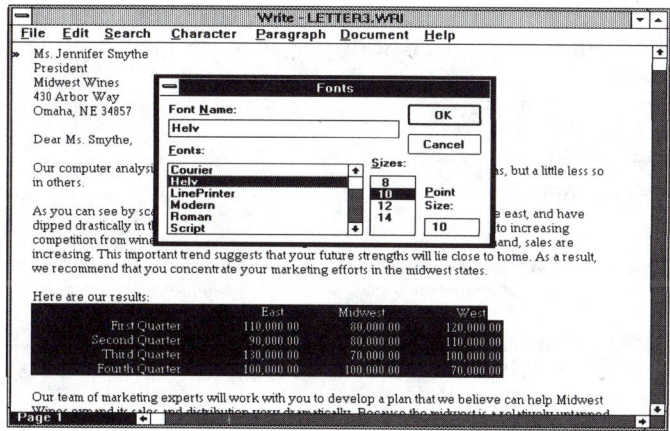

The Fonts dialog box appears.

3. Select the font you want from the **Fonts** list box (scroll the list if necessary). The selected font appears in the Font **N**ame text box.

4. From the **Sizes** list box, select the point size you want. Or type in the **P**oint Size box the size you want.

5. Choose OK.

Changing Alignment, Spacing, and Indents

9

The changes you make to the appearance of a document are called *formatting*. Write provides three levels of formatting. In a previous section, "Enhancing the Text," you learned how to format text at the character level, using the **Character** menu. Character-level formatting applies to blocks of text as small as one character. In this section, you learn about paragraph formatting with the **Paragraph** menu. Paragraph-level formatting applies to entire paragraphs—and remember, a paragraph is any block of text that ends when you press the Enter key. In the next section, you learn about document-level formatting, which applies to an entire document.

You can format paragraphs in two ways: with the **Paragraph** menu or with the ruler. The ruler has icons that illustrate the type of formatting you are

193

selecting; for example, the icon for centered text looks like several lines of centered text. To use the ruler, you must first display it.

To display the ruler, follow these steps:

1. Choose the **Document** menu.

2. Select the **Ruler On** command.

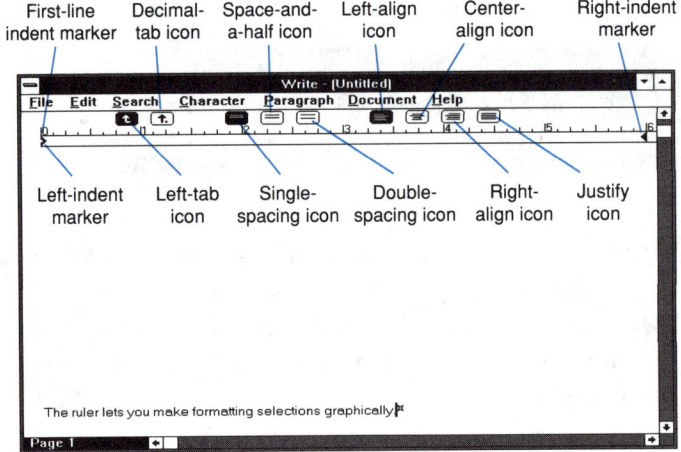

The ruler enables you to make selections graphically with the mouse.

When the ruler is displayed, the **Ruler On** command in the **Document** menu changes to **Ruler Off**. Choose the **Document** menu and select **Ruler Off** to hide the ruler.

Changing Paragraph Alignment

Paragraphs of text can be aligned at the left margin, the right margin, or both margins (justified). Or paragraphs can be centered between margins.

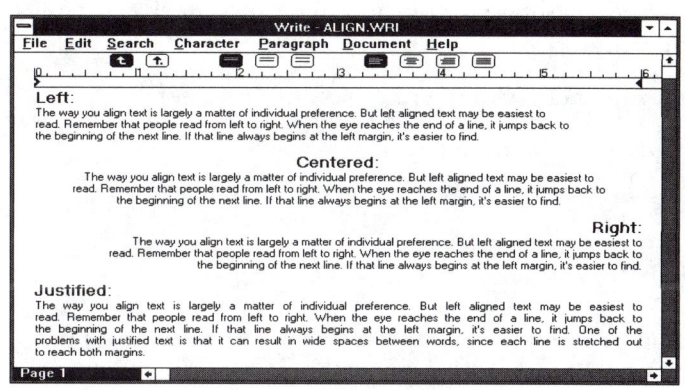

Write's default is left-alignment, but you can easily change the alignment for any paragraph you select.

To change paragraph alignment, follow these steps:

1. Select the paragraph(s) you want to align.
2. Choose the **P**aragraph menu.

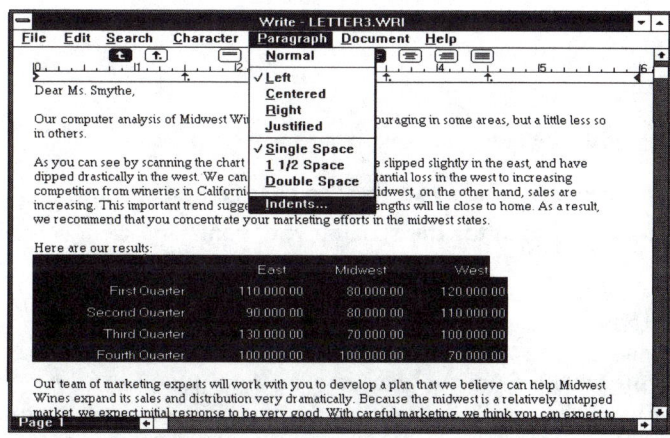

The **P**aragraph menu offers several formatting and alignment commands.

3. Select one of the alignment commands:

> **Left**
> **Centered**
> **Right**
> **Justified**

The current paragraph formatting selection appears with a check mark to its left in the **P**aragraph menu.

To change paragraph alignment with the ruler, follow these steps:

1. Select the paragraph(s) you want to align.
2. Click on the alignment icon for the alignment you want.

Changing Line Spacing

Paragraphs can be single-spaced (with no extra spacing between lines) or double-spaced (with a full line of space between lines). Or lines in paragraphs can be separated by a space and a half.

To change line spacing, follow these steps:

1. Select the paragraph(s) for which you want to change line spacing.
2. Choose the **P**aragraph menu.
3. Select one of the line-spacing commands:

    Single Space
    1 1/2 Space
    Double Space

To change line spacing with the ruler, follow these steps:

1. Select the paragraph(s) for which you want to change line spacing.
2. Click on the line-spacing icon for the spacing you want.

Changing Indents

Indenting means moving text in from the margin. You can indent just the first line of a paragraph, or you can indent either the left or the right edge of a paragraph (or both edges). If you want all your paragraphs to have a first-line indent, set the first-line indent before you start typing. Every time you press the Enter key, the indent will be carried over to the next paragraph.

To indent a paragraph, follow these steps:

1. Select the paragraph(s) you want to indent.

9

2. Choose the **P**aragraph menu and select the **I**ndents command.

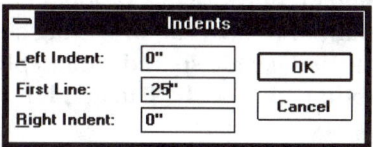

The Indents dialog box appears.

3. Type an indent distance (in decimal numbers) in the **L**eft Indent, **F**irst Line, or **R**ight Indent text box.

4. Choose OK.

Setting indents with the ruler—especially first-line indents—requires good hand-eye coordination. The ruler contains three indent markers. The black triangle on the left side of the ruler is the left-indent marker. The first-line indent marker is a small black square under the ruler. (When the first-line indent marker is on top of the left-indent marker, the marker appears as a small white square.) The black triangle on the right represents the right indent. To set an indent, drag an indent marker to a new position on the ruler.

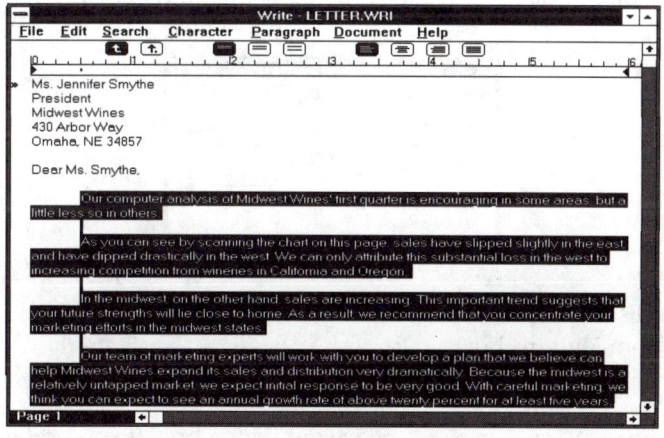

Dragging the first-line indent marker to the half-inch mark on the ruler indents the first line of selected paragraphs.

9

To indent a paragraph with the ruler, follow these steps:

1. Select the paragraph(s) you want to indent.

2. Drag the indent marker to a new position on the ruler.

Removing Paragraph Formatting

You can always change the alignment, line spacing, or indents for any selected paragraph. But if you want to remove all formatting at once and revert to Write's default of left-aligned, single-spaced paragraphs with no indents, then select the paragraph(s), choose the **P**aragraph menu, and select the **N**ormal command.

Changing Margins and Tabs

In Write, margin and tab settings apply to an entire document. Write starts out with default settings: tabs every half inch, left and right margins of one and one-quarter inches, and top and bottom margins of one inch. You can change margins and tabs through the **D**ocument menu, and you can change tabs with the ruler.

Changing Margins

To change a document's margins, follow these steps:

1. Choose the **D**ocument menu and select the **P**age Layout command.

The Page Layout dialog box appears.

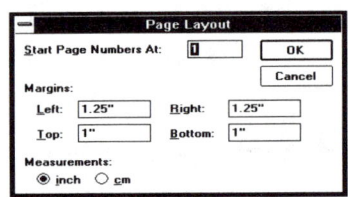

2. Type a margin distance (in decimal numbers) in the **L**eft, **T**op, **R**ight, and **B**ottom Margins boxes.

3. Choose OK.

You can make two other changes in the Page Layout dialog box. If you prefer working with centimeters rather than inches, choose the **cm** Measurements button. The ruler and dialog boxes will then show centimeters. Additionally, you can change the starting number for automatic page numbers in the Start

198

Page Numbers At box. Automatic page numbering (explained in the section "Adding Headers and Footers") starts with that number.

Changing Tabs

In all word processing programs, using tabs is a two-part process: setting the tab stops and pressing the Tab key. When you press the Tab key while you are typing, the insertion point moves to the next tab stop. In Write, you set the tab stops with either the Tabs dialog box or the ruler. There are two types of tab stops: left and decimal. Left tabs align text on the left side of the tab stop, and decimal tabs align text on a period (useful for decimal numbers).

In the Tabs dialog box, you must type the location for each tab stop, measured in decimal inches from the left margin. For example, if you want tab stops every quarter inch, you must set tabs at 0.25, 0.5, 0.75, and so on.

To set tabs in a document, follow these steps:

1. Choose the **Document** menu and select the **Tabs** command.

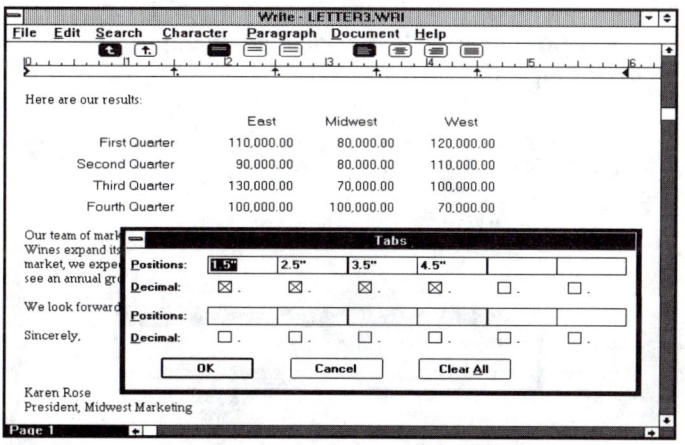

The Tabs dialog box appears.

2. In the **Positions** boxes, type the positions where you want tab stops, measured in decimal inches from the left margin.

9

3. If you want any tab to be a decimal tab, select the **Decimal** box below the appropriate **Positions** box so that an X appears inside the **Decimal** box.

4. Choose OK.

If you want to clear all the existing tab stops so that you can start over, choose Clear **All** in the Tabs dialog box.

Adding Headers and Footers

Headers and footers are strings of text that appear at the top or bottom of each page of a document (although you can exclude them from the first page if you prefer). Headers and footers appear inside the margins. For instance, if your top margin is one inch, a header will appear above one inch. Headers and footers don't appear on the computer screen—you see them when they print. One handy feature of headers and footers is that they can include automatic page numbers.

To create a header or footer, follow these steps:

1. Choose the **Document** menu and select the **Header** or the **Footer** command. The Page Header or Page Footer dialog box appears, and your document disappears.

9

The document is replaced by a special window for typing the text of your header or footer.

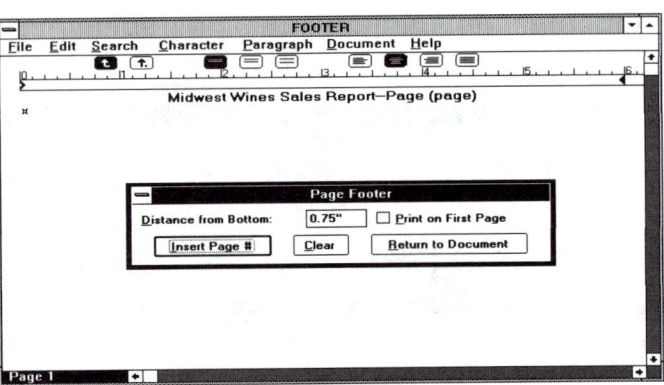

2. Type the text of the header or footer, formatting it any way you want. Move between the dialog box and the header or footer window by clicking on the location or by pressing [Alt]+[F6].

3. In the **D**istance from Bottom box or the **D**istance from Top box, type (in decimal numbers) the distance from the edge of the page that you want the header or footer to appear.

4. Choose **P**rint on First Page if you want the header or footer to appear on page 1 of the document.

5. Choose Insert Page # to include automatic page numbering at the current location of the insertion point.

6. Choose **R**eturn to Document to accept the header or footer.

If you include automatic page numbering, you'll see (page) on the header or footer screen; (page) will be replaced with the correct page number when you print the document. To change the starting page number, choose the **D**ocument menu and select the **P**age Layout command. When the Page Layout dialog box appears, type the starting page number in the **S**tart Page Numbers At box. You might want to change the starting page number, for example, if your document is the second chapter of a multichapter report and you want sequential page numbering throughout the report.

If you are rewording an old header or footer, you can clear out the old before you start the new by choosing **C**lear in the Page Footer or Page Header dialog box.

Inserting Page Breaks

9

Write inserts automatic page breaks in a document, based on the size of the type, the width of margins, the line spacing, and so on. If you want page breaks to appear in specific places, you must insert them manually.

To insert page breaks, follow these steps:

1. Choose the **F**ile menu and select the **R**epaginate command. The Repaginate Document dialog box appears.

2. Select Confirm Page **B**reaks and choose OK. The Repaginating Document dialog box appears. Suggested page breaks appear as double arrows in the left margin.

3. Choose **Up** or **Down** to move the suggested page breaks up or down. You can move a page break down only if you've moved it up earlier.

4. Choose **Confirm**.

Adding Pictures or Graphics

You may think that you don't want to put pictures or graphics in your documents. But you may change your mind when you find out how much fun another Windows accessory program, Paintbrush, is to use, or how helpful a chart you created in the spreadsheet program Excel can be.

To get a picture or graphic into Write, you must use the Clipboard to copy the picture from the program you used to create it, and then paste the picture into Write. After that, you can use special Write commands to move the picture or change its size. But first you must select the picture—select it just as though it were text, or point to the picture and click the mouse button.

To move a picture, follow these steps:

1. Select the picture.

2. Choose the **Edit** menu and select the **Move Picture** command.

A dotted line outlines the picture, and a double-square icon appears inside the outline.

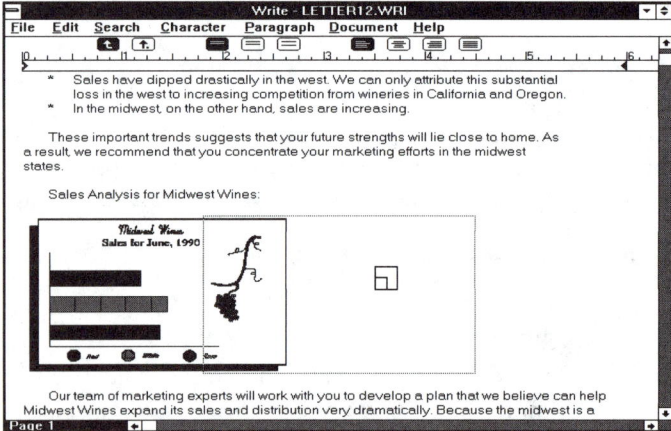

3. Move the outline left or right by dragging the mouse to the left or right, or by pressing ← or →.

4. Drop the picture into its new location by clicking the mouse button or pressing ↵Enter.

To change the size of a picture, follow these steps:

1. Select the picture.

2. Choose the **Edit** menu and select the **S**ize Picture command.

   A dotted line outlines the picture, and a double-square icon appears inside the outline—just as for moving a picture.

3. Move the double-square icon to the outline's edge or corner that you want to move. To move the icon, drag the mouse or press the arrow key that points to the edge you want to move. (You will need to press the arrow key only once.)

4. Size the picture by moving the edge or corner to a new position. To move the edge or corner, drag the mouse or press the arrow key. For example, if you want to move the edge or corner to the left, either drag the mouse to the left or press ←.

5. Accept the new size by clicking the mouse button or pressing ↵Enter.

Printing a Document

9

Printing a document requires two steps. First, you must select the printer; after you've done this, you never have to do it again until you change printers. Second, you select the **P**rint command.

To select a printer, follow these steps:

1. Choose the **F**ile menu and select the P**r**inter Setup command.

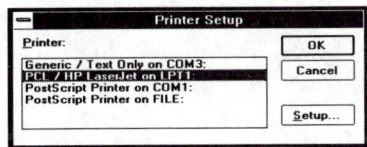

The Printer Setup dialog box appears, listing all the installed printers.

2. From the **Printer** list box, select the printer you want.

3. Choose OK.

The Printer Setup dialog box contains another choice, **Setup**. When you choose **Setup**, you get another dialog box; its appearance depends on the printer you selected. You can use this second dialog box to change other settings, such as paper source, size, and orientation, as well as the available fonts.

To print a document on the selected printer, follow these steps:

1. Choose the **File** menu and select the **Print** command.

The Print dialog box appears.

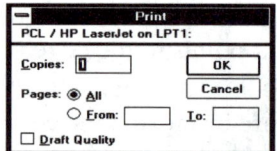

2. In the Copies box, type the number of copies you want to print.

3. If you want to print all the pages of the document, select **All**.

   Or, if you want to print a range of pages, select From. In the From box, type the first page you want to print. In the **To** box, type the last page you want to print.

4. Choose OK.

In the Print dialog box, you can select the **Draft Quality** option if your printer supports draft printing. Many dot matrix printers support draft printing, but laser printers do not.

Quitting Write

After you've created, saved, and printed your document, you are probably ready to call it a day (and with a little luck, it's quitting time). This is the easiest part of all.

To quit Write, follow these simple steps:

1. Choose the **File** menu.

2. Select the **Exit** command.

If you have made changes to your document since you last saved it, Write prompts you to save them.

Summary

Write is a simple but powerful word processing program you can use to do much of your work. Although Write contains all of the most important word processing features, it lacks some advanced tools, such as a spelling checker, automatic tables of contents, and footnoting. If you find your needs expanding, you can easily move to a more powerful program like Word for Windows. Many of Write's commands are the same as those in Word for Windows, and your existing Write files are compatible with Word for Windows files.

Important features in Write include the capability to format text (for example, with bold and italic), to cut and paste, and to search for text. Like all Windows programs, Write works well with other Windows programs, using the Clipboard to transfer selections, such as pictures and graphics, between programs.

Some of Write's most important concepts and procedures are the following:

- Write shows you how the document will appear when printed, except for headers and footers.
- Turning on the ruler enables you to reformat a document quickly and easily using the mouse.
- Write accepts graphics, pictures, charts, and screen shots pasted from the Clipboard using **Edit Paste**.
- Write files, the ruler, shortcut keys, and some commands are compatible with the more powerful Word for Windows word processor.

9

The next chapter, "Using Windows Paintbrush," shows you how to use the simple graphics program that is included in the Windows package among the accessories. You can use Paintbrush to illustrate your work or to create computer drawings just for fun.

Using Windows Paintbrush

You may wonder why you would ever need a program like Windows Paintbrush. You may think that you're not the artistic type, and what's more, you may think that you don't have time for Paintbrush because you have *real* work to do. What does drawing pictures have to do with work?

Plenty. Think about a long report filled with statistical facts and lots of numbers—but no illustrations. How many people would want to read that report? But imagine the same report spiced up with a few well-placed charts and graphs. Those illustrations would not only make the report more inviting to readers, but also help clarify many points that might otherwise seem abstract.

Windows Paintbrush is a simple program you can use to create all kinds of illustrations—from free-form drawings to precise charts and graphs. You can copy the illustrations into many other Windows accessory programs, such as Write, Cardfile, or Notepad. Or you can use the illustrations in Windows programs like Word for Windows (a powerful word processing program), PageMaker (a desktop publishing program), or PowerPoint (a slide-show presentation program).

Key Terms in This Chapter

Draw	To draw a line, box, circle, or polygon in Paintbrush
Paint	To paint a free-form line or shape in Paintbrush
Toolbox	The box that is on the left of the Paintbrush screen and contains all the tools used for drawing and painting
Line-width box	The box that is at the bottom left of the Paintbrush screen and from which you can select a width for lines, for the borders of shapes, and for some tools
Palette	The palette of colors (if you have a color monitor) or shades (if you have a monochrome monitor) that you can use in your Paintbrush drawings
Zoom in or out	To enlarge a drawing so that you can edit it dot by dot, or to reduce the drawing so that you can see the whole page
Font	An alphabet of letters in a particular style

Paintbrush is a simple program, but at the same time, it's powerful enough to illustrate your reports, presentations, newsletters, instruction manuals, or training guides—whatever you create on your computer.

10

Paintbrush is a useful business tool. And besides, it's fun.

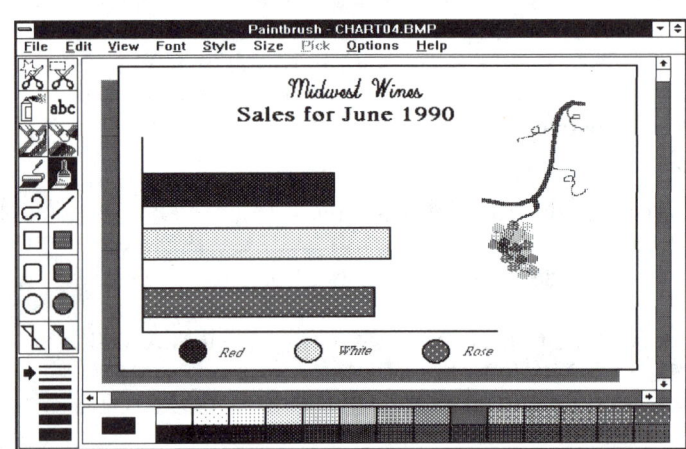

Starting Windows Paintbrush

To start Paintbrush, you must have already started Windows. (Refer to Chapter 2, "Getting Started," if you need help starting Windows.) When you first start Windows, a window called the Program Manager appears on the screen. The Program Manager contains at least three program groups: Main, Accessories, and Games. (Because you can create your own program groups, you may see more than three groups on your screen.) The program groups can appear as icons (pictures) or as open windows.

You can open a program group icon, such as Accessories, into a window by double-clicking on the icon; or press Ctrl+Tab enough times to select the Accessories icon, and then press Enter. When the Accessories program group is open as a window, you can see the programs it contains. Windows Paintbrush is a Windows accessory program located in the Accessories program group.

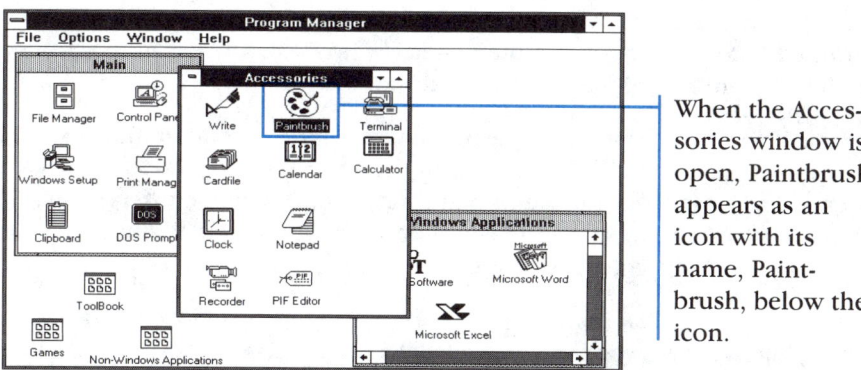

When the Accessories window is open, Paintbrush appears as an icon with its name, Paintbrush, below the icon.

10

To start the Paintbrush program, double-click on the Paintbrush icon; or, with the Accessories window selected, press Tab enough times to select the Paintbrush icon, and then press Enter. (This procedure is the same one you use to start any Windows program.)

209

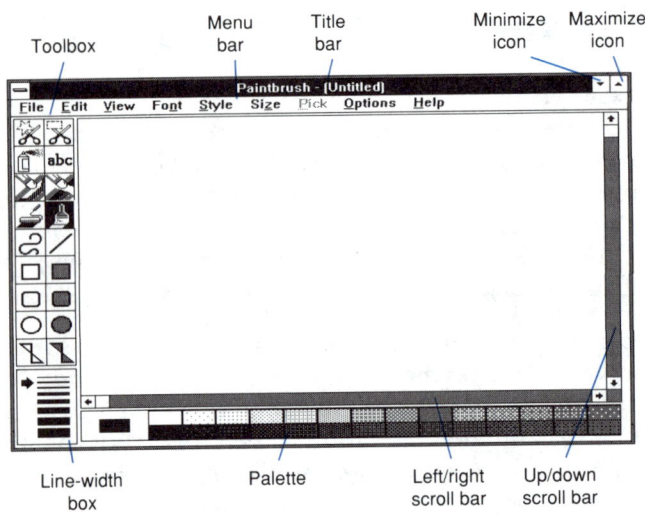

Toolbox   Menu bar   Title bar   Minimize icon   Maximize icon

Line-width box   Palette   Left/right scroll bar   Up/down scroll bar

When you first open Paintbrush, a new window appears, containing a blank Paintbrush document.

Some parts of the window are like those in other windows. A title bar across the top tells you the name of the program and the name of the document (untitled until you name it). A menu bar is below the title bar. And scroll bars are located on the right and bottom sides of the window.

Besides these familiar window parts, Paintbrush has several unique features. A *toolbox* appears on the left side of the screen, containing the tools you use to create a Paintbrush drawing or painting. At the bottom left is a *line-width box*, which you use to select the width of lines. A *palette* at the bottom of the screen contains the colors or shades you use to fill shapes.

Also on the screen is a pointer that roams around as you move the mouse. The pointer may appear as a crosshair (after you select a drawing tool), as a special tool (when you select an eraser tool or a painting tool), as an arrow (when you move the pointer over a menu name or scroll bar), or as an I-beam (when you are typing text).

Understanding How Paintbrush Works

Before you plunge into using Paintbrush, you should understand how the program works.

10

The middle, white area of the screen is the drawing area—it's where you create your Paintbrush masterpiece. To draw or paint, you must first select a tool by pointing to its icon in the toolbox and clicking the mouse button. For example, if you want to draw a straight line, you must select the Line tool. After you have selected a tool, you move the pointer into the drawing area, where the pointer becomes a crosshair or another drawing (or painting) icon.

Though the procedure varies from tool to tool, you generally draw or paint by holding down the mouse button, dragging the mouse, and then releasing the mouse button. To draw a line, for instance, you position the crosshair where you want the line to begin, hold down the mouse button, drag the crosshair to where you want the line to end, and release the mouse button.

The line-width box (below the toolbox) and the palette (at the bottom of the screen) function as accessories to the tools. For instance, when you draw a line, it appears in a certain width. You determine that width by selecting one from the line-width box. Similarly, when you draw a filled shape, its fill pattern is determined by the color or shading choices you make in the palette.

You can make additional refinements to a drawing by selecting commands from the Paintbrush menus. For example, you can select a type style or size for any text you add to the drawing. You can also tilt, flip, or shrink objects in the drawing.

Using the Keyboard with Paintbrush

Paintbrush is easiest to use if you have a mouse. But if you don't, you can still use the program. In this chapter, the instructions assume that you have a mouse; if you're using the keyboard, use the following keystrokes in place of the equivalent mouse actions:

Mouse Action	*Keyboard Equivalent*
Click left mouse button	Press Ins
Click right mouse button	Press Del
Double-click left mouse button	Press F9 + Ins
Double-click right mouse button	Press F9 + Del
Drag	Press arrow keys

10

211

You also can move around the Paintbrush screen using the keyboard. You may find that some of these techniques work as shortcuts, even if you have a mouse:

Keystroke(s)	Action
Tab⇄	Move among drawing area, toolbox, line-width box, and palette
← → ↑ ↓	Move in direction of arrow
Home	Move to top of drawing area
End	Move to bottom of drawing area
PgUp	Move up one screen
PgDn	Move down one screen
⇧Shift + ↑	Move up one line
⇧Shift + ↓	Move down one line
⇧Shift + Home	Move to left edge of drawing area
⇧Shift + End	Move to right edge of drawing area
⇧Shift + PgUp	Move left one screen
⇧Shift + PgDn	Move right one screen
⇧Shift + ←	Move left one space
⇧Shift + →	Move right one space

Using the Paintbrush Menus

As in all Windows programs, Paintbrush's first two menus are **File** and **Edit**.

10

The **File** menu contains commands for saving your drawing to a computer file, for opening a new file, and for printing.

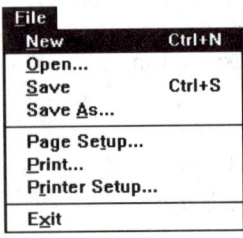

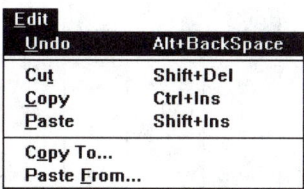

The Edit menu contains commands for cutting, copying, and pasting.

The third menu, **View**, contains commands for zooming in for a close look at a drawing and then zooming back out.

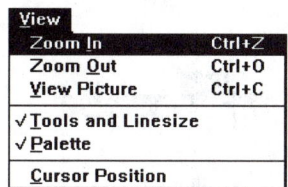

The **View** menu also enables you to hide the toolbox, the line-width box, and the palette so that you can make the drawing area larger.

The next three menus—**Font**, **Style**, and **Size**—are used to control the appearance of text in your drawing.

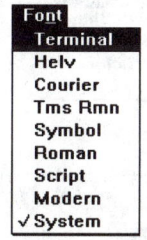

Use the Font menu to choose type that has a different appearance.

10

The **Style** menu includes commands for enhancing fonts or returning them to normal.

213

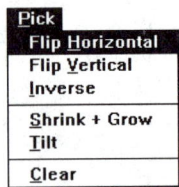

You can select a
different type size
in the Size menu.

The **P**ick menu is quite unique. You can use it only after you select an object
with one of the two cutout tools, Scissors or Pick (which both look like
scissors).

With the **P**ick
menu, you can
flip, inverse, tilt,
grow, or shrink
the selected
object.

The **O**ptions
menu lets you
change the size of
the drawing area,
change your col-
ors, or change the
brush shapes.

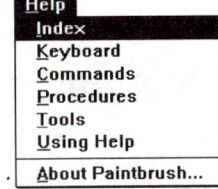

10

Like any Windows
Help menu, the
Paintbrush **H**elp
menu comes in
handy when you
can't remember a
definition or
procedure.

Using the Paintbrush Toolbox

The toolbox is the heart of Paintbrush, containing all the tools you need to create the lines and shapes that make up a drawing.

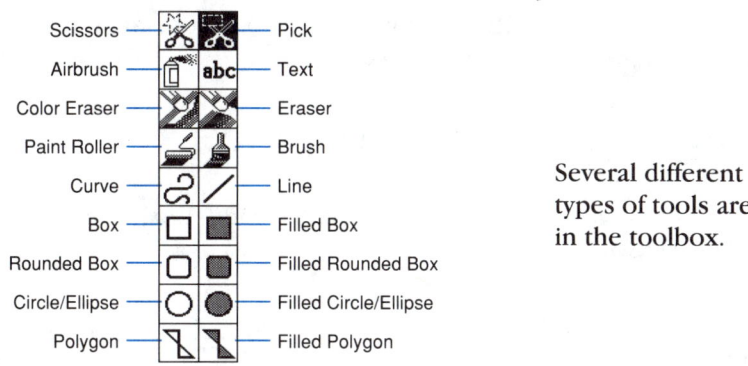

Several different types of tools are in the toolbox.

You use the Scissors and Pick tools to select objects in a drawing, or to select areas within the drawing that contain several objects.

The Airbrush, Paint Roller, and Brush tools are for painting. The Airbrush tool splatters a transparent mist of paint. The Paint Roller tool fills a shape with paint. And the Brush tool paints a line of color. Before using any of these tools, make sure that the color or shade you want to paint with is selected in the palette.

With the Text tool, you can add text to a drawing. You use the Font, Style, and Size menus to control the appearance of text.

The Curve and Line tools are for drawing lines. The Curve tool draws curved lines, and the Line tool draws straight lines. Be sure to choose a line width from the line-width box before you draw a line.

The Box and Rounded Box tools draw boxes. The Box tools (filled and unfilled) draw boxes with right-angle corners; the Rounded Box tools (filled and unfilled) draw boxes with rounded corners. Before you draw any box, choose a line width to define the width of its borders. If you are drawing a filled box, select a fill color or shade from the palette.

10

215

You use the Circle/Ellipse tools (filled and unfilled) to draw circles and ovals. To draw a perfect circle, hold down the Shift key as you draw. Select a line width before you draw a circle or ellipse, and if it's to be filled, select a color or shade from the palette.

The Polygon tools (filled and unfilled) draw multisided objects with straight sides. Select a line width before you draw a polygon, and if it's to be filled, select a color or shade from the palette.

Using the Line-Width Box

At the bottom left of your screen is the line-width box, containing eight lines of different widths.

An arrow points to the selected line width.

The selected line width controls the width of the lines you draw, as well as the width of the borders around boxes, circles, and polygons. If, for example, you select the thin line width at the top of the box, the next line that you draw will be thin. The selected line width also controls the width of some tools, such as the Airbrush, Brush, and Eraser tools. Note that selecting a line width doesn't change the width of any lines you've already drawn.

To select a line width, follow these steps:

1. Move the pointer over the line width you want to select.
2. Click the left mouse button.

Using the Paintbrush Palette

At the bottom of the Paintbrush screen is a palette containing the colors or shades you use to draw, paint, and fill objects. If you work in color, the palette shows colors; if you work on a monochrome system, the palette shows shades of gray. You must select the colors or shades you want to use.

10

216

The palette at the bottom of the Paintbrush screen.

Selected foreground color

Selected background color

You actually get two choices in the palette: a *foreground* color and a *background* color. The foreground color is the color you draw with, using the line or shape tools, and it is the color you paint with whenever you use one of the painting tools (Airbrush, Paint Roller, or Brush). The foreground color is also the fill color that goes inside filled shapes. The *background* color is the color of the border around the edges of filled shapes, and also the background color of your screen whenever you start a new Paintbrush file.

If you look at the left end of the palette, you see a rectangle within a rectangle. These rectangles show you the colors or shades currently selected. The *inside* rectangle is the foreground color; the *outside* rectangle is the background color.

To select foreground and background colors or shades, follow these steps:

1. Move the pointer on top of the foreground color or shade you want to select, and click the *left* mouse button.

2. Move the pointer on top of the background color or shade you want to select, and click the *right* mouse button.

Drawing Lines and Shapes

Paintbrush has two line tools for straight and curved lines, and eight shape tools for filled and unfilled boxes, circles and ellipses, and polygons. You use a similar process when you draw with each of these tools: select a tool, select a line width, select foreground and background colors, move the pointer into the drawing area (where the pointer becomes a crosshair), and draw the line or shape.

Lines and unfilled shapes are always drawn in the selected line width and selected foreground color. Filled shapes are filled with the selected foreground color and bordered with the selected background color. (If you want a filled shape with no border, select a background color that is the same as the foreground color.)

10

Although you draw lines and shapes with the left mouse button, you use the right mouse button for a special purpose with the line tools. To undo the line you are drawing, click the right mouse button before you release the left mouse button.

Straight Lines

The Line tool draws a straight line in the foreground color (or shade) and in the selected line width. While you're drawing the line, it appears as a thin black line. But when you release the mouse button to complete the line, it has the width and color (or shade) you've selected.

To draw a straight line, follow these steps:

1. Select the Line tool from the toolbox.

2. Select a line width and foreground color.

3. Move the pointer into the drawing area, where the pointer becomes a crosshair.

4. Position the crosshair where you want the line to start.

5. Press and hold down the left mouse button.

6. While holding down the mouse button, drag the crosshair in any direction to draw a line.

7. Release the mouse button to complete the line.

10

The Line tool draws straight lines; you can hold down the Shift key as you draw to make the lines vertical, horizontal, or at a 90-degree angle.

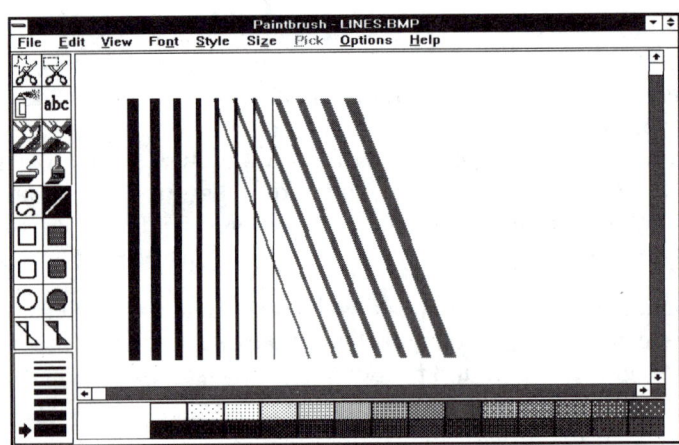

Curved Lines

 The Curve tool doesn't draw "free-form" curves; instead, it draws precise curves that are C-shaped or S-shaped.

Using the Curve tool requires a series of three press, hold, and drag movements. First, you press-hold-drag to draw a straight line. Second, you move to one side of the line and press-hold-drag to pull the line into a curved shape. Third, you complete the line in either of two ways: move to the opposite side of the line and press-hold-drag again to pull the line in the opposite direction (to make an S shape), or click on the end of the line to set the line in its current shape (a C shape).

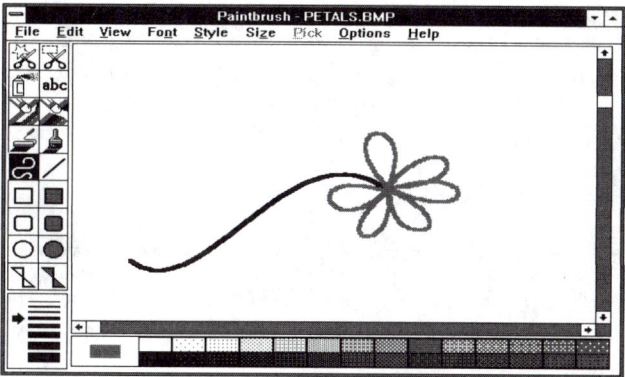

The line you draw shows the selected width and color (or shade) only when you complete the line with the third press-hold-drag movement or with a click at the end of the line.

To use the Curve tool, follow these steps:

1. Select the Curve tool from the toolbox.

2. If necessary, select a line width and foreground color.

3. Move the pointer into the drawing area, where the pointer becomes a crosshair. Position the crosshair where you want the line to start.

4. Press and hold down the left mouse button, drag the mouse to draw a straight line, and then release the mouse button. The line appears as a thin black line.

5. Move the crosshair to one side of the line you drew.

10

6. Press and hold down the left mouse button, and then drag the crosshair away from the line to pull it into a C-shaped curve. Release the mouse button when you're done.

7. If you want the line you have created to remain a C-shaped curve, click the end of the curve to complete the operation.

   Or, if you want to change the line to an S-shaped curve, press and hold down the left mouse button on the opposite side of the line, and then drag the crosshair away from the line to pull the line in the opposite direction.

Boxes

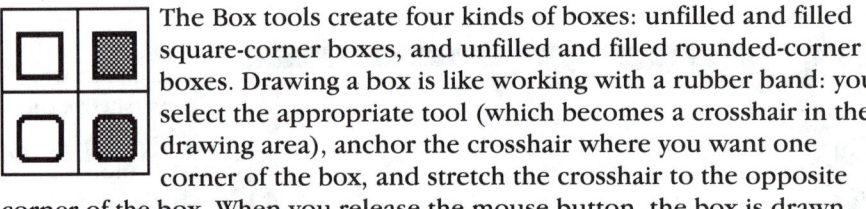 The Box tools create four kinds of boxes: unfilled and filled square-corner boxes, and unfilled and filled rounded-corner boxes. Drawing a box is like working with a rubber band: you select the appropriate tool (which becomes a crosshair in the drawing area), anchor the crosshair where you want one corner of the box, and stretch the crosshair to the opposite corner of the box. When you release the mouse button, the box is drawn (and filled, if it's a filled box).

Be sure to select the line width, foreground color, and background color before you start.

To draw a box, follow these steps:

1. From the toolbox, select the filled or unfilled Box tool, or the filled or unfilled Rounded Box tool.

2. Move the pointer into the drawing area of the screen, where the pointer becomes a crosshair.

3. Position the crosshair where you want to anchor one corner of the box.

4. Press and hold down the left mouse button.

10

5. While holding down the mouse button, drag the crosshair in any direction to draw the box. Until you finish, the box appears as a thin black line.

6. Release the mouse button when the box is the shape you want. The box has the selected line width and color or shade.

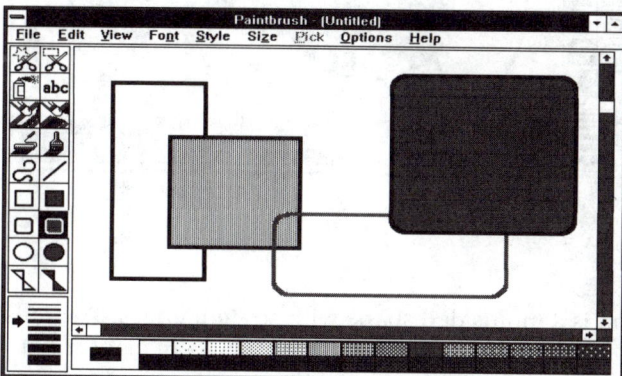

If you want to draw a square box, hold down the Shift key as you draw.

Circles and Ovals

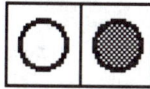 The Circle/Ellipse tools draw circles and ovals, either filled or unfilled. Both of the Circle/Ellipse tools draw an oval shape by default; if you want a perfect circle, hold down the Shift key as you draw the shape.

To draw a circle or oval, follow these steps:

1. Select the filled or unfilled Circle/Ellipse tool from the toolbox.

2. Move the pointer to the drawing area, where the pointer becomes a crosshair.

3. Press and hold down the left mouse button where you want to start the circle or oval.

4. Drag the crosshair away from the starting point in any direction.

5. Release the mouse button to complete the circle or oval.

10

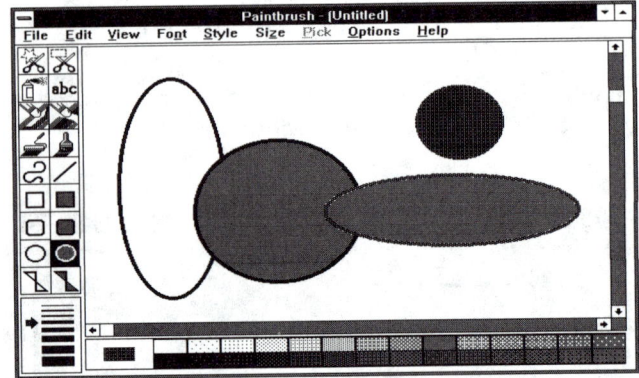

The circle or oval appears as a thin black line until you release the mouse button.

Polygons

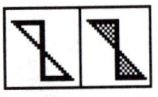

A polygon is a multisided shape with straight edges. The most familiar example of a polygon is a stop sign—an eight-sided polygon. A stop sign is symmetrical, but your polygons can be much more exciting, in any shape and with as many sides as you want.

Drawing a polygon is different from drawing a line or box. First, you draw a side of the polygon just as though you were drawing a line. Second, you click the mouse button once to define each of the polygon's remaining corners. Finally, you double-click the mouse button to close the polygon by connecting the first point to the last point.

To draw an unfilled or filled polygon, follow these steps:

1. Select the filled or unfilled Polygon tool from the toolbox.
2. Move the pointer into the drawing area, where the pointer becomes a crosshair.
3. Press and hold down the left mouse button to start the polygon.
4. Drag the crosshair to draw the first side of the polygon, and release the mouse button when the line is finished.
5. Position the crosshair where you want the polygon's next corner to appear. Then click the mouse button.
6. Create the polygon's remaining corners by positioning the crosshair where you want them and clicking the mouse button.

10

7. To complete the polygon, double-click the mouse button to connect the first point to the last point.

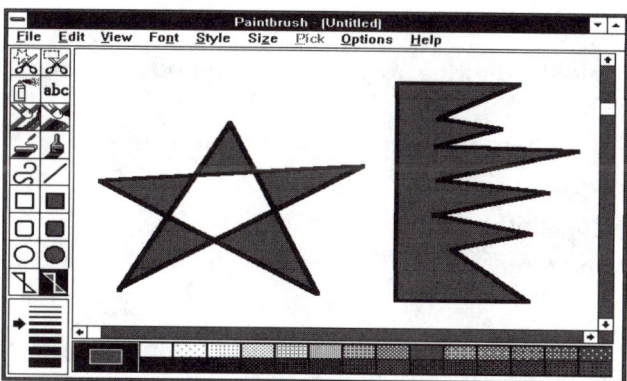

If you want straight horizontal, vertical, or diagonal sides, hold down the Shift key as you draw.

Using the Painting Tools

The Paintbrush drawing tools are rather constraining. You can draw straight lines, precise curves, and obedient shapes. But you can't draw anything freeform. If your nature is a little freer, you'll appreciate Paintbrush's painting tools, which you can use to draw more imaginative shapes. All the painting tools "paint" in the selected foreground color or shade. Before you start, remember to select the color or shade you want by pointing to it and clicking the left mouse button.

The Airbrush Tool

The Airbrush tool is a lot like a can of spray paint—it sprays a transparent mist of color instead of painting a solid color. If you select the Airbrush tool and click the left mouse button once, you get a round dot of misty color. But if you drag the mouse, you get a misty line.

You control the diameter of an airbrush dot or line by selecting the line width you want from the line-width box: a thin line produces a small dot or thin line; a thicker line produces a larger dot or thicker line. You control the

10

223

density of the mist by how fast you drag the mouse: a fast drag produces a light line; a slow drag produces a much denser airbrushed line.

To use the Airbrush tool, follow these steps:

1. Select the Airbrush tool.
2. Move the pointer into the drawing area, where the pointer becomes a crosshair.
3. Position the crosshair where you want to start the airbrush stroke.
4. Press and hold down the left mouse button.
5. Drag the crosshair to paint the airbrush stroke.
6. Release the mouse button.

Unlike other painting tools, the Airbrush tool sprays a transparent mist of color.

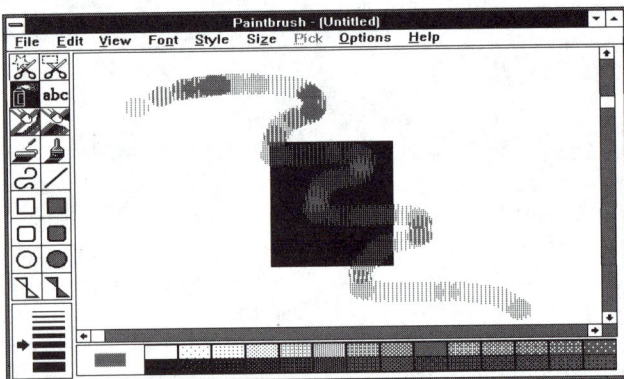

The Paint Roller Tool

 The Paint Roller tool fills a shape with a color or shade. The shape you fill can be an open shape or one that is already filled. In either case, the Paint Roller tool fills the shape with the selected foreground color or shade.

When you select the Paint Roller tool and move the pointer into the drawing area, the pointer turns into a tool which looks like a paint roller that is spreading paint. The pointed tip of this tool is where paint flows out to fill a shape. Because the tip is pointed, you can fill a very small shape with this tool.

10

Be careful when you fill a shape with the Paint Roller tool. If the shape is not completely closed, the paint leaks out, filling the entire screen. If that happens, choose the **Edit** menu and select the **Undo** command; then close the shape and try again. If you can't see the leak clearly, use the **View Zoom In** command to "blow up" the painting so that you can patch the leak dot by dot. (The **View Zoom In** command is explained in the section "Editing a Drawing" later in this chapter.)

To fill a shape with the Paint Roller tool, follow these steps:

1. Select the Paint Roller tool from the toolbox.

2. Select a foreground color or shade from the palette by clicking on the color or shade you want with the left mouse button.

3. Position the pointed tip of the Paint Roller tool inside the shape you want to fill.

4. Click the left mouse button.

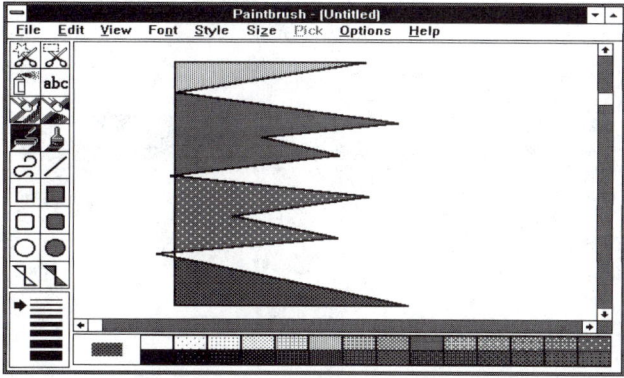

You can use the Paint Roller tool to fill any shape with the selected foreground color or shade.

10

The Brush Tool

The Brush tool paints an opaque stroke of the selected foreground color or shade. You can modify this versatile tool in two ways: by selecting a line width and by selecting a different brush shape. (Six brush shapes are available; if you don't choose one, you get the default square brush shape.) Like the other painting tools, the Brush tool enables you to paint free-form shapes.

225

To use the Brush tool, follow these steps:

1. Select the Brush tool from the toolbox.
2. Select a foreground shade or color from the palette.
3. Select a line width from the line-width box.
4. Press and hold down the left mouse button where you want the brushstroke to begin.
5. Drag the brush to paint a brushstroke.
6. Release the mouse button.

Using a line-shaped Brush tool, you can draw a line of variable width.

To change the brush shape, follow these steps:

1. Choose the Options menu and select the **Brush Shapes** command.

The Brush Shapes dialog box shows six different brush shapes.

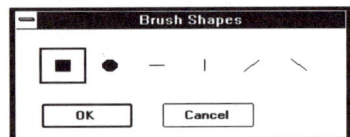

2. Select the brush shape you want to use.
3. Choose OK or press ↵Enter .

Adding Text

abc A picture may be worth a thousand words, but sometimes words can help clarify your message. Using the Text tool, you can type text in your drawing by using any of several fonts, styles, sizes, and colors or shades.

Typing with Paintbrush has some limitations. Unlike a word processing program, Paintbrush doesn't allow you to edit your text after you've finished typing. You can press the Backspace key to correct typing errors *while* you are typing, but after you click the mouse button, you can no longer use the Text tool to edit your text. Paintbrush also lacks a word-wrap feature; when you reach the edge of the screen, you must press Enter to move the insertion point to the next line.

When you type, text appears in the selected font, style, size, and foreground color. You can change any font and color selections before you start typing. Or you can change the selections while you type—before you click the mouse button. The changes will apply to all the text you have typed.

To type text, follow these steps:

1. Select the Text tool from the toolbox.
2. Move the pointer into the drawing area, where the pointer becomes an I-beam.
3. Position the I-beam where you want to start typing, and then click the left mouse button. (The I-beam turns into a flashing cursor or insertion point.)
4. Type the text.

10

227

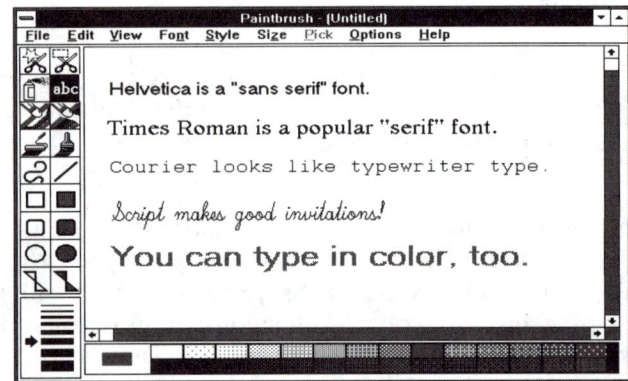

You can type text in black or in any color or shade— whatever you've selected as the foreground color.

Selecting a Font

A font is an alphabet of characters having the same appearance. Common fonts include Times Roman, Helvetica, and Courier.

The selected font has a check mark to its left.

10

To select a font, follow these steps:

1. Choose the Font menu.

2. Select the font you want to use.

When you select a font, that font applies to any new text you type as well as to any text you are currently typing, if you haven't clicked the mouse button.

Selecting a Type Style

A type style is a variation of the selected font. Paintbrush offers several type styles: Normal, **Bold**, *Italic*, Underline, Outline, and Shadow. You can use as many styles as you like at the same time. For example, you can type a title that is both bold and underlined. Select the Normal style to return to the plain (unadorned) font.

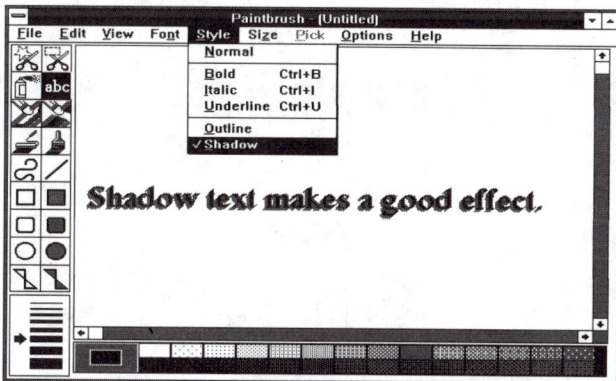

Typed text appears in the selected foreground color, with one exception: shadow text adds a shadow in the selected background color.

To select a type style, follow these steps:

1. Choose the **Style** menu.

2. Select one of the following styles:

   Normal
   Bold
   Italic
   Underline
   Outline
   Shadow

3. Repeat the process to select additional styles for the same text.

10

Selecting a Type Size

You can type your text in a variety of sizes. Type sizes are measured in points, 72 points per inch. Text you read in magazines, newspapers, and books appears in fairly small sizes—usually 9, 10, or 11 points. Larger text for headlines may be 18, 24, or 36 points.

In Paintbrush, different sizes are available for different fonts; unusable font sizes are dimmed in the Size menu. Some sizes have asterisks to their right. These sizes will give you the best printed results.

The size you se-
lect appears with
a check mark to
its left.

Size			
6	24	44	66
8	26	45	70
10	28 *	48	72
12	30	50	74
15 *	32	52	75
16 *	✓ 36 *	54	76
18	37	56	78
19 *	38	57	80
20	40	60	84
22 *	42	64	

To select a type size, follow these steps:

1. Choose the Size menu.
2. Select the size you want.

Editing a Drawing

10

A drawing can be modified in many ways. You can edit single objects, or you can change the whole picture. The simplest edit you can make is to use the Undo command, which undoes your most recent action (or series of actions). You can erase part of a drawing or change its colors. You can move or duplicate objects. And you can resize or tilt objects. For many editing procedures, you must first use either the Scissors or Pick tool to select the object (or objects) you want to modify.

Using the Undo ("Oops") Command

Everyone makes mistakes. When you do, you'll find a useful ally in the Undo command. Undo erases everything you've done since you last selected the tool you're using, used a scroll bar, opened another program, or resized the window. To avoid undoing something accidentally, reselect your tool each time you draw a line or shape you want to keep. That way, the next time you choose Undo, you'll undo your work only back to that point.

To undo your work, follow these steps:

1. Choose the **Edit** menu.
2. Select the **Undo** command.

Erasing

 Paintbrush has two tools you can use to erase—or recolor— parts of a drawing. The eraser tool on the *left* in the toolbox is the Color Eraser tool, which you can use to change the colors in the drawing. The eraser tool on the *right* in the toolbox is the Eraser tool, which changes everything to the background color. Selecting either tool produces a square "eraser." To erase, just drag the square eraser across the drawing. The size of the eraser depends on the selected line width; you get a small eraser with a thin line width, or a large eraser with a thick line width.

The Color Eraser Tool

The Color Eraser tool isn't really an eraser; it's a color switcher. It works two ways, and both ways depend on the foreground and background colors you've selected from the palette (this tool works only with colors, not shades):

- Drag the Color Eraser tool across an area in your drawing. Every occurrence of the *selected* foreground color changes to the selected background color.

- Double-click on the Color Eraser tool in the toolbox. Every occurrence of the *selected* foreground color in the visible area of your drawing changes to the selected background color. (The Color Eraser tool changes only the *selected* foreground color, whereas the Eraser tool, described next, changes *all* foreground color.)

10

231

Remember that the foreground color is the color in the *center* of the rectangle at the left end of the palette. You select the foreground color by clicking on the color you want with the *left* mouse button. The background color is the *outer* color in the rectangle in the palette box. You select the background color by clicking with the *right* mouse button.

To use the Color Eraser tool on part of your drawing, follow these steps:

1. Select the Color Eraser tool.
2. Select from the palette a foreground color (the color you want to change).
3. Select from the palette a background color (the color you want to change the foreground color to).
4. Move the pointer into the drawing area, where the pointer turns into a square eraser.
5. Press and hold down the left mouse button.
6. Drag the Color Eraser tool across the part of the drawing that you want to change from the selected foreground color to the selected background color.
7. Release the mouse button.

The Eraser Tool

The Eraser tool "erases" by changing every part of your drawing that it touches to the selected background color or shade. If the background color is white, passing the Eraser tool over an area turns it white. (If the background color is not white, the Eraser tool works more like a paintbrush than an eraser; everything you drag the tool over turns to the background color.)

To use the Eraser tool, follow these steps:

1. Select the Eraser tool from the toolbox.
2. If necessary, select a background color from the palette.
3. Move the pointer into the drawing area, where the pointer becomes a square eraser.
4. Press and hold down the left mouse button.
5. Drag the Eraser tool across the part of the drawing that you want to change to the background color or shade.
6. Release the mouse button.

10

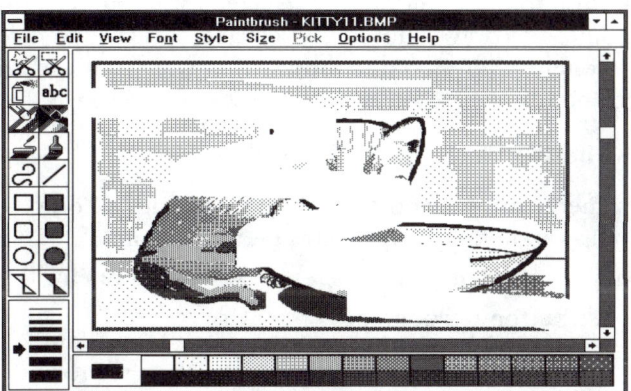

If the background color is white, passing the Eraser tool over an area turns it white.

You can use the Eraser tool to erase your *entire* drawing by double-clicking the Eraser tool in the toolbox. When you do, Paintbrush closes the current file but first asks whether you want to save changes. Choose **Yes** if you want to save them; otherwise, choose **No**.

Zooming In and Out

When you are doing detailed work, you can zoom in to get a close-up look at your drawing. To get an overview, you can zoom out to see the whole page.

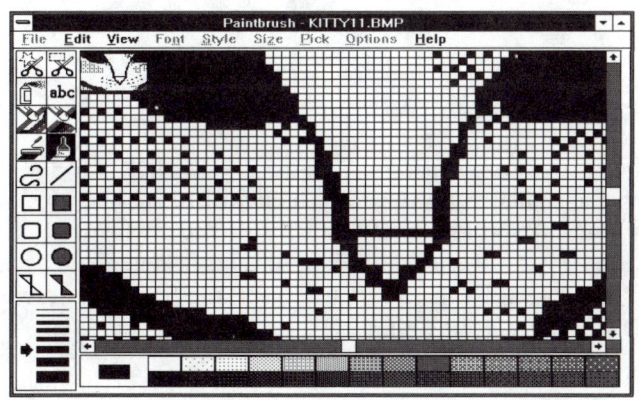

10

When you zoom in, you can edit the drawing dot by dot.

233

Click the *left* mouse button to draw a dot in the selected foreground color; click the *right* mouse button to draw a dot in the selected background color. You can use the Paint Roller tool in Zoom In mode if you want to fill an area with the foreground color.

To zoom in for a close-up view of a drawing, follow these steps:

1. Choose the **View** menu and select the Zoom **In** command. A Zoom box appears to help you define where you want to zoom in.
2. Position the Zoom box over the spot where you want to zoom in.
3. Click the left mouse button to zoom in.

To zoom back out to the regular editing view, choose the **View** menu and select the Zoom **Out** command. If you're in the regular editing view, Zoom Out shows you a reduced picture of the entire page.

Viewing More of a Drawing

If your drawing is larger than your computer screen, you can see more of the drawing by hiding all toolboxes, menus, and scroll bars. You can only view in this mode; you can't edit the drawing.

To view more of a drawing, follow these steps:

1. Choose the **View** menu and select the View **P**icture command.
2. To return to the regular editing view, click the mouse button or press Esc.

Selecting Objects in a Drawing

 With the two cutout tools, the Scissors (on the left) and the Pick (on the right), you can draw an enclosure around any part of your Paintbrush drawing. What's inside the enclosure is then "selected," and can be moved, cut, copied (and then pasted elsewhere), resized, tilted, flipped, or inverted. The left cutout tool, the Scissors, draws a free-form enclosure. The right cutout tool, the Pick, draws a rectangular enclosure.

10

To draw an enclosure with the Scissors tool, follow these steps:

1. Select the Scissors tool from the top *left* of the toolbox.
2. Move the pointer into the drawing area, where the pointer becomes a crosshair.
3. Press and hold down the left mouse button where you want to begin the enclosure.
4. Drag the mouse to draw a line around the area you want to select.
5. Release the mouse button at the same place you started drawing the line.

Press the left mouse button if you want to cancel the cutout.

With the Scissors tool, you can select an irregular shape; in this example, the kitten's head is selected.

To draw an enclosure with the Pick tool, follow these steps:

1. Select the Pick tool from the top *right* of the toolbox.
2. Move the pointer into the drawing area, where the pointer becomes a crosshair.
3. Press and hold down the left mouse button where you want to begin the enclosure.
4. Drag the mouse to draw a rectangle around the area you want to select.
5. Release the mouse button.

10

235

With the Pick tool, you can se-lect a rectangular shape; in this ex-ample, a dashed line surrounds the entire drawing.

Moving Objects

You can move an object, or groups of objects, to a different place in the drawing. First, you must select the objects with the Scissors or Pick tool.

To move an object, follow these steps:

1. Select the Scissors or Pick tool.
2. Draw a selection enclosure around the object you want to move.
3. Move the pointer inside the selection enclosure, where the pointer appears as an arrow.
4. Press and hold down the mouse button to "pick up" the selection.
5. Drag the selected object where you want it.
6. Release the mouse button.

You can move the selection as a transparent object by dragging it with the *left* mouse button. You can move the selection as an opaque object by dragging it with the *right* mouse button.

Duplicating Objects

Once you have selected an object, you can use the Scissors or Pick tool to duplicate it. The procedure is as simple as "copy and paste." When you paste

10

the object, it arrives, still selected, at the top left of the screen. You can move the object where you want it while it's still selected.

To select and copy an object, follow these steps:

1. Select the Scissors or Pick tool.
2. Draw a selection enclosure around the object you want to copy.
3. Choose the **E**dit menu and select the **C**opy command.
4. Choose the **E**dit menu and select the **P**aste command.

To move the pasted object, move the crosshair inside the selection enclosure, where the crosshair turns into an arrow. Press and hold down the mouse button, drag the object where you want it, and release the mouse button.

Using Special Effects

Using the **P**ick menu, you can perform all kinds of tricks with objects you have selected with either of the cutout tools (Scissors or Pick). You can flip, invert, shrink, enlarge, or tilt your selection.

Flipping a Selection

A selection can be flipped in two ways: horizontally (left to right) and vertically (top to bottom). To flip a selection, follow these steps:

1. Use the Scissors or Pick tool to select the object you want to flip.
2. Choose either the **P**ick Flip **H**orizontal command or the **P**ick Flip **V**ertical command.

10

Inverting Colors

You can invert the colors in your drawing, changing each one to the opposite color on the red/green/blue color wheel. For example, in an inverted black-and-white drawing, black becomes white, and white becomes black. In an inverted green-and-yellow drawing, green becomes magenta, and yellow becomes purple.

To invert colors, follow these steps:

1. Use the Scissors or Pick tool to select the object or area you want to invert.

2. Choose the **Pick Inverse** command.

Shrinking and Growing a Selection

You can use the **Pick Shrink + Grow** command to reduce or enlarge your selection. The procedure is a little unusual. Once you've selected the object and chosen the command, you drag the mouse to "draw" a box that is the size you want the resized image to fit. When you release the mouse button, the object drops into the box you drew, and the box disappears.

If you choose the **Pick Clear** command before you choose the **Pick Shrink + Grow** command, Paintbrush clears your original selection when you create the new, resized image. If you don't choose **Pick Clear**, you'll create a duplicate of your original.

To shrink or grow a selection, follow these steps:

1. Use the Scissors or Pick tool to select the object or area you want to shrink or grow.

2. Choose the **Pick** menu and select the **Shrink + Grow** command.

3. Move the crosshair where you want the new larger or smaller image to appear.

4. Press and hold down the mouse button, and then drag the mouse to draw a box that is the size you want for the duplicate image.

5. Release the mouse button.

To keep the new image proportional to the original, hold down Shift as you press, hold, drag, and release the mouse button.

Tilting a Selection

The **Tilt** command works a little like the **Shrink + Grow** command. Once you've selected the object and chosen the command, you drag the mouse to "draw" a box that is the angle you want the tilted image to drop into. When

10

238

you release the mouse button, the object appears, tilted, in the box you drew. The box disappears.

To tilt a selection, follow these steps:

1. Use the Scissors or Pick tool to select the object or area you want to tilt.

2. Choose the **Pick** menu and select the **Tilt** command.

3. Move the crosshair where you want the tilted object to appear.

4. Press and hold down the mouse button, and then drag the crosshair left or right to draw a tilted box.

5. Release the mouse button.

If you choose the **Pick Clear** command before you choose the **Pick Tilt** command, Paintbrush clears your original selection when you create the new tilted image.

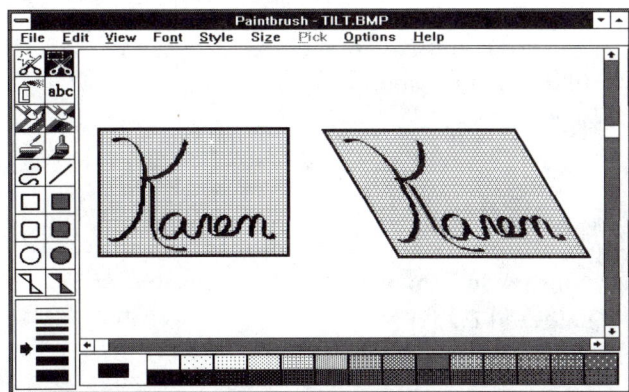

If you don't choose **Pick Clear**, you create a duplicate of your original.

Changing Margins, Headers, and Footers

Before you print your masterpiece, you may want to adjust its margins, or add headers or footers. Paintbrush starts out with default margins of one-half inch (0.50) on each side. If you want your drawing positioned differently on

10

the page, you can change the margins. Headers appear at the top of each printed page; footers appear at the bottom of each printed page. Headers and footers are centered between the left and right margins of the printed pages.

To change margins, headers, and footers, follow these steps:

1. Choose the **File** menu and select the **Page Setup** command.

The Page Setup dialog box appears.

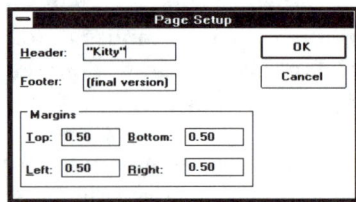

2. In the **Header** text box, type a header if you want one.

3. In the **Footer** text box, type a footer if you want one.

4. In the four Margins boxes (**Top**, **Bottom**, **Left**, and **Right**), type the margins you want (in decimal numbers).

5. Choose OK or press ⏎Enter.

Printing a Drawing

When it's time to print your drawing, many options are available with Paintbrush. For example, you can print a draft copy of the drawing to see a rough version of it, or you can print a final proof. You can print the whole drawing, or you can print only part of it—first selecting *which* part you want to print. You can print one or more copies of the drawing, and you can print the copies at a reduced or enlarged scale.

Paintbrush prints on the printer currently selected in Windows. If you've been printing with another Windows program, you probably won't have to select a printer in Paintbrush. But if this is your first time to print, or if you need to change printers, be sure to use the **Printer Setup** command to select a printer.

10

To select a printer, complete these steps:

1. Choose the **File** menu and select the **P**rinter Setup command.

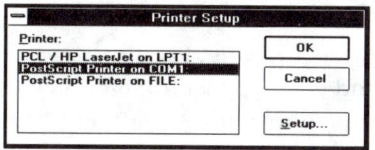

The Printer
Setup dialog box
appears.

2. Select a printer from the **P**rinter list box.
3. Choose OK or press ⏎Enter.

If you need to learn more about setting up a printer (such as changing fonts or paper orientation), refer to Chapter 6, "Customizing Your Work Area."

To print a Paintbrush drawing on the selected printer, follow these steps:

1. Choose the **File** menu and select the **P**rint command.

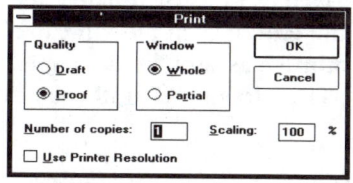

The Print dialog
box appears.

2. In the Quality box, select **D**raft to print a rough draft, or **P**roof to print a final version of the drawing.
3. In the Window box, select **W**hole to print the entire drawing, or **P**artial to print the portion you select.
4. In the **N**umber of copies box, type the number of copies you want to print.
5. In the **S**caling box, type a percent at which you want to print the drawing. For example, type **50** (for 50 percent) to print at half size.
6. Select the **U**se Printer Resolution check box to print at printer resolution rather than screen resolution.

10

If your drawing appears out of proportion the first time you print it, try selecting the Use Printer Resolution option and printing again. This option may correct the problem.

7. Choose OK or press ⏎Enter.

If you elected to print only part of the drawing, Paintbrush shows you a reduced version of the drawing and gives you a crosshair. Use the crosshair to draw a box around the area of the drawing you want to print.

Saving a Drawing and Quitting the Paintbrush Program

To avoid losing any of your work, you should save your files frequently. It's often a good idea to save several versions of your progressing drawing. For example, if you're creating a chart, you might name your successive files CHART01, CHART02, and so on. File names can contain up to eight characters.

Like most programs, Paintbrush saves files in its own native file format and assigns a three-letter extension to the end of each file (an extension is like a last name). The extension that Paintbrush assigns to file names is BMP. If, for instance, you assign the name PAINTING to a file, Paintbrush calls it PAINTING.BMP.

If you want to save a drawing to use in a different program, you can save the drawing in a different format. For example, many graphics and desktop publishing programs are compatible with the PCX format. You can save a Paintbrush drawing in PCX format; Paintbrush then assigns the extension PCX to the file name.

To save a Paintbrush file, follow these steps:

1. Choose the File menu and select the Save As command.

10

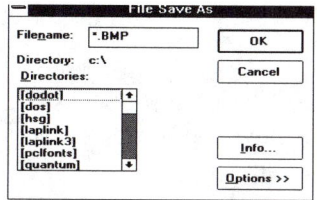

The File Save As
dialog box
appears.

2. Type a file name in the File**n**ame text box.

3. From the **Directories** list box, select the directory in which you want to save the file.

4. Select the **O**ptions >> box if you want the PCX file format; then select the **PCX** button.

5. Choose OK or press ⏎Enter.

To resave your file later, without changing its name, choose the **E**dit menu and select the **S**ave command.

When you are finished working with Paintbrush, quit the program by choosing the **F**ile menu and selecting the **E**xit command.

Summary

Paintbrush is a simple graphics program you can use to create illustrations for your work, or computer drawings just for fun.

When you start Paintbrush, you are presented with a toolbox, a line-width box, a palette, and a drawing area. The toolbox contains tools for drawing lines, boxes, circles, and polygons, as well as tools for drawing free-form lines and shapes. The line-width box offers a selection of line widths. The palette displays an array of colors if you have a color monitor, or a variety of gray shades if you have a monochrome monitor. To pick a tool or line width or to select a color, just point and click. When you move the pointer into the drawing area of the screen, the pointer turns into a crosshair, and you're ready to start creating.

You can type text on your drawing, selecting from a variety of fonts, sizes, and styles. You can perform many tricks with selected objects, such as flipping, reducing, enlarging, and tilting them. To improve your evolving drawing, you can erase and edit parts of it.

10

In this chapter, you learned the following important points about the Paintbrush tools:

- You use the Scissors and Pick tools to select objects in a drawing. You can then change, copy, or move the selected objects.

- The Airbrush tool sprays a fine mist of the color you selected from the palette.

- With the Text tool, you can type text in a drawing.

- The Color Eraser and Eraser tools change the colors in a drawing when you drag these tools across it. If you "erase" with white (and the background of the drawing is also white), the Eraser tool erases the portion you drag across.

- The Paint Roller tool fills a shape with a color or shade. The Brush tool paints a stroke of color or shade.

- You use the Curve tool to draw precise C-shaped or S-shaped curves, and the Line tool to draw straight lines.

- The unfilled Box tool draws empty boxes with right-angle corners. The filled Box tool draws filled boxes with right-angle corners. The unfilled Rounded Box tool draws empty boxes with rounded corners. And the filled Rounded Box tool draws filled boxes with rounded corners.

- The unfilled Circle/Ellipse tool draws empty circles and ovals. The filled Circle/Ellipse tool draws filled circles and ovals.

- The unfilled Polygon tool draws empty polygons. The filled Polygon tool draws filled polygons.

10

In the next chapter, "Using Desktop Accessories," you will learn about many more Windows accessory programs. Described in that chapter are Notepad, a text editing program that works like a simple word processing program; Cardfile, a computerized stack of name-and-address cards; Calendar, an automated appointment tracker; Calculator, a quick desktop calculator you can use side-by-side with your other programs; Terminal, an easy-to-use communications program to use with your modem; and Clock, a small but accurate desktop timepiece. In combination with Windows Write and Windows Paintbrush, you will find the desktop accessories to be valuable aids in your day-to-day work.

Using Desktop Accessories

One of the greatest advantages to using Windows is that you can run several programs at the same time. But instead of using your major programs side by side, you may want to work with only one of those programs—and keep small accessory programs close at hand. That's where the Windows accessory programs shine. For example, you may be working in Excel and want to jot down an idea in a quick memo. The Notepad accessory is perfect for the task. Or you may be working in Word for Windows and need to do a quick calculation. Open the Calculator accessory, add up your figures, and copy the total back into Word for Windows. At the end of the day, you may want to relax with a game. Challenge yourself with Solitaire.

The Windows accessory programs Notepad, Calendar, Cardfile, Calculator, and Clock are small, so they don't use much of your computer's memory. And they're simple, so they don't take much of *your* memory! They are good, useful companions to your primary programs.

11

Key Terms in This Chapter

Insertion point	The flashing vertical line where text appears when you type (sometimes called a cursor).
Scroll	To move up, down, left, or right in a document. Most programs have scroll bars to make scrolling easy.
Select	To highlight text for editing.
Cut/copy and paste	To move or copy text from one part of a document to another, or to move or copy text between programs.
Clipboard	The temporary file in Windows that stores any text you selected and then cut or copied. You can paste the contents of the Clipboard wherever you move the insertion point.
Search or find	To look through a document for a specific word or phrase.
View	To look at a document in a different way; for example, you can look at the Calendar in the Day view or Month view.

Four other Windows programs—Write, Paintbrush, Recorder, and PIF Editor—are considered Windows accessory programs as well. But because they are powerful enough to be used as primary programs, the first three are discussed in separate chapters, and the PIF Editor is covered in Chapter 13, "Running Non-Windows Programs." This chapter covers six accessory programs and two games:

- Notepad—a miniature word processor you can use to type quick notes and memos.
- Calendar—an "alarming" appointment calendar that lets you see daily or monthly views of your schedule. You can set an alarm to remind you of something important.

11

- Cardfile—a computerized "stack of cards" you can use to store names, addresses, phone numbers, and other information. You can quickly find the cards containing a specific word or phrase.

- Terminal—a communications program that lets your computer "talk" with another computer over a telephone line. (You must have a modem to take advantage of Terminal.)

- Calculator—a program that works just like a calculator, except that you don't need batteries.

- Clock—a clock that lets you be a clock-watcher as you stare at the screen. Even as an icon, Clock shows the time.

- Reversi—a little strategy game that will make you wonder how it got to be 1:00 a.m. so quickly.

- Solitaire—the classic card game to help you get tense about something other than work.

Starting the Windows Accessory Programs

All the Windows accessory programs are located inside the Accessories group window. Each accessory program appears as an icon with its name below it. To start any program, just double-click on its icon. Or select the Accessories window, press an arrow key to select the program item icon, and press Enter.

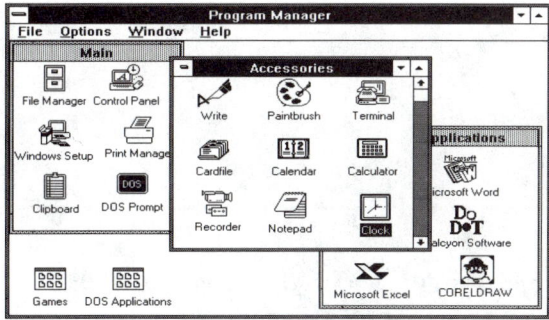

When the Accessories group icon is open as a window, you can see the programs it contains.

After you start the accessory programs, you may want to minimize them as icons at the bottom of the screen until you need to use them.

11

Writing in Notepad

The Notepad program is like a miniature word processor. Although Notepad has limited functions compared to Windows Write or Word for Windows, Notepad is ideal for many purposes. Just as you use a notepad on your desk, you can use Notepad to take notes on-screen alongside other Windows programs, such as Excel.

As a bonus, Notepad includes a feature for logging time. You can therefore use Notepad as a time clock to let you know when you opened a file or to monitor the time you spend on a project.

Notepad retrieves and saves files as ASCII text. (ASCII is a computer's most basic file format.) For this reason, you can transfer Notepad files into almost any word processing program.

Opening Notepad and Typing Text

Open the Notepad program just as you open any Windows program—by double-clicking on the Notepad icon in the Accessories group window, or by pressing the arrow keys to select the icon and then pressing Enter. A new Notepad file with a blank screen appears.

As soon as you open a Notepad file, you can begin typing.

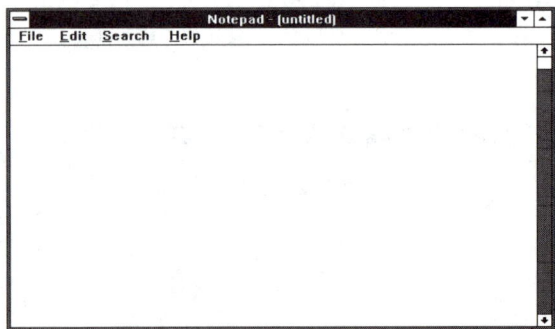

Each character you type appears to the left of a blinking vertical line called the insertion point. Unlike most word processing programs, Notepad does not wrap text automatically to the next line. If you want text to wrap (so that you don't have to press Enter each time you reach the end of a line), choose the Edit menu and select the **Word Wrap** command.

248

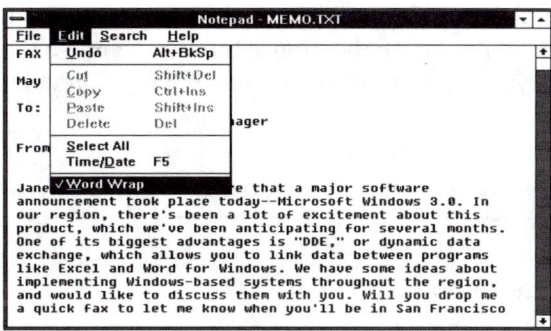

11

When you select
the Word Wrap
command, a
check mark ap-
pears to its left.

With word wrap selected, text wraps to fit the width of the Notepad window, no matter how wide the window is. If you make the window wider, the text will be wider also (and may stretch past the right edge of the window). With automatic word wrap turned off, lines can be as long as 160 characters.

Note: A Notepad document can hold about 50,000 characters—maybe 10 or 15 pages. To see how many characters a document contains, choose the **Help** menu and select the **About Notepad** command. The `Characters in File` message at the bottom of the About Notepad window tells you how many characters the document contains. If the number gets too high, you risk losing your work. Start a new file or transfer your work into a word processing program such as Windows Write or Word for Windows.

Moving and Scrolling on the Notepad Page

To edit text in a Notepad file or to add new text, you must learn to scroll the page and move the insertion point. The Notepad page scrolls just like other Windows programs. The horizontal and vertical scroll bars represent the entire Notepad document, and a white box, the *thumb*, represents your current position within the document. With the mouse, scroll the Notepad page by clicking the up and down arrows in the vertical scroll bar, or the left and right arrows in the horizontal scroll bar. With the keyboard, scroll the page by pressing the PgUp and PgDn keys, or the up- and down-arrow keys.

Another way to move around on the Notepad page is to move the insertion point, using either the mouse or the keyboard. As in any word processing program, you cannot move the insertion point beyond where you've already typed.

11

To move the insertion point with the mouse, position the I-beam where you want the insertion point, and then click the mouse button. To move the insertion point with the keyboard, use the keystrokes described in table 11.1.

Table 11.1
Keystrokes for Moving the Insertion Point

Keystroke(s)	Action
↑	Moves the insertion point up
↓	Moves the insertion point down
←	Moves the insertion point left
→	Moves the insertion point right
End	Moves the insertion point to the end of a line
Home	Moves the insertion point to the beginning of a line
Ctrl + Home	Moves the insertion point to the beginning of the document
Ctrl + End	Moves the insertion point to the end of the document

Opening an Existing or New Notepad File

If you have already opened the Notepad program, you can open an existing Notepad file—one you created earlier. When you open an existing Notepad file, the Notepad file you are currently working on closes, offering you the option to save your changes.

To open an existing Notepad file, follow these steps:

1. Choose the **File** menu and select the **Open** command.

The File Open dialog box appears.

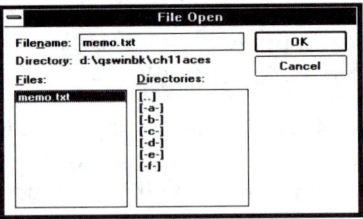

250

11

2. From the **Directories** list, select the directory containing the file you want to open.

3. From the **Files** list, select the file you want to open.

4. Choose OK.

If you want to open a new Notepad file, choose the **File** menu and select the **New** command. If you haven't saved the Notepad document you're currently working on, Notepad asks whether you want to save the document. Choose **Yes** if you want to save the file, or **No** if you don't. Refer to the section "Saving and Printing Notepad Files" later in this chapter to learn more about saving a file.

Selecting and Editing Text in Notepad

Selecting and editing text in Notepad is exactly the same as selecting and editing text in Write and other word processing programs.

The simplest way to edit is to insert and delete text one character at a time. To insert text, move the insertion point to the new text location and start typing. Delete a single character by moving the insertion point to the left of the character and pressing the Del (Delete) key, or by moving to the right of the character and pressing the Backspace key.

To make more extensive edits, you must first select text. To select text with the mouse, drag the I-beam across the text you want to select while holding down the mouse button. To select text with the keyboard, hold down the Shift key while you then press any arrow key. You can select all the text at once in your Notepad document by choosing the **Edit** menu and selecting the **Select All** command.

To delete text, select the text to delete, choose the **Edit** menu, and select the **Delete** command. Or select the text to be deleted and press the Del key.

11

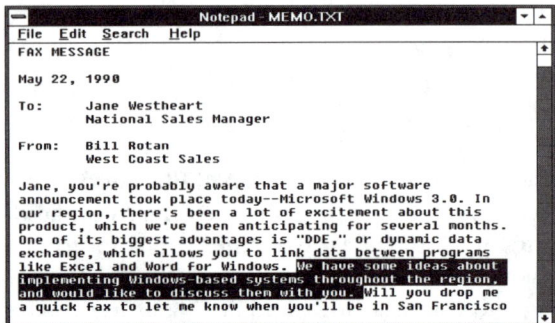

You can replace
selected text by
simply typing the
new text.

If you make a typing error, you can correct it by choosing the Edit menu and selecting the Undo command. Remember that you can undo only the most recent "Oops!"

Copying and Moving Text in Notepad

Notepad's **Edit** commands enable you to copy or move selected text from one place to another. As in any Windows program, text to be copied or moved is stored in the Clipboard, a temporary file that holds only one selection. Text is then pasted from the Clipboard into the document at the insertion point.

To copy or move text, follow these steps:

1. Select the text you want to copy or move.
2. Choose the **E**dit menu and select the **C**opy command to copy text. Or choose the **E**dit menu and select the **Cu**t command to move text.
3. Move the insertion point where you want to copy or move the text.
4. Choose the **E**dit menu and select the **P**aste command.

You can paste text from the Clipboard as many times as you like. Because the Clipboard holds only one item at a time, though, be sure to paste text as soon as you copy or cut it; the next item you copy or cut replaces what is currently in the Clipboard.

Searching through a Notepad Document

11

Notepad's Search menu contains commands for finding and selecting any word or phrase. When Notepad finds the word you are looking for, the program closes the Find dialog box and selects the word or phrase found.

To search for text, follow these steps:

1. Choose the **Search** menu and select the **Find** command.

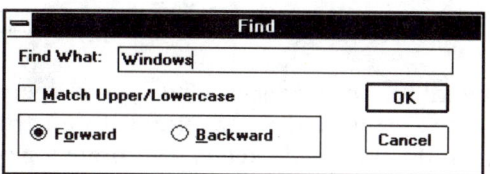

The Find dialog box appears.

2. In the **Find What** text box, type the text you want to find.

3. Select the **Match Upper/Lowercase** box if you want to find text that matches upper- and lowercase letters.

4. Select **Forward** to search forward from the insertion point, or **Backward** to select backward from the insertion point.

5. Choose OK.

Creating a Time-Log File with Notepad

Using a special but simple code, Notepad automatically enters the time and date at the end of a document each time you open it. This feature is convenient if you need to monitor your time or calculate the amount of time you spend on a project.

To create an automatic time log in your document, follow these steps:

1. Move the insertion point to the left margin of the first line in your Notepad document.

2. Type the command **.LOG** in capital letters.

253

11

Each time you open a file that has .LOG as its first line, Notepad logs the current time and date.

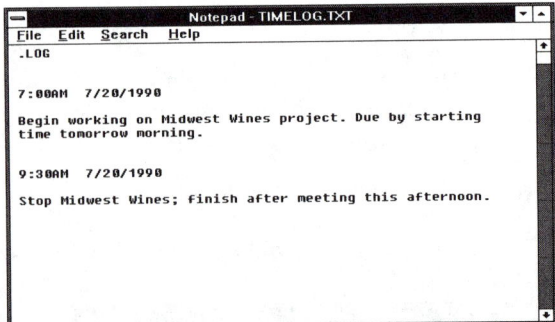

Now you can type a note describing your project. When you reopen the Notepad file, the time and date are inserted automatically. By entering notes describing your work between the times, you keep an accurate log of how you are spending your time.

Another way to create a time log is to insert the current time and date manually.

To insert the time and date in your document, follow these steps:

1. Move the insertion point where you want the time and date entered.
2. Choose the **E**dit menu and select the Time/**D**ate command.

Saving and Printing Notepad Files

To save a Notepad file and give it a name, follow these steps:

1. Choose the **F**ile menu and select the Save **A**s command.

The File Save As dialog box appears.

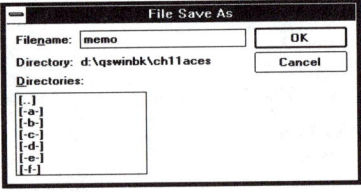

254

2. From the **D**irectories list box, select the directory in which you want to save the file.

3. Type a name (up to eight characters) in the **F**ilename text box.

4. Choose OK.

Notepad adds the extension TXT to the file name. For example, if you call the file MEMO, Notepad names it MEMO.TXT. To save a file with the name it already has, choose the **F**ile menu and select the **S**ave command. The current file replaces the original version.

You can print a Notepad file on the currently selected printer. When you print the file, you will see a message box on the screen, telling you that the document is printing. To cancel the print, choose the Cancel button in the Notepad dialog box. (For more information about selecting a printer, refer to the section "Adding and Setting Up Printers" in Chapter 6.)

To print a Notepad file, follow these steps:

1. Make sure that the Notepad file you want to print is displayed on-screen.

2. Choose the **F**ile menu and select the **P**rint command.

Closing a File and Exiting Notepad

You can close a Notepad file in two ways: open a new file or exit the Notepad program. To open a file, choose the **F**ile menu and select the **O**pen command. (You can even use this technique to reopen the currently open file—for example, to log the current time and date.) To exit the Notepad program, choose the **F**ile menu and select the Exit command.

Tracking Appointments with Calendar

The Windows Calendar program is a computerized appointment book you can use to record appointments, mark special dates, and even set an alarm to remind you of an important event. Calendar operates in two views: Day and Month.

11

Opening Calendar

Open the Calendar program as you open any Windows program—by double-clicking on the Calendar icon in the Accessories group window, or by pressing the arrow keys to select the icon and then pressing Enter. A new Calendar file appears, displayed in the Day view.

Calendar's Day view is marked in hourly intervals. You can scroll through the times and type appointments for each hour.

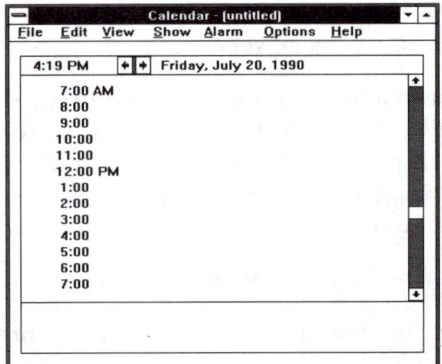

Below the Calendar window's menu bar is a status bar showing the current time and date. (If they are wrong, refer to Chapter 6, "Customizing Your Work Area," to learn how to reset them through the Control Panel.) The status bar is shared between Calendar's two views, Day and Month.

Typing Appointments in the Day View

When you open the Calendar window, you see the Day view for the current time and date. On the left are listed times, and on the right is room to type appointments. To type an appointment, move the insertion point to the correct time and then type the text. You can type about 80 characters on each line.

To move the insertion point with the mouse, point to any time by clicking the I-beam where you want to type. With the keyboard, just press the up- or down-arrow key.

Although only part of the day is displayed in the Calendar window, 24 hours are available. To enter an appointment at a time not displayed, use the scroll

256

bar on the right side of the Calendar window to scroll up or down to the time you want. Or from the keyboard, use the up- and down-arrow keys, or the PgUp and PgDn keys, to scroll up and down.

To type an appointment in a Calendar file, follow these steps:

1. Scroll the Calendar window to display the time you want.

2. Move the insertion point to the time of your appointment.

3. Type the appointment.

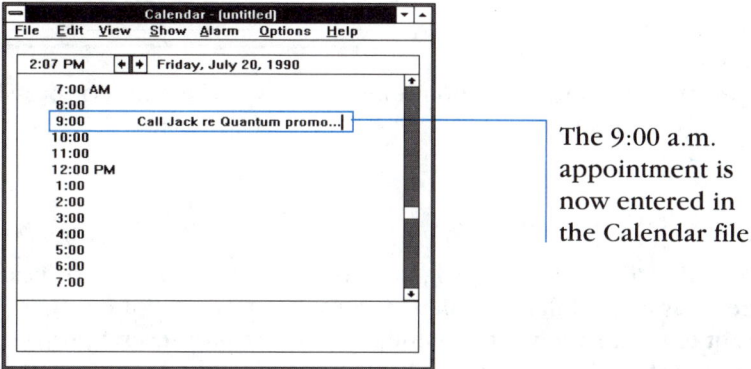

The 9:00 a.m. appointment is now entered in the Calendar file.

4. Press Enter to move the insertion point to the next line.

At the bottom of each daily or monthly Calendar window is a three-line scratch pad in which you can type notes. A note stays attached to its date; whenever you turn to that date, the note appears in the scratch pad.

To type a note in the scratch pad, follow these steps:

1. Move to the scratch pad by clicking in it or pressing [Tab⇄].

2. Type the text of your note.

11

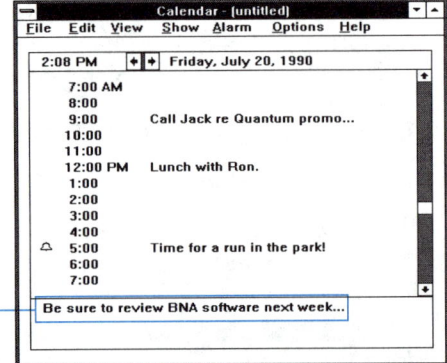

A note is attached to the date for which it is typed.

3. Move back to the appointment area by clicking in it or pressing Tab ⇆ again.

Opening an Existing Calendar File

Calendar, like any other program, creates and stores files. You can therefore create as many different Calendar files as you want. For example, you may want to create a separate Calendar file for each of several projects. You can open each of the Calendar files as you need them.

To open an existing Calendar file, follow these steps:

1. Choose the **File** menu and select the **Open** command.

The File Open dialog box appears.

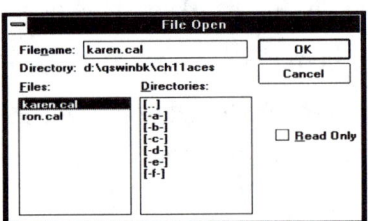

2. In the **Directories** list, select the directory containing the Calendar file you want to open.

3. In the **Files** list, select the Calendar file you want to open.

4. Choose OK.

258

Editing and Moving Calendar Appointments

11

You can edit text in either the appointment area or the scratch pad just as you edit text in any Windows program. For instance, you can select text and then press the Backspace key or the Del (Delete) key to delete it. To add text, you can position the insertion point where you want the new text, and then type it. You can also copy or move appointments from one time or date to another time or date.

To copy or move appointments or notes, follow these steps:

1. Select the text you want to copy or move.
2. Choose the **E**dit menu and select the **C**opy command to copy the text. Or choose the **Cut** command to move the text.
3. Move the insertion point to the new time or date.
4. Choose the **E**dit menu and select the **P**aste command.

Removing Appointments from a Calendar File

Old appointments take up disk space, and you probably don't want them cluttering up your Calendar files. Fortunately, you can remove appointments for an individual day or for a range of days. (You remove appointments only in the currently open Calendar file.)

To remove appointments from the currently open Calendar file, follow these steps:

1. Choose the **E**dit menu and select the **R**emove command.

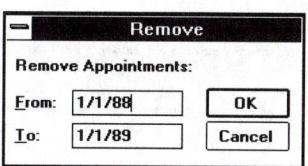

In the Remove dialog box that appears, you can specify a range of dates to remove.

2. In the From box, type the first date you want to remove, using the format mm-dd-yy or mm/dd/yy.

11

3. In the **To** box, type the last date you want to remove, using the
format mm-dd-yy or mm/dd/yy.

4. Choose OK.

If you want to remove appointments from just one date, type the date in the
From box and type nothing in the **To** box.

Setting an Alarm

To remind yourself of an important appointment, you can set an alarm that
alerts you when the time for the appointment arrives. You can set alarms for
as many appointments in a Calendar file as you like.

To turn on the alarm, follow these steps:

1. Move the insertion point to the time when you want the alarm to
sound.

2. Choose the **Alarm** menu and select the **Set** command.

To turn off the alarm, follow the same procedure.

When you set the
alarm, a small
bell appears to
the left of the ap-
pointment time
in the Calendar
window.

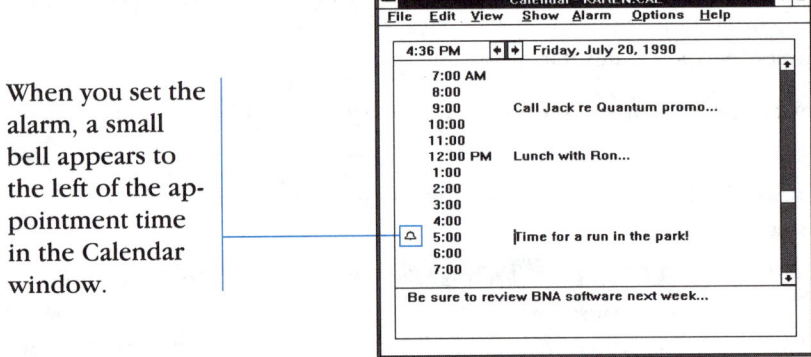

When the appointed time arrives, an alarm sounds a beep (unless you have
inactivated the sound), and the Alarm dialog box flashes to remind you of
your appointment.

260

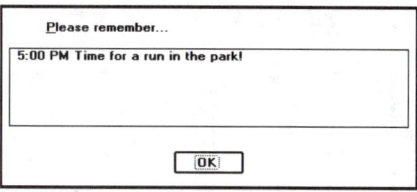

To continue
working, you
must respond
to the Alarm
dialog box.

11

If the Calendar is inactive when the alarm goes off, the Calendar title bar or
icon flashes instead. You must activate Calendar so that you can respond to
the Alarm dialog box. To turn off the Alarm dialog box, choose OK in the
dialog box.

Using Calendar's Two Views

As indicated previously, Calendar has two views, Day and Month. The Day
view shows you the details of each day's appointments. The Month view
shows you an overview of the whole month.

Switching between the views is easy. To switch to the Month view, choose
the View menu and select the **Month** command. To switch to the Day view,
choose the View menu and select the **Day** command.

If you have a mouse, you can double-click on the date in the status bar to
switch between the Month and Day views.

Viewing the Calendar by Month

Like the Day view, Calendar's Month view shows the current time and date in
a status bar below the menus. The day selected in Calendar's Month view is
the same day you were on when you switched from the Day view.

11

In the Month view, the current date (today's date) appears in angle brackets (> <).

```
┌─────────────────────────────────────────────────┐
│ ─           Calendar - KAREN.CAL          ▼ ▲     │
│ File  Edit  View  Show  Alarm  Options  Help      │
│ ┌───────────────────────────────────────────┐   │
│ │ 4:45 PM    ◆ ◆   Friday, July 20, 1990      │   │
│ │                   July 1990                 │   │
│ │   S     M     T     W     T     F     S     │   │
│ │   1     2     3     4     5     6     7      │   │
│ │   8     9    10    11    12    13    14      │   │
│ │  15    16    17    18    19   > 20 <  21     │   │
│ │  22    23    24    25    26    27    28      │   │
│ │  29    30    31                             │   │
│ │ Be sure to review BNA software next week... │   │
│ └───────────────────────────────────────────┘   │
└─────────────────────────────────────────────────┘
```

Notice that the scratch pad for the selected day in the Month view is the same as the scratch pad for that day in the Day view. You can move into the scratch pad to type or edit text by either pressing the Tab key or clicking the mouse button in the scratch pad.

To select a different day in the Month view, press any arrow key to move one day in that direction, or click on the day you want to select. You can make other moves in the monthly calendar just as you move in the daily calendar; these moves are listed in table 11.2 in the section "Displaying Different Dates and Times."

Marking Important Days

In the Month view, you can mark a date to remind you of a special event, like a report due date, a project completion date, or your sister's birthday. (It's a good idea to make a note in the scratch pad area reminding you *why* the occasion is marked.)

You can use any of five symbols to mark a date in Calendar's Month view.

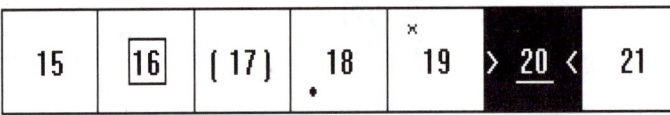

To mark a date in Calendar's Month view, follow these steps:

1. Select the date you want to mark by clicking on it or pressing the arrow keys.

2. Choose the **O**ptions menu and select the **M**ark command.

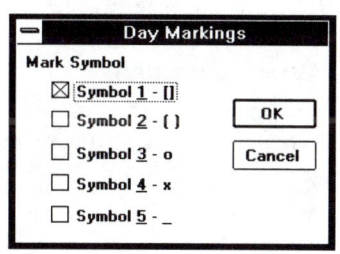

The Day Markings dialog box appears.

3. Select one of the following:

> Mark Symbol **1** - [ ]
>
> Mark Symbol **2** - ( )
>
> Mark Symbol **3** - o
>
> Mark Symbol **4** - x
>
> Mark Symbol **5** - _

4. Choose OK.

Displaying Different Dates and Times

Whenever you open a new or an existing Calendar file, you will always see the current date in the Day view, or the current month in the Month view. But you can move between different dates and times by using the techniques listed in table 11.2. Many of the techniques include commands in the **S**how menu.

263

11

Table 11.2
Moving in a Calendar File

Action(s)	*Result*
Choose the **Sh**ow menu and select the **Pr**evious command	Moves to the previous day or month
Click the left arrow in the date/time status bar	Moves to the previous day or month
Choose the **Sh**ow menu and select the **N**ext command	Moves to the next day or month
Click the right arrow in the date/time status bar	Moves to the next day or month
Choose the **Sh**ow menu and select the **T**oday command	Moves to today's date
Choose the **Sh**ow menu, select the **D**ate command, type the date (such as 1/1/91), and press Enter	Moves to a specific date
Press the up- or down- arrow key	Moves to a different time (Day view) or day (Month view)
Press PgUp or PgDn	Moves to a different time (Day view) or month (Month view)
Click the scroll bar arrows	Moves to a different time (Day view only)
Tab	Moves between the scratch pad and the appointment area (Day view) or date (Month view)

Saving a Calendar File

You can save as many different Calendar files as you like—for different projects, resources, clients, and so on. The first time you save a Calendar file, you must name it.

To save a new Calendar file, follow these steps:

1. Choose the **F**ile menu and select the Save **A**s command.

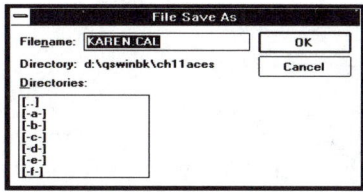

The File Save As
dialog box
appears.

2. In the **Filename** text box, type a file name (up to eight characters).

3. From the **Directories** list box, select the directory in which you want to save the file.

4. Choose OK.

To save an existing Calendar file without changing its name, choose the **File** menu and select the **S**ave command.

Printing Appointments from a Calendar File

You can print appointments for a day or a range of days from the currently open Calendar file. Pages are printed on the currently selected printer. (See Chapter 6, "Customizing Your Work Area," to learn how to select a printer.)

To print a range of appointments, follow these steps:

1. Choose the **F**ile menu and select the **P**rint command.

2. In the **F**rom box, type the first appointment day to print.

3. In the **T**o box, type the last day to print, using the format mm-dd-yy or mm/dd/yy.

4. Choose OK.

If you want to print just a single date, type the date in the **F**rom box and type nothing in the **T**o box.

Closing a Calendar File and Exiting the Program

You can close a Calendar file in two ways: open a new file or close the Calendar program. To open a new file, choose the **F**ile menu and select the **N**ew command. To close the Calendar program, choose the **F**ile menu and select the E**x**it command.

11 Storing and Retrieving Information in Cardfile

The Cardfile program is a good place to store names, addresses, phone numbers, and even graphics—any information you want to access quickly. Each "card" in a Cardfile file has two parts: an index line at the top, and an area for text (or graphics) below. Cards are always arranged alphabetically by index line, and the active card is the one displayed on top of the stack.

Cardfile is like a computerized stack of three-by-five index cards.

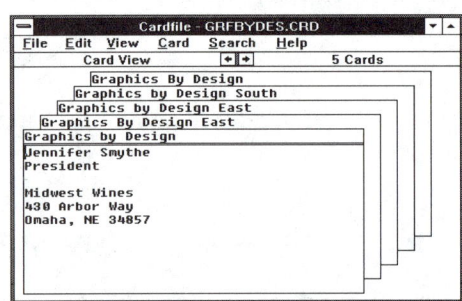

You can create as many separate Cardfile files as you want. For example, you may want a separate file for each of your major clients or projects, or you may want separate files for home and office.

Starting Cardfile

You open the Cardfile program the way you open any Windows program—by double-clicking on the Cardfile icon in the Accessories group window, or by pressing the arrow keys to select the icon and then pressing Enter.

An empty Cardfile appears when you start the Cardfile program.

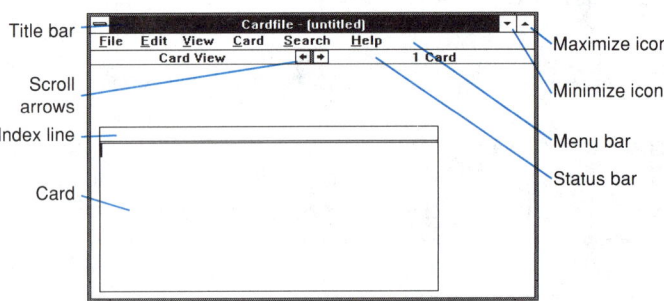

266

11

Once the Cardfile program is running, you can open an existing Cardfile. When you open an existing Cardfile, the file you are using is closed. If necessary, a dialog box asks whether you want to save the current changes. Choose **Yes** to save the current changes, **No** to discard them, or Cancel to return to your file.

To open an existing Cardfile, follow these steps:

1. Choose the **File** menu and select the **O**pen command.

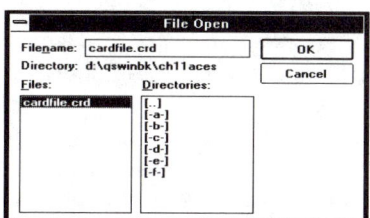

The File Open dialog box appears.

2. From the **Directories** list, select the directory containing the file you want to open.

3. From the **Files** list, select the file you want to open.

4. Choose OK.

After you've already started the program, you can also open a new Cardfile by choosing the **File** menu and selecting the **New** command.

Entering Information into a Cardfile Card

When you open a new Cardfile, you see a single blank card. The card's index line is at the top of the card, and the card's body is below the index line. The insertion point flashes in the top left corner of the body of the card, just below a double line. You type information—such as a name, an address, and a phone number—in the body of the card. To enter the information, simply begin typing. When you reach the right edge of the card, text automatically wraps to the next line.

The index line at the top of the card is important because Cardfile arranges cards alphabetically by index lines. Creating an index line is different from

11

typing text in the body of the card. You must choose a menu command before you can type an index line.

To create an index line and type text in it, follow these steps:

1. Choose the **Edit** menu and select the **Index** command.

The Index dialog box appears.

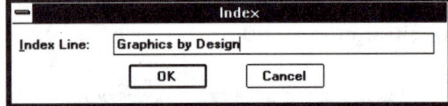

2. In the **Index Line** text box, type the text for the index line.

3. Choose OK.

Using the Index command is the only way to enter—or change—an index line in an existing card. (To change an existing index line, follow the same steps as for creating a new index line. Instead of typing new text, edit the existing text in the index line.) A shortcut for displaying the top card's index line is to double-click on the index line.

Adding a Card

Adding new cards to an existing Cardfile is easy, but the procedure is a little different from starting with a brand new Cardfile. When you add a new card, you type the index line before you type the text on the card.

To add a new card to an existing Cardfile, follow these steps:

1. Choose the **Card** menu and select the **Add** command.

The Add dialog box appears.

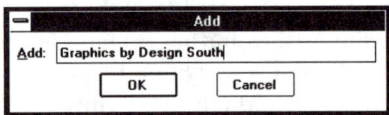

2. In the **Add** text box, type an index line for the new card.

3. Choose OK.

268

The new card with the index line you just typed is displayed on top of the stack of cards. The insertion point is at the top left of the card, ready for you to type the card's contents.

Scrolling through the Cards

Once you have added many cards to a Cardfile, you need a way to display the card you want to see by bringing it to the top of the stack. The Cardfile program provides several ways to scroll through your cards to display the one you want.

You can scroll through the cards one by one. At the top of the Cardfile window is a pair of arrows, one facing left and one facing right. Click on the left arrow to scroll backward one card; click on the right arrow to scroll forward one card. The PgUp and PgDn keys perform the same tasks. But perhaps the easiest way to display a card is to click on its index line. These and additional methods of scrolling in a Cardfile are summarized in table 11.3.

Table 11.3
Scrolling in a Cardfile

Action(s)	*Result*
Click the left arrow in the Cardfile window or press PgUp	Scrolls backward one card
Click the right arrow in the Cardfile window or press PgDn	Scrolls forward one card
Click on the card's index line	Scrolls to a specific card
Press Ctrl + Home	Scrolls to the first card
Press Ctrl + End	Scrolls to the last card
Press Ctrl + *letter*	Scrolls to the card with an index beginning with *letter*

Searching through the Cards

Another way to find a specific card, besides scrolling, is to search for a card containing a certain word or phrase. You can search through text in the body

11

of the cards, or you can search the index lines—there's a different command for each type of search. An additional command lets you quickly repeat your most recent search.

To search through index lines in a Cardfile, follow these steps:

1. Choose the **Search** menu and select the **Go** To command.

The **Go** To dialog box appears.

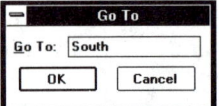

2. In the **Go** To text box, type any portion of the index line you want to find (even a partial word will do). It doesn't matter whether you use upper- or lowercase letters.
3. Choose OK.

When you choose OK, the next card whose index line contains the text you're searching for jumps to the top of the stack. If no index line has the text you're searching for, you get a dialog box advising you that Cardfile cannot find the text. Choose OK and try again.

To search through text in the body of the cards, follow these steps:

1. Choose the **Search** menu and select the **Find** command.

The **Find** dialog box appears.

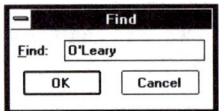

2. In the **Find** text box, type any portion of the information you want to search for (a partial word will do).
3. Choose OK.

Choosing OK brings to the top of the stack the next card that contains the text for which you are searching.

To repeat your most recent find, choose the **Search** menu and select the Find **Next** command. (Find **Next** works only with the **Find** command, not with the **Go** To command.)

Editing and Moving Text

11

You can change, add, or delete text from a card or its index line. And you can move text or graphics from one card to another. You can even transfer data between cards or to other programs.

To edit the text in the body of a card, follow these steps:

1. Display the card you want to change.
2. Use normal editing techniques to edit the text in the body of a card: move the insertion point where you want to make a change by positioning the I-beam and clicking the mouse button, or by pressing the arrow keys.
3. Press ◆Backspace or Del (Delete) to delete text, or just type to insert text.

You can select longer blocks of text to edit by pressing the mouse button and dragging across the text, or by holding down the Shift key and pressing the arrow keys. Just type new text to replace the selected text, or press Del or Backspace to remove the text.

To edit an index line, follow these steps:

1. Display the card containing the index line you want to edit.
2. Choose the **E**dit menu and select the **I**ndex command.

A mouse shortcut is to double-click on the index line of the top card. This command displays the Index Line dialog box, where you can make changes.

To copy or move text between cards or to other programs, follow these steps:

1. Display the card containing the text you want to copy or move.
2. Select the text.
3. Choose the **E**dit menu, and then select the **C**opy command to copy text or the **Cut** command to move text.
4. Position the insertion point where you want to copy or move the selected text.
5. Choose the **E**dit menu and select the **P**aste command.

11

Two more useful editing features are the **U**ndo and the **R**estore commands. Cardfile "remembers" your most recent single edit and will undo it—as long as you use Undo before you make another change. Cardfile remembers also the information that was on the displayed card before you began editing it, and will restore the card to its original condition as long as you have not turned to another card since you began editing.

To undo your most recent edit, follow these steps:

1. Choose the **E**dit menu.
2. Select the **U**ndo command.

To restore a card to its original condition, follow these steps:

1. Choose the **E**dit menu.
2. Select the **R**estore command.

Duplicating and Deleting Cards

Sometimes the information on two cards is so similar that duplicating the current card and making minor edits to it are faster than typing a whole new card. For example, you may want to create two separate cards for two people in the same company—the names and phone numbers are different, but the company name and address are the same.

To duplicate a card, follow these steps:

1. Bring the card you want to duplicate to the top of the stack.
2. Choose the **C**ard menu and select the **Du**plicate command.

Edit the text on the duplicated card with the usual Windows text-editing procedures. If you want to edit the index line, choose the **E**dit menu and select the **I**ndex command.

To delete a card, follow these steps:

1. Bring the card you want to delete to the top of the stack.
2. Choose the **C**ard menu and select the **D**elete command.

272

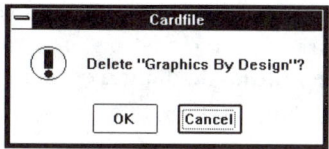

The dialog box that appears asks whether you want to delete the card.

11

3. Choose OK.

Viewing a List of Index Lines

When you look at a Cardfile on your screen, you can see the top card in its entirety, and you can see the index lines for several more cards. To make it easier to see *all* the index lines in the Cardfile, there's a special List view.

To view a list of the index lines, follow these steps:

1. Choose the **View** menu.

2. Select the **List** command.

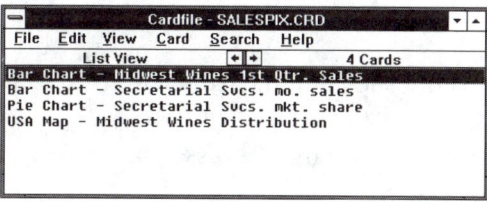

You can edit an index line in the List view, just as you edit an index line in the Card view.

Simply double-click on the line you want to edit. The Index dialog box appears, and you can edit the index line.

To restore a full view of the cards, choose the **View** menu and select the **Card** command.

Dialing a Phone Number with Cardfile

If your computer is connected to a modem and you include phone numbers on your cards, you can use Cardfile to dial the phone numbers for you.

When you choose the command for automatic dialing, Cardfile dials the *first* number listed on the *top* card in the stack. Unfortunately, that may be either

11

a ZIP code or a phone number that is different from the one you want to dial. If the number you want to dial isn't listed first on the card, select the phone number before choosing the automatic dialing command. Or just type the correct phone number in the Autodial dialog box.

When you type a phone number on a card, be sure to include the area code (if it's different from your own). Don't use spaces or parentheses; Cardfile doesn't understand them. Hyphens won't interfere with autodialing, so a good format for your phone numbers might be this: 707-538-1737.

To dial a phone number automatically, follow these steps:

1. Display the card containing the phone number you want to dial. If that number is not the first one listed on the card, select the number you want to dial.

2. Choose the **Card** menu and select the Autodial command.

The Autodial dia-
log box appears.

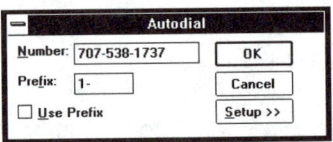

3. If the correct number is not shown in the **Number** box, type the phone number you want to dial.

4. Select **Prefix** and type a dialing prefix if necessary (a prefix is useful for long distance calls).

5. Select **Use Prefix** if you want to begin dialing with the prefix (you won't need this for local calls).

6. Choose OK.

A Cardfile dialog
box instructs you
to pick up the
phone.

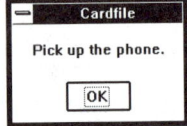

7. Pick up your phone receiver as instructed by the dialog box.

8. Choose OK or press ⏎Enter to complete the connection.

274

The first time you dial automatically, check the dial settings—dial type, port, and baud rate—that are available. Once you establish these settings, they stay set, and you shouldn't have to change them.

To change the automatic dialing settings, follow these steps:

1. Choose the **Card** menu and select the Autodial command.

2. Select **Setup**.

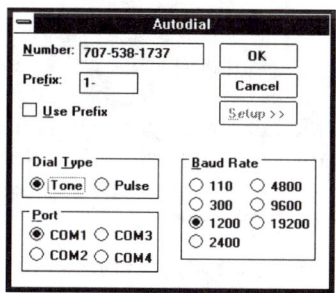

The Autodial dialog box expands to display Dial Type, **Port**, and Baud Rate settings.

3. Make the appropriate dialog box selections:

- In the Dial **Type** box, select Tone or Pulse, depending on which type of phone you have. (If you hear different tones while dialing, you have a touch-tone phone; if you hear clicks, you have a pulse phone.)

- In the **Port** box, select COM1, COM2, COM3, or COM4, depending on which port your modem is connected to.

- In the **Baud** Rate box, select 110, 300, 1200, 2400, 4800, 9600, or 19200, depending on your modem's baud rate.

4. Choose OK.

Printing a Cardfile

Printing a Cardfile is simple. You just choose a print command, and your cards are printed on the selected printer. You can choose one command to print the top card only, or a different command to print all your cards. Printed cards from a Cardfile look like real cards, and they are the right size to cut out and paste onto a rotary file. (To learn more about selecting a printer, refer to Chapter 6, "Customizing Your Work Area.")

11

To print the top card in the stack, follow these steps:

1. Choose the **File** menu.
2. Select the **P**rint command.

To print all the cards in a Cardfile, follow these steps:

1. Choose the **File** menu.
2. Select the Print **A**ll command.

Saving and Naming a Cardfile

When you save Cardfile files, Cardfile automatically assigns them the extension CRD. You can create as many different Cardfile files as you want.

To save and name a Cardfile, follow these steps:

1. Choose the **File** menu and select the Save **A**s command.

The File Save As
dialog box
appears.

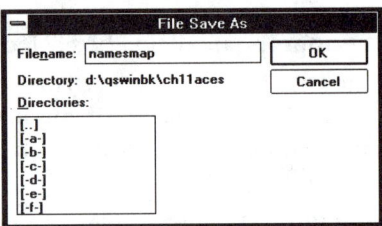

2. Type a file name (up to eight characters) in the Filename text box.
3. From the **Directories** list box, select the directory in which you want to save the file.
4. Choose OK.

To save an existing Cardfile, choose the **File** menu and select the **S**ave command. The new version of the file replaces the old version.

Closing a Cardfile and Exiting the Program

You can close a Cardfile in two ways: open a new Cardfile or exit the Cardfile program. To open a new Cardfile, choose the **File** menu and select the New

11

command. To exit the Cardfile program, choose the **File** menu and select the **Exit** command.

Using Terminal

Personal computers give a great deal of power to the individual. But sometimes individual power isn't enough. People need to be able to communicate with other people, as well as with other computers. You can use your computer to exchange files with other computers; to get data from corporate mainframe computers; or to "talk" with on-line services (such as CompuServe), which offer free software, databases of publicly available information, and "conversation" with other computer users.

Windows Terminal is a communications program that controls a modem, which connects your computer—by telephone line—to another computer. Terminal has several jobs. First, it establishes the settings which ensure that the computers on both ends of the phone line can understand one another. Second, it dials the telephone to make the connection. Third, it transfers or receives data over the open communication line.

To establish the settings that enable your computer to communicate with other computers, you must know quite a bit about your computer, your modem, and your communications package—for instance, the speed at which data is transferred, or the baud rate. You will need similar information about the computers you plan to communicate with, and you'll need to know the phone numbers. The good news is that you need to learn these settings only once, because Terminal saves the information as files you can open later. (The better news is that your company's personal computer coordinator can probably create these settings for you.) The Terminal settings are not included in this book; if you need to learn more about them, refer to the more comprehensive Que book, *Using Microsoft Windows 3*, 2nd Edition.

Starting Terminal

You start the Terminal program the same way you start any other Windows program—by double-clicking on the Terminal icon in the Accessories group window, or by pressing the arrow keys to select the icon and pressing Enter. If this is the first time you have ever used Terminal, you'll see a message box

11

named Default Serial Port. The box wants to know which port your modem is connected to and proposes a port. (Use the Windows Control Panel to change the serial port settings after you have used Terminal the first time.)

Opening a Terminal Settings File

If someone has set up your computer for you, some Terminal settings files have probably been created and are available for you to use. These settings files contain the information you need to communicate with other computers. For example, if you regularly send files by modem to your San Francisco office, you might have a settings file called SF.TRM (TRM is the extension Terminal assigns to files).

To open an existing Terminal settings file, follow these steps:

1. Choose the **File** menu and select the **Open** command.

The File Open dialog box appears.

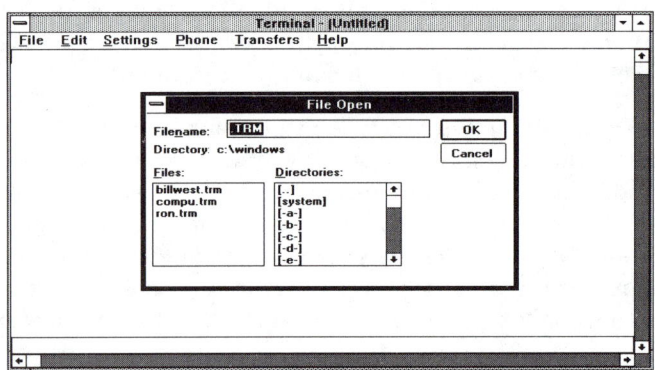

2. From the **Files** list box, select the settings file you want to open. (Change to a new directory, if necessary, by selecting a directory from the **Directories** list and choosing OK.)

3. Choose OK.

When you open a settings file, your screen won't look any different, but the settings will be in place.

Creating and Saving a New Settings File

When you first start the Terminal program, you see a new, untitled file. At that time, you can create your own settings file. The Settings menu contains many commands for establishing settings. If you are familiar with these commands, you can use them, but if you would like to learn more about the settings, refer to the chapter "Using Windows Terminal" in the Que book *Using Microsoft Windows 3*, 2nd Edition. Once your settings files are in place, you will most frequently change phone numbers.

To set a phone number in a new or existing Terminal settings file, follow these steps:

1. Choose the Settings menu and select the Phone Number command.

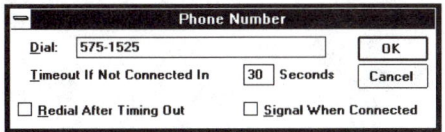

The Phone Number dialog box appears.

2. Select the Dial box and type the phone number (include the access number and area code for a long distance number).

3. Choose OK.

After you have entered a phone number (and established any other needed settings), save your settings file and give it a descriptive name. Terminal automatically assigns the extension TRM.

To save a Terminal settings file, follow these steps:

1. Choose the File menu and select the Save As command.

2. If you want the file placed in a different directory, select the directory from the Directories list and choose OK.

3. Select the Filename text box and type a file name (up to eight characters).

4. Choose OK.

11

Dialing the Phone

After you have opened a settings file, you are ready to make the connection to a remote computer. Since the settings file already contains the phone number for the computer you want to "talk" to, all you have to do is instruct your computer to dial. To dial a remote computer, choose the **P**hone menu and select the **D**ial command.

The screen displays a message box telling you that the remote computer is being dialed.

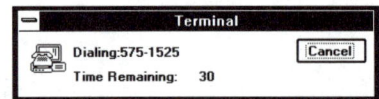

Making the Connection

Dialing the phone opens the pathway for communicating with another computer; what you do after you dial depends on the type of communication you plan. In many cases, the computer you connect with will control the session. For example, after you dial CompuServe, you are prompted for your user ID number and password. To respond, follow the instructions that appear on your screen. Other remote communications programs behave in much the same way; simply respond to the directions you see on-screen.

Sending a File

Your Terminal session may include sending previously created files to a remote computer. You can send two types of files: text and binary. The process is similar for both.

To send a text or binary file, follow these steps:

1. Choose the **T**ransfers command and select either the **S**end Text File command or the Send **B**inary File command.

11

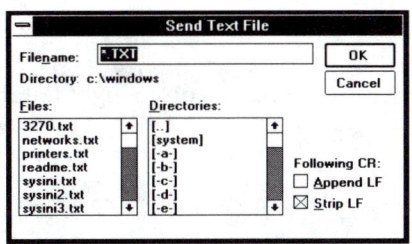

The Send Text (or Binary) File dialog box appears.

2. From the **Files** list box, select the file you want to send. (Use the **Directories** list and the OK button to change directories, if necessary.)

3. Choose OK.

Note: Use the text-file mode to send and receive text-only files, such as those created by Notepad. Use the binary-file mode to send or receive files created by most programs, such as Windows Write, Excel, or Word for Windows.

Receiving a File

If you will be receiving a file from the remote computer, you must select the directory into which the file will be received, and you must give the file a name. As with sending files, you can receive either text or binary files, and the process for both is the same.

To receive a text or binary file, follow these steps:

1. Choose the **Transfers** menu and select either the **R**eceive Text File command or the Receive Binary **F**ile command.

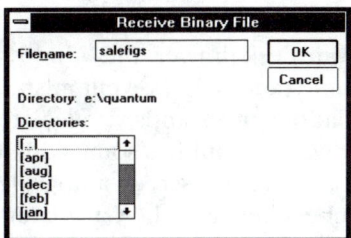

The Receive Binary (or Text) File dialog box appears.

281

2. From the **Directories** list box, select the directory in which the file is to be received.

3. In the File**n**ame text box, type a file name (up to eight letters).

4. Choose OK.

Hanging Up (Disconnecting)

After your communication session is complete, be sure to hang up the phone to avoid excess on-line or long-distance phone charges. Hanging up doesn't happen automatically—you must use the **H**angup command to disconnect the modem.

To hang up (disconnect), choose the **P**hone menu and select the **H**angup command.

Exiting Terminal

When your Terminal session is complete, you can exit the Terminal program. If you have established or changed settings, Terminal asks whether you want to save them. Choose **Y**es if you want to save the settings; otherwise, choose **N**o.

To exit the Terminal program, choose the **F**ile menu and select the Exit command.

Making Desktop Calculations with the Windows Calculator

Like the calculator you keep in your desk drawer, the Windows Calculator is small, but it can save you much time (and help prevent mistakes, too). The Calculator performs all the calculations of a standard calculator—addition, subtraction, multiplication, and division—but has some added advantages. For example, you can keep the Calculator on-screen alongside other programs, and you can copy numbers between the Calculator and other programs you work with.

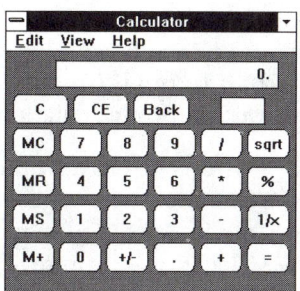

11

The standard Windows Calculator works so much like a pocket calculator that you will need little help in getting started.

The Calculator's "keypad" contains familiar number keys, along with memory and math keys. A display window just above the keypad shows the numbers you enter and the results of calculations. The Scientific view of the Calculator (described in a later section) performs more advanced calculations.

Although you cannot change the size of the Calculator, as you can other Windows programs, you can minimize the Calculator to an icon so that it's easily available as you work in another program.

Opening and Closing the Calculator

Open the Calculator program just as you open any Windows program—by double-clicking on the Calculator icon in the Accessories group window, or by pressing the arrow keys to select the icon and then pressing Enter. The Calculator opens in whichever view (Standard or Scientific) was displayed the last time you used it.

To close the Calculator program, choose the Control menu (on the keyboard, press Alt and then the space bar) and select the Close command. But if you plan to use the Calculator frequently, minimize it to an icon instead of closing it; that way, you can access it quickly when you need it.

Using the Calculator

Operating the Windows Calculator is nearly the same as operating a desk calculator—you "press" the appropriate buttons (by selecting them) and see the result displayed at the top of the Calculator.

11

Using the mouse to select numbers and math functions on the Calculator, simply click on the appropriate number and math keys, just as you press buttons on a desk calculator. Numbers appear in the display window as you select them, and results appear after you perform calculations.

Operating the Calculator with the keyboard is just as easy. Enter numbers with either the numeric keypad or the numbers across the top of your keyboard. To calculate, press the keys on the keyboard that match the Calculator's keys. For example, if the Calculator button reads +, press the + key on your keyboard.

The simple math functions are easy to perform. For instance, to add two plus two, select 2, select +, select 2, and finally select =. These selections produce the formula 2+2=.

To use the Calculator to add (+), subtract (–), multiply (*), or divide (/), follow these steps:

1. Select the first number on which you want to perform a calculation. The number appears in the display area at the top of the Calculator.

2. Select a mathematical function (+, –, *, or /).

3. Select the second number to calculate. This number now appears in the display area.

4. Select the = button on the Calculator, or press = on the keyboard. The result appears in the display.

The other three math functions—finding a square root, calculating a percentage, and inverting a number (the 1/× button on the Calculator)— operate differently.

To find a square root, follow these steps:

1. Select the number for which you want to find a square root.

2. Select the sqrt button or press the @ key.

To calculate a percentage, follow these steps:

1. Select the number of which you want to calculate a percent.

2. Select the * button (for multiply) or press the * key.

3. Select the percentage amount.

4. Select the % button or press the % key to display the result.

For example, to find 15% of 80, select 80*15%. The result, 12, is displayed in the Calculator's display area.

Note: Be sure to press the C button to clear all numbers and functions after calculating a percent.

Inverting a number means dividing that number into the number 1.

To invert a number, follow these steps:

1. Select the number you want to invert.
2. Select the 1/× button or press the R key.

The Calculator can work with positive or negative numbers. A negative number is indicated with a minus (–) sign to its left. To change any number's sign, select the number so that it is displayed and then select the +/– button or the F9 function key.

Editing Numbers in the Calculator Display

Three buttons on the Calculator—C, CE, and Back—are used for editing a number or function. These buttons (and their keystroke alternatives) do the following operations:

Calculator Button	Keystroke Alternative	Action
C	Esc	Clears (erases) the Calculator of all numbers and functions
CE	Del (Delete)	Deletes the displayed value
Back	Backspace	Deletes the last number in the displayed value

Working with the Calculator's Memory

You can use the Calculator's memory to store numbers. The memory holds a single number, which starts as zero. You can add to, display, or clear that number; or you can store a different number in memory. You can display the number in memory at any time and perform calculations on the number, just as you can on any other number. Any time a number is stored in memory, the letter M appears in the box above the sqrt button on the Calculator.

11

Here are the Calculator's memory functions:

Calculator Button	Keystroke Alternative	Function
MS	Ctrl+M	Stores the displayed value in memory
M+	Ctrl+P	Adds the displayed value to memory
MR	Ctrl+R	Reveals (displays) the value in memory
MC	Ctrl+C	Clears (erases) the memory

One use for the Calculator's memory is to sum a series of subtotals. For example, you can sum the first series of numbers and then add that sum to the memory by clicking the M+ button or pressing Ctrl+P on the keyboard. Then clear the display and calculate the second subtotal. Add it to memory. Continue until you have added all the subtotals to memory; then display the value in memory by clicking the MR button or pressing Ctrl+R.

Copying a Number from the Calculator into Another Program

When working with many numbers or complex numbers, you are less likely to make mistakes if you copy the Calculator results into another program instead of retyping the results. The Calculator is easy to use with other Windows programs and DOS programs.

To copy a number from the Calculator into another program, follow these steps:

1. Perform the math calculations required to display the number in the Calculator's display area.
2. Choose the Edit menu and select the Copy command to copy the displayed value.
3. Activate the program in which you want to copy the number.
4. Position the insertion point where you want the number copied.
5. Choose the Edit menu and select the Paste command (or its equivalent in the new program).

Copying a Number from Another Program into the Calculator

11

You can copy a number from another program and paste it into the Calculator. Once the number is in the Calculator, you can perform calculations with the number and then copy the result back into the other program.

To copy a number from another program into the Calculator, follow these steps:

1. Select the number in the other program.

2. Choose the **Edit** menu and select the **C**opy command (or its equivalent for that program).

3. Activate the Calculator, choose the **Edit** menu, and select the **P**aste command.

Using the Scientific Calculator

If you have ever written an equation wider than a sheet of paper, you're a good candidate for using the Scientific Calculator. This special version of the Calculator offers many scientific functions.

To display the Scientific Calculator, follow these steps:

1. Activate the Calculator.

2. Choose the **V**iew menu and select the **S**cientific command.

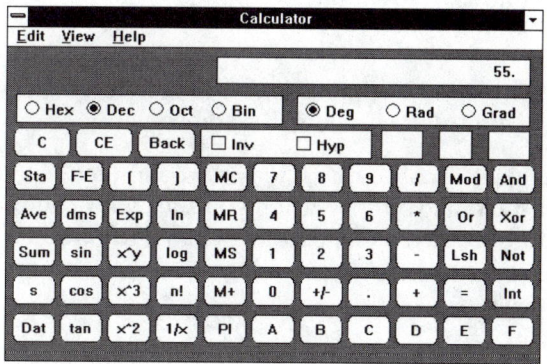

The Scientific Calculator works the same as the Standard Calculator but contains many advanced functions.

11

The advanced functions of the Scientific Calculator aren't described here, but they're well documented in the Calculator's **Help** command. To learn more about using the Help feature, refer to Chapter 3, "Operating Windows."

Watching the Clock

Windows comes equipped with a standard clock, which you can display on the computer screen in almost any size by simply resizing the clock's window. And when you minimize the Clock program to an icon at the bottom of the screen, the hands are still readable.

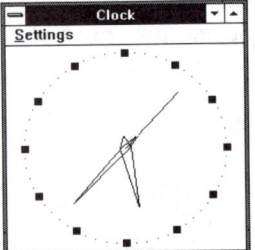

The Clock, even when reduced to a small icon, tells you the time.

The Clock program has one menu—the **Settings** menu—and two commands: **Analog** and **Digital**. The Analog view shows a round clock face with ticking hands; the Digital view shows a numerical readout of the time (including seconds). Windows remembers the setting you choose and displays that setting the next time you start the Clock program.

To change the clock face, follow these simple steps:

1. Choose the **Settings** menu.
2. Select the **Analog** command to display a clock with hands. Or select the **Digital** command to display a clock with numbers.

The time displayed by the clock is based on either your computer's internal clock (if you have one) or the time you type when you start your computer. If the time on the clock is inaccurate, use the Control Panel to reset the clock. (To learn more about the Control Panel, refer to Chapter 6, "Customizing Your Work Area.")

Developing Your Strategic Skills with Reversi and Solitaire

11

Reversi and Solitaire are included at the *end* of the chapter for a good reason: many Windows users have been kept up until the wee hours of the morning trying to beat the computer at a challenging game of Reversi or Solitaire! And now you have a good excuse for playing these games; you can claim that you're developing your strategic skills.

Opening and Closing Reversi and Solitaire

Open either game by double-clicking on its icon in the Program Manager. Both games are included in a group window called Games, rather than in the Accessories group window, which contains the other Windows accessory programs. Close either game by choosing Exit from the **G**ame menu.

Playing Reversi

Reversi's game board presents a grid with four dots in the center—two for you and two for the computer—in two colors. If you have a monochrome monitor, your dots are white, and the computer's dots are black. If you have a color terminal, yours are red, and the computer's are blue.

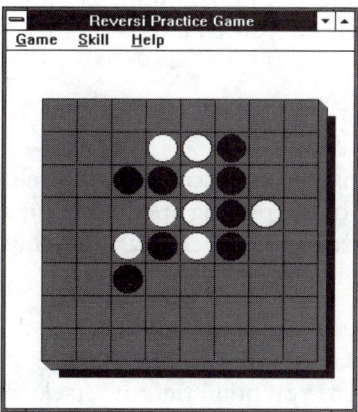

The object of the game is to fill the grid with more of your white (or red) dots than the computer's black (or blue) dots.

289

You win points by "capturing" the computer's dots, turning them into your color. To capture a dot, enter one of your dots anywhere you can "surround" the computer's dots in a straight line. You enter a dot on the board by clicking on the square you want to select. With the keyboard, move the pointer to the square you want to select (by pressing the arrow keys), and then press the space bar.

When you select a square, two things happen. First, a dot in your color appears in that square. Second, any of the computer's dots that fall between two of your dots turn to your color.

The pointer arrow turns into a cross on squares where you can make a legal move. If you cannot make a legal move, you have to choose the **Game** menu and select the **Pass** command, forfeiting your turn.

As soon as you make your move, of course, the computer retaliates with its move (usually winning back *lots* of dots).

Reversi has four levels of skill. To change skill levels, choose the **Skill** menu and select the **Beginner**, **Novice**, **Expert**, or **Master** command. The selected level of skill is checked in the menu.

If you cannot decide which move to make, let the computer give you a hint; just choose the **Game** menu and select the **Hint** command.

When the game is over, you see a message at the top of the game board that reads something like this: `You lost by 4.` (There may be a message that says you've won, but we've never seen it.) If you want to start a new game, choose the **Game** menu and select the **New** command.

Playing Solitaire

When you start the Solitaire game, you see a screen with three active areas: the deck in the upper left corner of the playing area, four suit stacks in the upper right corner of the playing area (the stacks start out empty), and seven row stacks in the bottom half of the screen.

The object of the game is to move all the cards out of the deck, onto the row stacks in the bottom half of the playing field, and from there into the suit stacks at the top right of the screen. You build the row stacks downward, in alternating colors; you build the suit stacks upward, in sequential order, from Ace to King, one suit per stack. To start a suit stack, you need an Ace.

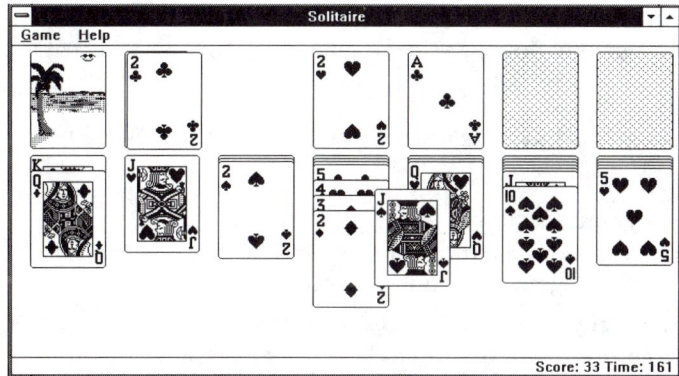

This Solitaire screen shows a game in progress.

To move cards between the stacks, or from the deck to the stacks, click on the card you want to move, and then drag it. In the lower stacks, you can move either a single card at a time or a group of cards.

To get new cards, click on the deck to turn over the top card, or move cards off of downturned cards in the lower stacks. Click on downturned cards to turn them over.

Solitaire offers several options. Choose the **G**ame menu and select the Deck command to choose a different deck illustration. Choose the **G**ame menu and select the **O**ptions command to select the draw (one or three cards) and scoring options. Solitaire even has an **U**ndo command in the **G**ame menu to undo your last action.

When you're finished playing and want to start a new game, choose the **G**ame menu and select the **D**eal command. To learn the rules of Solitaire, browse through the information in the **H**elp command.

Summary

The Windows desktop accessories are so convenient to use that they can quickly become a part of your daily business tools. The Calendar and Cardfile are useful every day. After checking appointments and a To Do list, you can minimize these accessories to icons or close them if you need maximum memory. Notepad is a great way to keep track of telephone conversations, as well as notes while you're working on various projects. Terminal links your computer to other computers so that you can exchange files or send and receive messages. The Calculator is a handy tool for quick mathematical functions. And the Clock, even when minimized as an icon, tells you the time. Reversi and Solitaire can challenge you to a little fun at the end of the day.

In this chapter, you learned the following information about the Windows accessories:

- The Notepad program is a simple text processor you can use to type quick notes and memos. Notepad saves files in ASCII (text) format, which most programs can understand.

- Calendar displays daily or monthly views of your appointment schedule. You can use this accessory to keep track of appointments and to remind yourself of important deadlines.

- Cardfile is a computerized "stack of cards" for storing names, addresses, phone numbers, and other information. You can quickly flip through the cards to find the one containing the information you need, or even search through the cards automatically if you're looking for a specific name or number not listed at the top of a card. If your computer has a modem, you can use Cardfile to dial phone numbers for you.

- Terminal is an easy-to-use communications program. With Terminal and a modem, you can exchange files or messages with other computers.

- The Calculator program works just like a calculator, except that you don't need batteries. You use it to add, subtract, multiply, divide, calculate percentages, and compute square roots. You can copy results from the Calculator into other programs.

- The Clock program lets you be a clock-watcher as you stare at the screen. Clock has two views: analog (showing hands) and digital (showing a numerical readout).

- Reversi is a simple strategy game that you'll find hard to outwit.

- Solitaire challenges you with the classic card game. Watch the deck while you play—you may discover that the dealer has something up her sleeve, or that the sun comes out in a laughing sort of way!

In the next chapter, you learn how to automate tasks by creating and using macros. A macro is a set of "memorized" commands or keystrokes you can play back as often as you like. If you perform repetitive tasks, macros can save you a great deal of time and work.

Creating Macros

With the Windows Recorder, you can automate many tasks that you now do repeatedly by hand. The Recorder keeps track of keystrokes you type, shortcut keys you press, and mouse actions you make—saving them all in a *macro* you can play back later. When you play back thè macro, Windows repeats the keystrokes and mouse movements exactly as you made them the first time. Macros can therefore save you a great deal of work whenever you retype phrases, reuse a formatting sequence, or regularly copy data from one program and paste it into another program.

You can use the Windows Recorder with any Windows program or group of Windows programs. Even with such powerful programs as Excel and Word for Windows, which have their own built-in macro recorders, you will find the Windows Recorder useful for integrating the work you do in multiple programs.

12

Recording a Macro

Before you begin recording a macro, you should have a good idea of what you want to do. You may find it helpful to practice a few times the procedure to be recorded before you actually record it. During this practice, you will often think of a shorter or better way to do the procedure.

The macro you create is stored in a Recorder file with the extension REC. Each Recorder file can contain multiple macros. After you start the Recorder and open a Recorder file, you'll see within the file the macros it contains.

Each of the macros available in a Recorder file shows a shortcut key and descriptive name.

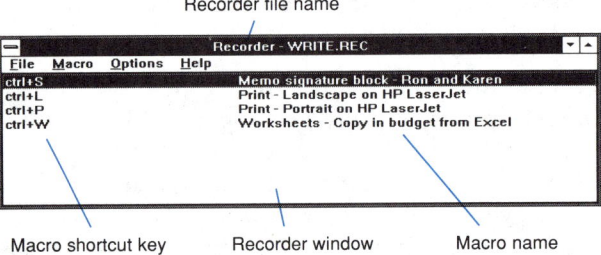

Recorder file name

Macro shortcut key   Recorder window   Macro name

Note: Macros do not work with non-Windows programs. When you use a macro with the Windows Terminal program, the macro works until you are connected to another computer.

Before recording a macro, you need to prepare your Windows programs. (Your macro may involve one or more windows and programs.) To prepare your programs for a recording, follow these steps:

294

1. Open the programs and documents for the recording.
2. Practice the task to be recorded.
3. Position the program and document windows as you want them for the recording.

If the procedure that you want to record is long, divide it into segments and record each segment as a separate macro. Making small macros that you can run separately is easier than making and repairing one large macro.

Note: If you want a macro to work on text or graphics that you select before playing back the macro, select a representative piece of text or graphics before you start the Recorder. If you wait until after the Recorder is on to select the text or graphics, the Recorder will always try to select the same text or graphics you selected during the original recording.

In the example described in this section, the Recorder records a macro that supplies a name and signature block in a Windows Write document.

To prepare the Recorder for recording, first position all the program windows to be used during the recording in their correct locations on-screen. Then follow these steps:

1. Open the Program Manager and open the Accessories group window.

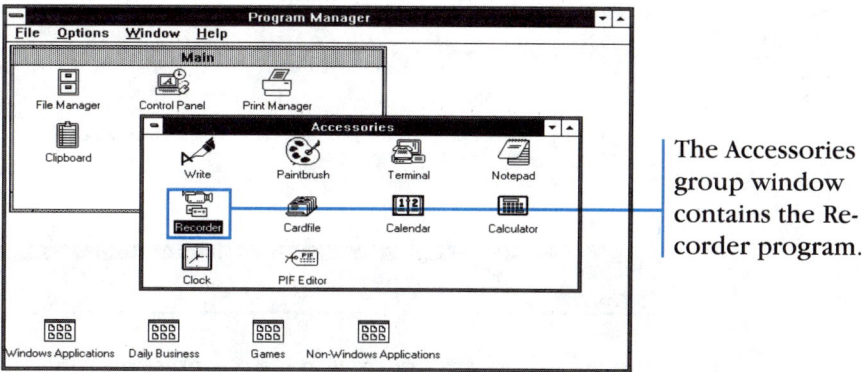

The Accessories group window contains the Recorder program.

2. Start the Recorder program. (This action does not start *recording* your steps, but only opens the Recorder program.) Then minimize the Program Manager so that it's out of the way.

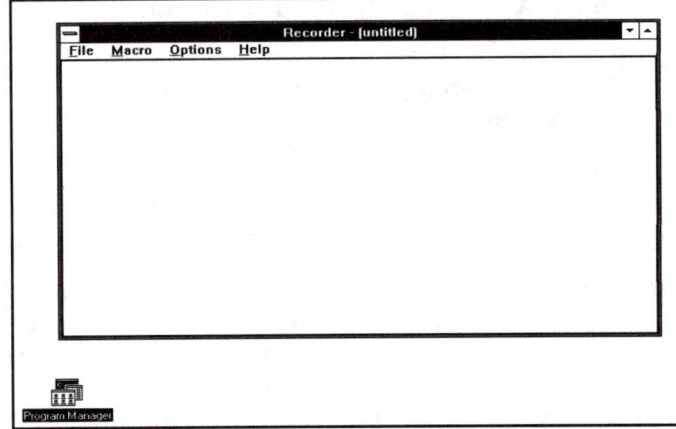

12

The Recorder window appears, and the Program Manager is mini- mized to an icon at the bottom of the screen.

3. Activate the first Windows program to be involved in the recording.

4. Select text or graphics, or position the insertion point where you want it when the macro starts.

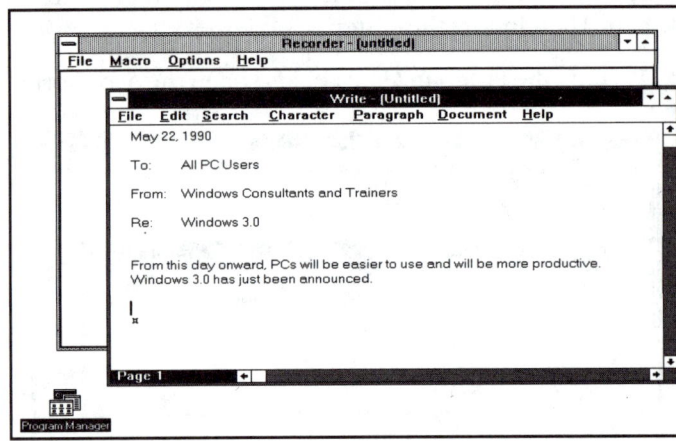

In this screen, the insertion point is posi- tioned where it will be when the macro starts recording.

5. Activate the Recorder window by clicking on it or by pressing Alt + Tab ⇄ until it is the topmost window.

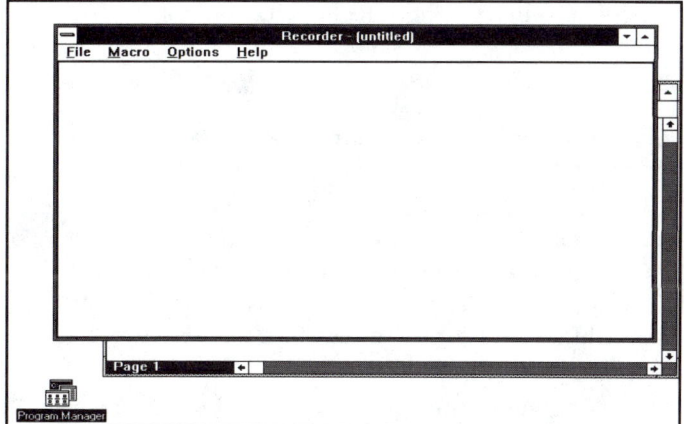

With the Recorder window active and the other windows positioned, you are ready to begin recording.

12

Follow these steps to record the macro:

1. Choose the **M**acro menu and select the Re**c**ord command.

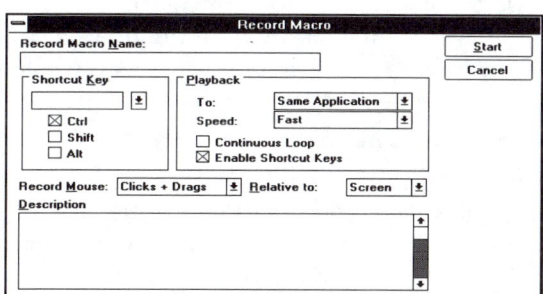

The Record Macro dialog box appears. You use this dialog box to determine what is recorded and how your macro plays back.

Note: Some dialog boxes, such as the Record Macro dialog box, have options and check boxes you cannot select directly with Alt-key combinations. In these cases, press Alt+*letter* to select the group enclosed by a box. Watch for the enclosing dashed line that tells you which option is the *focus*. Move the focus by pressing Tab or Shift+Tab. Select or deselect at the current focus by pressing the space bar. Open a drop-down list box—indicated by a down arrow to the right of a text box—by moving the focus to the text box and then pressing Alt+down arrow.

2. Type a macro name of up to 40 characters in the Record Macro Name text box. You will use this name later to identify the macro you want to run.

297

3. To control how the macro plays back, select one of the options described in table 12.1.

12

Table 12.1
Options for Controlling How Macros Play Back

Option	Description
Shortcut **Key**	Specifies the key you press to activate the macro. Type a single letter in the text box or choose a special key from the drop-down list. Select Ctrl, Shift, or Alt to use in combination with the shortcut key.
Playback To	Determines the applications in which the macro runs. Select Same Application to run the macro only in the application in which it was recorded. Select Any Application to run the macro in any application.
Playback Speed	Determines the speed of the macro. Select Fast to play back the macro at maximum speed. Select Recorded Speed to play back the macro at the speed at which you recorded it.
Playback Continuous Loop	Repeats the macro continuously. Press Ctrl+Break to stop the macro.
Playback Enable Shortcut Keys	Enables you to press shortcut keys that run other macros while you record a new macro. You therefore can nest one macro inside another.
Record **Mouse**	Determines the type of mouse actions that are recorded (described later in this chapter).
Relative to	Determines how mouse movements appear in the macro. Select Screen to make mouse movements relative to the screen position. Select Window to make mouse movements relative to the active window.
Description	Provides room for you to type a description of what the macro does and which applications it works with.

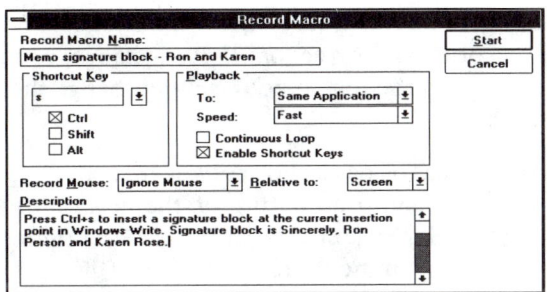

This filled-in dialog box describes the macro to be recorded and determines how it will play back when run.

12

4. Choose the Start button.

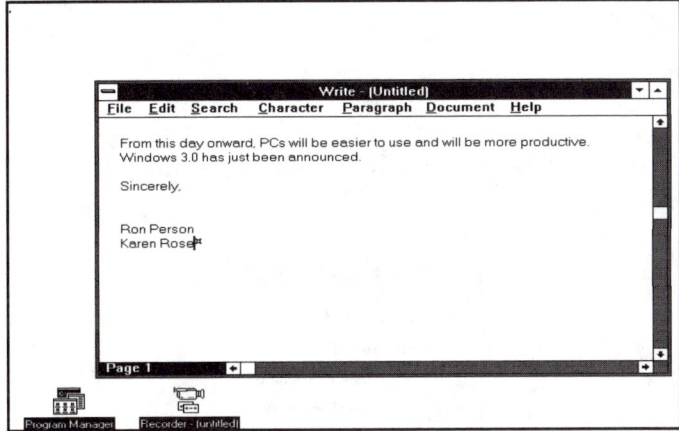

The Recorder becomes an icon at the bottom of the screen.

The Recorder icon flashes while the Recorder is recording. You may not be able to see this icon if it is behind a window.

5. Perform the steps you want recorded in the macro.

Using keystrokes during recordings is usually preferable to using mouse actions. A recording of keystrokes will play back as expected, but mouse actions may not produce the same results as in the original recording. A problem may arise because the Recorder repeats the exact screen location of the mouse pointer when a mouse action was recorded. If on playback, the windows are in different locations or the screen has a different resolution, the mouse pointer may be incorrectly positioned to make the selection or give the command you want. You should therefore use keystrokes to give commands, change windows, and select text or objects during the recording.

12

If you make a mistake during a recording, just correct the mistake and continue. The macro will record your correction. If, for instance, you make selected text italic but you wanted the text in bold, simply change the italic to bold while the Recorder is on.

Note: If one of your Recorder macros has a shortcut key that conflicts with a key combination in another program, you can turn off the Recorder's shortcut key by deselecting the **P**layback Enable Shortcut Keys option for the macro that conflicts. You can still run the Recorder macro by giving it a different shortcut key, or by choosing the **M**acro **R**un command and selecting the macro's name.

Stopping the Recorder

To stop the recording, follow these steps:

1. Click on the Recorder icon or press [Ctrl]+[Break]. (Break is usually located on the same key as Pause or Print Screen, depending on your keyboard.)

The Recorder dia-
log box appears.

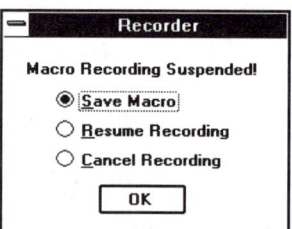

2. Choose one of the following buttons from the Recorder dialog box:

Button	*Description*
Save Macro	Saves the macro you have recorded
Resume Recording	Continues from where you stopped
Cancel Recording	Cancels but does not record what you have done

3. Choose OK or press [↵Enter].

Recording Multiple Macros in a File

The macro you recorded and saved with the procedures just described should now appear as a line item within the Recorder window. Each macro in the Recorder window shows as a line containing the macro shortcut key and the macro name.

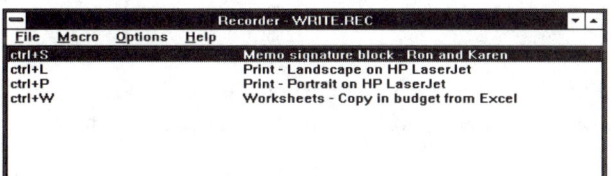

You can record and store multiple macros in one file. Here the file is named WRITE.REC.

You can record additional macros by repeating the same procedures. The new macros will be added to the current file. A later section, "Saving Macros," explains how to save the Recorder file containing your recordings. And the section "Opening Macro Files' shows you how to open existing Recorder files that contain other macros. Although you can have many different Recorder files on disk, only one Recorder file can be open in the Recorder at a time.

An easy way to look at Recorder files is to think of them as libraries that contain collections of similar macros. For example, you might have one file for use when typing letters in Windows Write, another file for copying and deleting files in the File Manager, and another file for transferring data between Excel and Word for Windows.

Recording a Macro in an Existing Macro File

A macro is stored in a Recorder file. You can have more than one Recorder file on disk, and each file can contain multiple macros.

Suppose that you have already created a file that contains other macros, and you now want to put your new macro recording into the existing file. Follow these steps:

1. Start the Recorder program as described at the beginning of this chapter.

301

2. Choose the **File** menu and select the **Open** command.

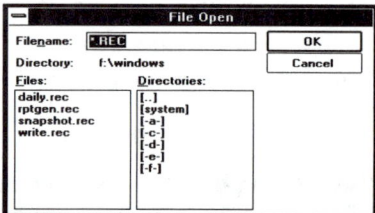

The File Open
dialog box
appears.

3. Select a Recorder file from the Files list and choose OK. When the macro file opens, the Recorder window displays a list of the macros contained in the file.

4. Proceed with the steps outlined in earlier sections for recording a macro. The macro you create will be stored in the file you opened in step 3.

Stopping or Pausing during Recording

During the recording of a macro, you can stop or pause—or even quit in the middle. Just click on the Recorder icon or press Ctrl+Break to stop the Recorder. When it stops, you will see the dialog box shown earlier in the section "Stopping the Recorder." Choose one of the buttons to save the macro in the current file, to continue recording, or to cancel and erase the recording.

Recording a Macro with Mouse Actions

With the Recorder, you can choose which types of actions to record. If you select the Record **M**ouse drop-down list box from the Record Macro dialog box, you will see the following options:

Option	Description
Ignore Mouse	Records keystrokes only. Select this option if you want to use the macro across multiple programs with windows in varying positions, or if you want to copy the macro to computers with different graphics resolutions.

302

Option	Description
Everything	Records keystrokes and mouse actions. Press Ctrl+Break to stop the recording when this option is selected.
Clicks+Drags	Records keystrokes and those mouse actions that result when you press a mouse button, such as choosing a menu or selecting a command.

Recording a macro with the Everything option selected may result in a macro that does not always work. As indicated earlier, the mouse actions recorded in the macro may not work during playback if the windows are moved to a different location, or if the screen resolution is different from that during the original recording.

Controlling How a Macro Plays Back

If you have a macro that should be used only with a specific program, select the Playback To drop-down list box when the Record Macro dialog box appears. Then select Same Application. If you want the macro to run with any program, select Any Application.

If the macro is already recorded, you can change this setting so that the macro will run only with the original application or with any program. Later in this chapter, the section "Editing and Changing Macros" explains how to make this change.

Saving Macros

When you record a macro, the recording is placed along with other macros in the current file within the Recorder. If you do not save this file, you will lose the macros you have recorded since the last time the file was saved.

To save your new macros, follow these steps:

1. Choose the **File** menu and select the Save **As** command.
2. Use the existing file name or type a new one.
3. Choose OK or press ⏎Enter.

You can use the File Manager to see the macro files on disk. Files containing macros have the extension REC.

12 Playing Back a Macro

You can play back any of the macros in the file currently loaded in the Recorder. Just press the appropriate shortcut key, or select the macro's name from the list in the Recorder window and choose **R**un from the **M**acro menu.

Opening a Recorder File

After you have saved a file containing one or more macros, you can retrieve the file and use those macros. Because you can have only one file at a time open in the Recorder, you can use only the macros within the open file.

To open a file, follow these steps:

1. Start the Recorder.
2. Choose the **F**ile menu and select the **O**pen command.
3. In the File Open dialog box that appears, type the file name or select the directory and file containing the macros you want to use.
4. Choose OK or press ↵Enter.

Running a Macro

You can run a macro by pressing the appropriate shortcut key or choosing the macro name from the list in the Recorder window. When you run a macro, it will react in one of two ways with the currently loaded programs in Windows:

- If the macro is the type that runs with any program, the macro will play back.
- If the macro is the type that runs in a specific program, the Recorder activates that program's window when the macro runs. If the program has not been started or if the program is an icon, the macro does not play back.

304

To run a macro with a shortcut key, follow these steps:

1. Start the Recorder program and open the file containing the macro you want to run.
2. Activate the program in which you want the macro to run, and then position the insertion point or select the appropriate text or graphics.
3. Press the shortcut key assigned to the macro.

If you want the Recorder to reduce to an icon during playback, choose the **Options** **M**inimize on Use command from the Recorder before you play back the macro.

A macro that you run by choosing its name is useful if you have too many macros to assign conveniently to shortcut keys, or if macros are complex and you need a reminder about their actions.

To run a macro by choosing its name, follow these steps:

1. Start the Recorder program. Then choose the **F**ile menu and select the **O**pen command.
2. Choose the file containing the macro you want to run.
3. Activate the program in which you want the macro to run, and then position the insertion point or select the appropriate text or graphics.
4. Click on the Recorder window to activate the Recorder so that it is the topmost window.

   Or press Alt + Tab↹ until the Recorder is on top.
5. Choose the macro you want to run by double-clicking on its name.

   Or select the name by pressing ↑ or ↓ and then selecting the **R**un command from the **M**acro menu.

When the macro runs, the Recorder window shrinks to an icon so that it is out of the way.

Stopping a Macro

To stop a macro, press Ctrl+Break. You can specify that a macro not be stopped with Ctrl+Break by choosing the **O**ptions Ctrl+Break Checking

12

command. If no check mark appears next to the command, you cannot turn off the macro by pressing Ctrl+Break; you must wait for the macro to finish. If you have Ctrl+Break turned off for a continuously running macro, you must restart the computer to stop the macro. You can do this without turning off the electricity; just press Ctrl+Alt+Del.

Continuously Playing a Macro

To create a demonstration, a tutorial, or an action that repeats continuously, you will want to know how to make a macro repeat continuously. You select the **P**layback Continuous Loop check box from the Record Macro dialog box before you record the macro. If you have already recorded the macro, you can use the **Macro P**roperties command to change a normal macro to one that loops.

Stop a continuously playing macro by pressing Ctrl+Break. If Ctrl+Break checking has been turned off, you will need to restart the computer to stop the macro.

Editing and Changing a Macro

You cannot change the steps a recorded macro performs. But you can change some of the properties of a recorded macro, such as its shortcut key, whether the macro works with a specific program or any program, or the macro plays back continuously.

The Macro Properties dialog box enables you to change the way in which a macro that you've already recorded works. For example, you can change the shortcut key combination that runs the macro, or you can change another property so that the macro will run with any program rather than with only a specific program. The following procedure does not enable you to change or edit the keystrokes or mouse actions that were recorded.

To change a macro's properties, follow these steps:

1. Activate the Recorder.
2. Select the macro name whose properties you want to change by clicking on the name or by pressing ⬆ or ⬇.
3. Choose the **Macro** menu and select the **P**roperties command.

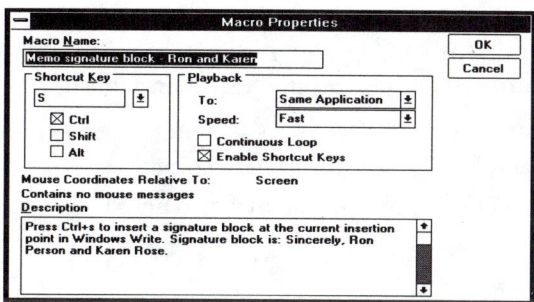

The Macro Properties dialog box appears.

12

Notice that the Macro Properties dialog box looks similar to the Macro Record dialog box. Many of the same items are changeable.

4. Select and change a property in the dialog box. For example, you can change a shortcut key by replacing the current one. If the macro's shortcut key interferes with another program's shortcut key, you can turn off the macro's shortcut key by deselecting the Enable Shortcut Keys option.

5. Choose OK or press ↵Enter.

The properties in the Macro Properties dialog box are described earlier in the section "Recording a Macro." You cannot change the Mouse Coordinates Relative To property, nor can you change the video display characteristics for the recording hardware. If the mouse was used in the recording, the screen resolution is shown underneath the text Mouse Coordinates Relative To:.

Managing Macros

Macros, like files, seem to expand and grow on their own. One moment, you have only two on your disk, and the next time you look, you have 159. No one knows how so many macros collected, but you can learn to manage them.

Deleting a Macro from a File

Delete a macro from its file in the Recorder by following these steps:

1. Activate the Recorder.
2. Choose the File menu and select the Open command.

12

3. Select the file containing the macro you want to delete, and choose OK or press ⏎Enter. After the file is loaded into the Recorder, the list of macros in that file will appear in the Recorder window.

4. Select the macro name you want to delete.

5. Choose the **Macro** menu and select the **Delete** command.

6. When asked to confirm that you want the macro deleted, choose OK or press ⏎Enter.

Merging Macros in Recorder Files

If you want to use one macro in multiple files, you need to merge files. Suppose, for example, that you have created a file of macros for use with invoices, a file of macros for memo writing, and a file of macros for worksheets. You may want to use in all of these files a macro you've made that enters your name and signature block.

Merging files brings the macros from a file on disk into the active file in the Recorder. If an incoming macro contains a shortcut key that is already in use, the macro merges anyway, but the shortcut key for the active file in the Recorder take precedence.

To merge the macros in two files, follow these steps:

1. Open a file in the Recorder or create a new file by making a new macro.

2. Delete unwanted macros or duplicate macros from the current file in the Recorder.

3. Choose the **File** menu and select the **Merge** command.

4. Select a new directory in the **Directories** box if necessary; then choose OK or press ⏎Enter.

5. Type the file name of the file you want to merge, or select the file name from the **Files** list.

The File Merge dialog box appears.

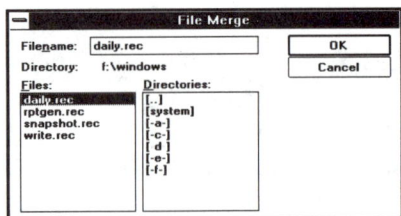

308

6. Choose OK or press ⏎Enter.

The file in the Recorder will now have the combined set of macros. You can save the file containing the old and merged macros to the same name by choosing the **F**ile menu and selecting the **S**ave command. Or you can save the file to a new name by choosing the **F**ile menu and selecting the Save **As** command.

12

Troubleshooting Macros

If you run a macro that cannot properly carry out its recorded instructions, the macro stops, and you see the dialog box named Recorder Playback Aborted! In that dialog box, the Error text box indicates the probable cause of the macro's stopping.

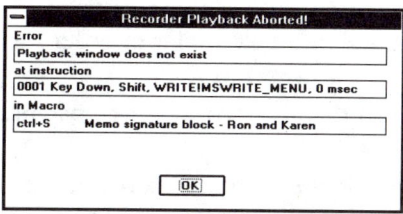

This error box indicates that the macro will not play because the Write program's window is not active.

The most common causes of macro failure are not having the correct programs running when you run the macro, and recording a macro that contains mouse actions but then playing back the macro with the windows in different locations.

If a macro fails, check to see whether it will run when you correctly position the windows involved. If the macro continues to fail, rerecord the macro with keystrokes. Note which programs are used by the macro. During macro operation, these programs must be running in windows. The first program used by the macro does not need to be in the active window; the macro will activate the windows as they are needed.

Use keystrokes whenever possible while recording your macros. Mouse actions require that screen resolution and window positions are the same each time the macro runs.

If a large macro fails, consider rerecording it as several smaller macros. Smaller macros are easier to troubleshoot and often can be used with other macros or programs.

12

Summary

Once you become familiar with Windows and with running a few Windows programs or accessories, you will want to make your work easier by creating macros to handle repetitive tasks. You can create macros by recording your keystrokes or mouse actions with the Recorder program, located in the Accessories group window. Macros can involve operations with one or more Windows programs but do not work with non-Windows programs.

The following important points were covered in this chapter:

■ A Recorder file with the extension REC may contain more than one macro. The file must be loaded in the Recorder in order for the macro to work.

■ Some macros are recorded so that they work with a specific program only.

■ After a Recorder file has been loaded, you can run a macro by activating the Windows program in which you want to run the macro, positioning the insertion point, and then pressing the shortcut key assigned to the macro.

■ You will have the best success in recording macros if you record keystroke actions. Mouse actions, which are recorded relative to screen resolution and window position, may not play back correctly when run on a different display or with window locations other than those used during the original recording.

The Windows environment adds a great deal of power to both Windows and non-Windows programs. To learn how to get the most from running one or more non-Windows programs in Windows, read Chapter 13, "Running Non-Windows Programs." To learn how to pass data between programs and how to integrate Windows programs so that they act as one program, read Chapter 14, "Integrating Programs."

Running Non-Windows Programs

Windows gives non-Windows programs, such as Lotus 1-2-3 and WordPerfect, more capabilities than they have running under DOS. With Windows, you can run more than one non-Windows program at a time, as well as copy and paste text or numbers to other programs.

Although non-Windows programs gain features under Windows, these programs do not have all the advantages of programs designed for Windows. Such features include standardized menus, dialog boxes for quick access to options, better memory use, or DDE links that automatically pass data between programs.

13

Key Terms in This Chapter

DOS program	A program that was not designed to take full advantage of Windows capabilities. DOS programs include 1-2-3 Release 2.2, 1-2-3 Release 3.1, WordPerfect 5.1, and dBASE IV.
Device contention	A conflict that occurs when two or more non-Windows programs need to use the same printer or modem at the same time.
PIF Editor	A program that enables you to control how a specific non-Windows program runs under Windows.
PIF file	A file containing the characteristics that determine how Windows should work when a specific non-Windows program is run.
Non-Windows program	A DOS program that has not been designed to take full advantage of Windows capabilities and does not use Windows menus or dialog boxes.

Running Non-Windows Programs under Windows

Windows controls memory, programs, and the hard disk so that you can run multiple non-Windows programs and copy information from one program to another. Windows uses different methods of operation in real, standard, and 386-enhanced modes.

Running Non-Windows Programs in Different Modes

Windows runs in one of three modes; real, standard, or 386-enhanced. The mode depends on the computer processor and the available memory.

In real or standard mode, non-Windows programs display across the full screen when they run. A full-screen display doesn't prevent you from loading multiple non-Windows programs. The inactive programs are minimized to icons and put on hold. The active program appears the same as when it runs without Windows.

In 386-enhanced mode, you can run non-Windows programs full screen or display them in windows. Displaying non-Windows programs in windows is convenient when you are copying and pasting between programs, or comparing results from two programs.

13

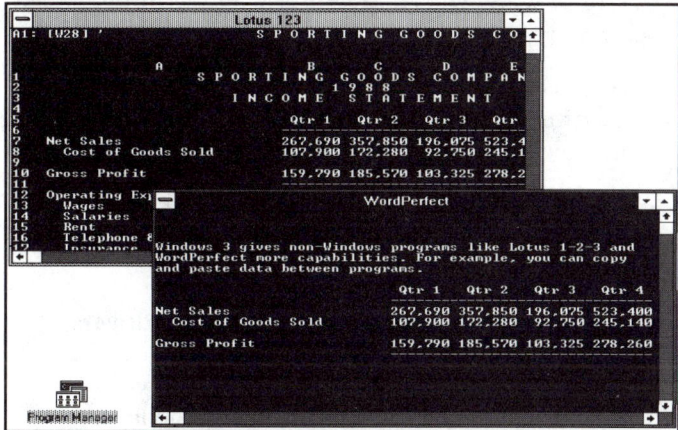

In 386-enhanced mode, you can run non-Windows programs, such as 1-2-3 Release 2.2 and WordPerfect 5.1, in separate windows.

When non-Windows programs run full screen under Windows, the computer display appears as though only a non-Windows program were running. Pressing Ctrl+Esc, however, takes you back to the Windows Task Manager. The non-Windows program is reduced to an icon at the bottom of the screen.

You can have multiple copies of the same non-Windows program running. Dots follow the name in the icon and window title for each additional copy.

During the Windows installation process, the Setup program automatically builds PIF files for the non-Windows programs you choose. PIF files are *Program Information Files* that tell Windows how to manage non-Windows programs.

Fitting Multiple Non-Windows Programs into Memory

In Windows standard mode, you can open more non-Windows programs than your computer memory normally allows. Each time you start a non-Windows program, Windows creates on your hard disk a temporary area, called the program swap file, to hold the program or data that is too large to fit into memory. While the program and data are active, they are in memory; while they are inactive, Windows switches them to the swap file whenever additional memory is needed. This capability makes your computer's available memory seem larger. When you exit the non-Windows program, Windows deletes the temporary swap file.

If you have a cluttered hard disk, a slow hard disk, or one with little free space, Windows may run slower. You may not be able to run as many non-Windows programs at one time.

Windows does not use program swap files while it runs in 386-enhanced mode. You must have sufficient memory, therefore, to hold each program you want to run simultaneously.

Note: Non-Windows programs use their own screen and printer drivers. Even if you will be running a non-Windows program under Windows, the program cannot use the screen or print drivers shared by Windows programs. Non-Windows programs cannot take advantage of the Print Manager's capability to queue printing jobs so that you can go back to work while the Print Manager controls printing.

Loading and Running Non-Windows Programs

You start non-Windows programs in the same ways you start Windows programs. Non-Windows programs can be started in one additional way: you can choose a PIF file from a directory window in the File Manager. A PIF file, ending with the extension PIF, tells Windows how to run a specific non-Windows program. If a PIF file has not been created for a non-Windows program, Windows runs the program with the default settings.

Starting a Non-Windows Program from the Program Manager

When you use Setup to install a non-Windows program, you can have Windows create program item icons for non-Windows programs and add those icons to the Non-Windows Application group. At that time, Setup also installs a PIF file for each program it recognizes in the Windows directory.

13

You can start a non-Windows program from a program group window in the Program Manager by choosing the program item icon, just as you start a Windows program. Starting a program from the program item icon is described in Chapter 4, "Grouping Programs and Documents."

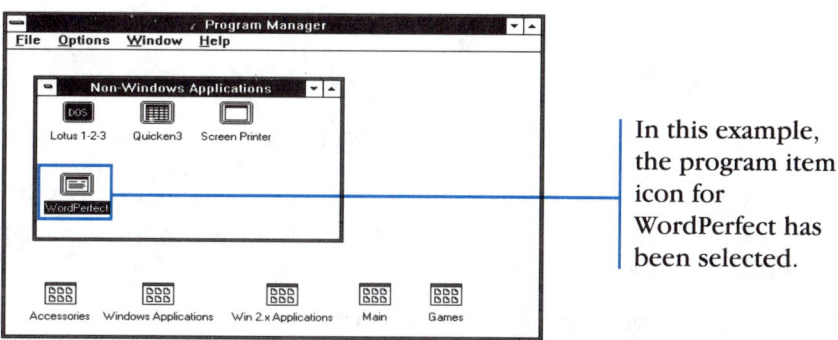

In this example, the program item icon for WordPerfect has been selected.

Note: While Windows is running, do not run non-Windows utilities or programs that modify files or the file allocation table. Such utilities and programs are used to unerase or undelete files and to defragment or compact your disk. When running, these programs modify temporary files that Windows leaves open for its use. If the temporary files are destroyed or modified, Windows may freeze, you may lose data, and you may need to reinstall Windows. Programs with this capability are Norton Utilities, Mace Utilities, PC Tools, and Vopt, as well as the DOS CHKDSK command when used with the /F argument. Such programs are extremely useful, but their commands that unerase or defragment files should not be used while Windows is running.

Starting a Non-Windows Program from the File Manager

You can start a non-Windows program from the File Manager also. Open the File Manager and then open a directory window onto the directory containing the program file or the PIF file created for the program.

13

Program file names have an extension of COM, EXE, or BAT. Once you can see the program file or the PIF file (with the same file name and the extension PIF), double click on the file name, or select the file and press Enter. In a few cases, Windows may not be able to run a non-Windows program with the default settings. For these programs, you must create a PIF file.

Running Multiple Non-Windows Programs

To run multiple Windows or non-Windows programs, start each program with the Program Manager or File Manager. To start other programs, activate the Task List by double-clicking on the desktop or pressing Ctrl+Esc. When the Task List appears, choose the Program Manager. When it opens, start your other programs.

You may switch between programs that have been loaded by using the Task List and choosing the programs, or by repeatedly pressing Alt+Tab until the desired program's title bar appears and then releasing both keys.

If memory or hard disk storage is not sufficient to start additional programs, a warning dialog box is displayed. To increase available memory, close unneeded data documents or programs. If you have insufficient disk space, erase or remove unneeded files from the hard disk.

Running DOS in a Window

As Setup installs program groups, it will install in the Main program group a DOS Prompt program item. Opening the DOS Prompt program item runs a copy of COMMAND.COM in full-screen mode. From the DOS prompt (for example, C: on that screen), you can run DOS internal and external commands—such as DIR, COPY, and FORMAT—just as you run them directly from DOS. To quit the DOS Prompt program, type **exit** and press Enter.

Running Memory-Resident (TSR) Programs

Some non-Windows programs are designed to be loaded into memory along with other non-Windows programs. These programs that co-reside are referred to as *terminate and stay resident* (TSR) programs. One of the more familiar TSR programs is SideKick.

You can start a TSR program as you would any program—by installing it in the Program Manager and then double-clicking on the program item icon. Once the TSR program is running, you can treat it as you would any other non-Windows program.

Switch to a TSR program by using the normal Windows methods instead of pressing the key combination that usually activates the program. For instance, double-click on the desktop or press Ctrl+Esc to display the Task List from which you can then activate the TSR program so that it's on top.

Understanding Why Windows Uses PIF Files

When you ask Windows to start a non-Windows program, Windows looks for the program's PIF file. A PIF file (Program Information File) tells Windows how much memory the program requires and how the program interacts with the keyboard and screen. If Windows cannot find a PIF file for a program, Windows starts the program with the standard settings. Because most non-Windows programs run correctly with the standard settings, many of these programs do not need PIF files created for them.

Sometimes a non-Windows program does not run correctly or does not run the way you want. In that case, you may need to modify the program's PIF file with the PIF File Editor. For instructions on using the PIF File Editor, see the section "Managing PIF Files" later in this chapter.

13

Controlling Non-Windows Programs

13

Windows enables you to run multiple non-Windows programs, switch from one program to another, and copy and paste text and numbers between programs. You can, for example, copy a table of numbers from 1-2-3 and paste the table into WordPerfect. Or you can copy a number from an accounting program like Quicken 3 and paste the number into 1-2-3.

Note: For information on copying and pasting text, numbers, or screen images with non-Windows programs, refer to Chapter 8, "Using the Clipboard To Copy and Paste."

Switching between Programs

Windows uses the same key combinations to switch between programs, whether they are Windows or non-Windows programs. To switch from an active non-Windows program to another program, follow these steps:

1. Hold down `Alt` and press `Tab↹`. Continue to hold down `Alt` and press `Tab↹` until you see the window or title bar of the program you want active.

2. Release both keys.

To minimize the non-Windows program to an icon and display the Task List so that you can select a different program to activate, just press Ctrl+Esc.

Once you are back in Windows, you can switch between programs by using the keyboard or mouse techniques described in Chapter 3, "Operating Windows."

Note: Some non-Windows programs may suspend the keyboard in some operating modes. During those times, Alt+Tab or Ctrl+Esc may not work. To switch back to Windows, return to the program's normal operating mode and then press Alt+Tab or Ctrl+Esc. If, for example, you are displaying a graph in 1-2-3 Release 2.2, press Esc to return to the spreadsheet or menu, and then press Alt+Tab.

318

Using the Control Menu

Non-Windows programs have a program Control menu similar to that of Windows programs. Use this program Control menu to copy and paste information and to move the icon. If you are using 386-enhanced mode, the Control menu controls whether the program runs full screen or in a window, and determines window size and temporary operating settings.

To activate the Control menu if the program is not in a window, press Alt, space bar. If the program is in a window, click on the Control menu at the top left corner of the window. A non-Windows program that has been reduced to an icon also contains a Control menu.

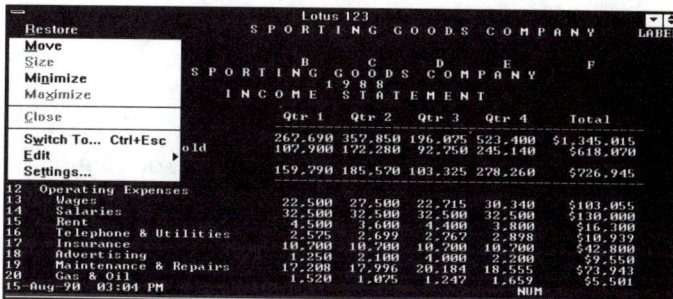

You will see on the Control menu the commands to **Re-store**, **Move**, or **Size** a non-Windows program window.

The program's icon also has a Control menu. You can restore or move the icon for a windowed or full-screen program. The Minimize command shrinks the program to an icon, and the Maximize command expands the program to a window or full screen.

Your non-Windows program may not have a Control menu available. In that case, you must quit the program to return to Windows.

Using a Mouse with Non-Windows Programs

If your non-Windows program has a mouse driver installed, you can use the mouse with the program while it runs full screen under Windows. If the program is in a window, the mouse operates under Windows control and can be used to select, copy, and paste areas, or to choose commands from the Control menu.

13

Sizing and Scrolling Non-Windows Programs

When you run Windows on an 80386 computer in 386-enhanced mode, non-Windows programs can be run in windows. When a non-Windows program is in a window, you can use the mouse with normal Windows techniques to maximize, minimize, or restore the window. You can resize the window by dragging a window's edge.

You can use the keyboard also to resize a window. Press Alt and then the space bar to display the Control menu, and then press the underlined letter for the Restore, Move, Size, Minimize, or Maximize command. If you choose Move, press the arrow keys to move the window, and then press Enter to fix its location. If you choose Size, press the arrow key that points toward the edge you want to change; then press the arrow keys to move that edge inward or outward.

When you reduce the size of a window containing a non-Windows program, portions of the program are left outside the window's edges. To see those hidden portions of the program, you must scroll the window. You cannot scroll the window over more information than would have appeared in the program's normal display screen.

To scroll with the mouse, use the mouse-scrolling techniques on the scroll bars. To scroll with the keyboard, select the Control menu by pressing Alt and then the space bar, select Edit, and choose Scroll. Then press the arrow keys, PgUp, PgDn, Home, or End to scroll the window. When you finish scrolling, press Esc or Enter.

Closing Non-Windows Programs

You quit non-Windows programs by using the method specific to the active non-Windows program you are quitting. Unlike Windows programs, each non-Windows program uses a different method of quitting. In a few cases, the screen might not return immediately to Windows; just press Alt and then the space bar to display the Control menu and then choose Close.

Note: If you are connected to a network while in a non-Windows program, disconnect from the network before you quit the program.

320

Setting Up Non-Windows Programs for 386-Enhanced Mode

When you have an 80386 computer and you run Windows in 386-enhanced mode, you can run a non-Windows program in a window. Non-Windows programs that are not in the active (topmost) window will continue to run.

This powerful capability enables your computer to work on more than one program at a time. For example, you can be typing a letter while a long spreadsheet recalculates in an inactive window. Problems may arise, though, when you decide how non-Windows programs should share computer power and the same printer.

Setting Multitasking Options

If you run multiple programs at the same time in 386-enhanced mode, and each program uses part of the processor's calculating power, the performance of all the programs will diminish. Processing takes longer. With the Control Panel, however, you can specify how much processor time is spent with each program. This decision becomes important if you are running a database report generator in the *background* (an inactive window) and calculating a spreadsheet in the *foreground* (the active window). If the two programs share processing power equally, the spreadsheet calculates more slowly than if it ran by itself. But if you don't need the database report quickly, you can schedule its processing for a smaller share of computing power. More calculating power is therefore available to the spreadsheet.

To schedule different amounts of processing power between Windows and non-Windows programs, follow these steps:

1. Open the Control Panel from the Main group window in the Program Manager.

2. Choose the 386 Enhanced icon from the Control Panel. (This icon appears only when you are in 386-enhanced mode.)

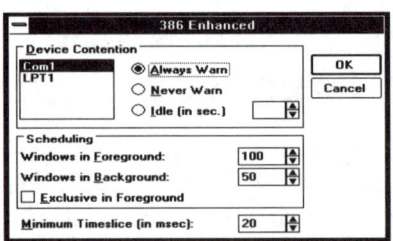

The 386 En-
hanced dialog
box appears.

13

3. Select one of these Scheduling options:

Option	Use
Windows in Foreground	Type a larger number than in the Windows in **Background** box if you want more processing power for the program in the active window. Use a number from 1 to 10,000. Usually, you will want this number to be much larger than in the Windows in **Background** box so that the active program operates faster and doesn't keep you waiting.
Windows in Background	Type a larger number than in the Windows in **Foreground** box if you want more processing power for the programs in the inactive windows. Use a number from 1 to 10,000. (This selection slows down the performance in the window in which you are working.)
Exclusive in Foreground	Select this box to ensure that Windows programs always get 100 percent of the processing time when a Windows program is in the active window. This selection leaves non-Windows programs on hold when they are in inactive windows.

4. Choose OK.

Managing Printing with Multiple Non-Windows Programs

When Windows programs need a printer or modem at the same time, Windows acts as a referee that decides which program comes first. Non-Windows programs are not so agreeable. If two or more programs want the same printer or modem at the same time, data may be lost. This problem is called *device contention*. Using the Control Panel, you can control how Windows solves device contention between non-Windows programs.

To control device contention, follow these steps:

1. Open the Control Panel from the Main group window in the Program Manager.

2. Choose the 386 Enhanced icon from the Control Panel.

3. From the **D**evice Contention list, select the port that may have a problem.

4. Select the way you want Windows to handle a device contention:

Option	Description
Always Warn	Displays a message when a problem arises. You are given the opportunity to select which program has priority over the port. Usually, you should select this option.
Never Warn	Allows any non-Windows program to use the port at any time. This option can cause contention problems.
Idle	Allows the port to remain idle the number of seconds you specify (1 to 999) before the next program can use the port without the warning message appearing. Select this option if you have a program that pauses between printing, such as a 1-2-3 print macro that prints multiple but separate pages; or a communication program that logs on to a database, downloads information, and then logs on a second time for additional information.

5. Choose OK.

13

323

13

Managing PIF Files

You use a PIF file to define how Windows works with a specific non-Windows program. A PIF file is separate from the program and contains characteristics that Windows uses when it starts the non-Windows program. These characteristics cover such questions as "Should this program run full screen or in a window?" and "How much memory should Windows reserve for this program?" In most cases, you do not have to create a PIF file for a non-Windows program. Windows creates PIF files for many popular non-Windows programs. If Windows cannot find the information about a program you want to run, Windows uses a default PIF file that is good for most non-Windows programs.

Letting Windows Make PIF Files for You

The simplest way to make a PIF file is to let the Install program or the Windows Setup program make a PIF file for a non-Windows program. When you first install Windows, you are asked whether you want Windows to look for programs on your hard disk and automatically set up those Windows and non-Windows programs. If you used this feature during installation, PIF files were created for the non-Windows programs you selected.

Note: Install and Windows Setup add PIF files for only recognized non-Windows programs. In some cases, you may need to create manually a PIF file for a non-Windows program.

If you have finished installation and you want to have one or more PIF files automatically created for you, use the Windows Setup program. To run Windows Setup and create PIF files, follow these steps:

1. Find your original or backup copies of the Windows 3 installation diskettes.
2. Open the Main group window in the Program Manager.

324

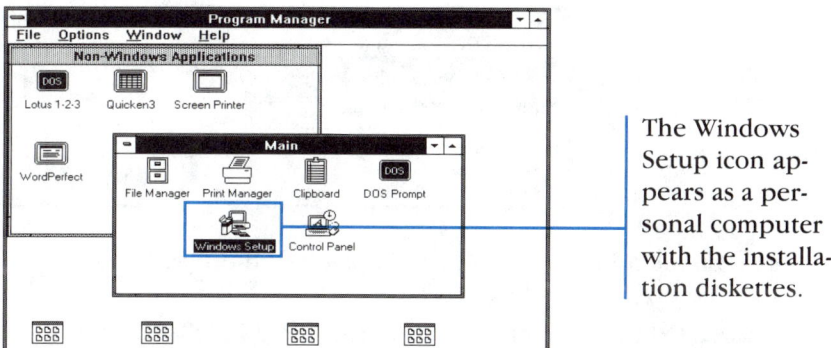

The Windows
Setup icon ap-
pears as a per-
sonal computer
with the installa-
tion diskettes.

3. Choose the Windows Setup program item icon.

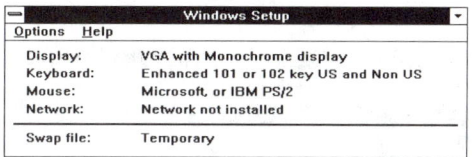

The Windows
Setup dialog box
appears.

4. Choose the **O**ptions menu and select the **S**et Up Applications
command. The Set Up Applications dialog box appears.

5. From the drop-down list box, select the drive(s) containing your
non-Windows programs. Then choose OK. (You may need to wait a
few minutes while Windows searches for programs on the drive or
drives you indicate.)

This example
shows that Win-
dows will search
on all drives.

6. When a second Set Up Applications box appears, select from the
left list box the non-Windows programs for which you want
program item icons and PIF files built. Use Shift+Click to select
more than one program at a time.

13

In this dialog box, three non-Windows programs have been selected.

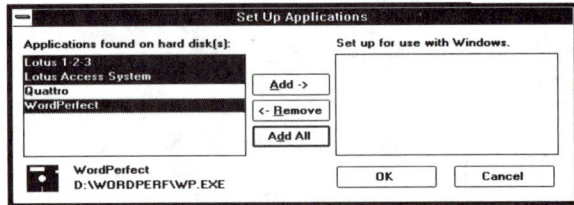

7. Choose the **Add ->** button to add the selected programs to the right list box.

8. Choose OK to create program item icons and PIF files for the programs listed in the right list box. The PIF files will be stored in the Windows directory.

9. Return to step 4 to select files from a different disk. Or choose Cancel to return to the Windows Setup dialog box.

Windows Setup creates a Non-Windows Application group window and program item icons in the Program Manager.

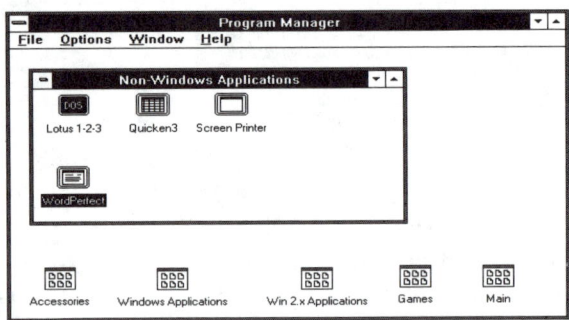

Within this group window are program item icons for each of the non-Windows programs you selected. A PIF file has been created also for each program and stored in the Windows directory. The discussion of the Program Manager in Chapter 4, "Grouping Programs and Documents," explains how to change the names and icons for each program item in the window.

To open the non-Windows Application group window in the Program Manager and to run a non-Windows program, select the program item icon for the program you want to run, and then double-click on it or press Enter.

Note: If the non-Windows program runs incorrectly when you start it or if it does not run at all, check its PIF file and its program item icon properties to be sure that they refer to the correct file name and directory. Changing the program item icon is described in Chapter 4, "Grouping Programs and Documents." Editing a PIF file is described in the following sections. Windows Setup may be unable to create a PIF file for a non-Windows program not recognized. You will need to create a PIF file manually for an unrecognized program if it will not run with the default PIF settings.

Editing a PIF File

As indicated earlier, Windows creates predefined PIF files for many popular non-Windows programs. When you use Windows Setup to install a non-Windows program, Setup automatically creates a PIF file for the program and stores the file in the Windows directory. If the program does not run as you want, you can edit the PIF file to make changes.

You edit PIF files with the PIF Editor, a program located in the Accessories group window of the Program Manager. In the PIF Editor, the contents shown for PIF files used in real and standard mode are different from the contents of PIF files used in 386-enhanced mode.

Note: Before you edit a PIF file, use the File Manager to make a backup copy of the original PIF file. For example, a WordPerfect PIF file, WP.PIF, might use the backup name of WP.BCK. If your edited PIF file gives you trouble, you can return to the preceding version by renaming the backup copy with the original name.

To edit a PIF file, follow these steps:

1. Choose the PIF Editor program from the Accessories group window.

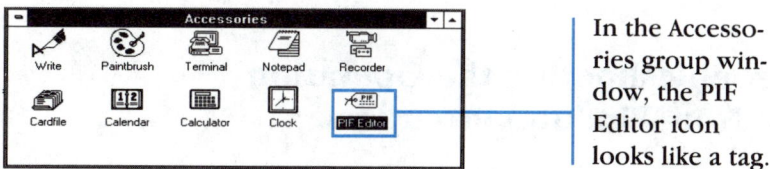

In the Accessories group window, the PIF Editor icon looks like a tag.

2. Choose **File Open** and change to the directory containing the PIF file to be edited. PIF files are usually in the Windows directory. Select and open the PIF file you want to edit.

327

3. The file appears, showing the current PIF settings for that program. Choose File Save **As** and save a backup copy of the PIF file with a BCK extension.

The PIF file shown here is for WordPerfect, running under Windows in 386-enhanced mode.

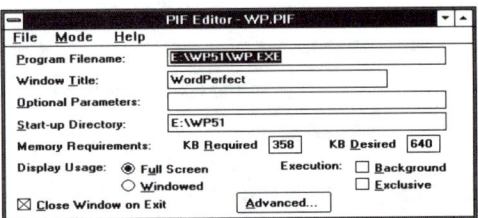

4. Make changes to the text boxes or selections in the PIF Editor window. (See the next section for detailed descriptions of the selections available.)

5. Choose File Save **As** and change the file name back to its original name with PIF as an extension. The PIF file root name must be the same as the program's root name—WP.EXE and WP.PIF, for example. Then choose OK.

6. Choose File **Exit** to quit the PIF Editor.

Save the data in other programs in Windows before you test a new PIF file. If the non-Windows program freezes the system, you can turn off your computer and restart it without losing data from other programs. Test the PIF file by starting the program and checking whether your changes have solved the problem.

Before you edit your own PIF files, look at tables 13.1, 13.2, and 13.3 to learn about the different parts of PIF files and the PIF Editor screen.

Troubleshooting the Operation of Non-Windows Programs

Some of the most common problems with PIF files, along with suggested changes, are the following:

Problem	*Change You Make in the PIF Editor*
Program file not found	Check the file name extension in the **P**rogram Filename text box.
Program file not found	Check the program path name in the **P**rogram Filename text box.
Associated files not found	Type the program's path name in the **S**tart-up Directory text box.
Insufficient memory to start	Increase the KB **R**equired.
Insufficient memory for documents	Increase the KB **D**esired or KB **L**imit.
Special keystrokes won't work	Use the Reserve Shortcut Keys group of options to reserve keystrokes for use in the non-Windows programs. (To see these options, choose the **A**dvanced button in a 386 PIF Editor screen.)

Making Basic Changes to PIF Files

The PIF Editor display for real and standard modes is nearly the same as for 386-enhanced mode. A few check boxes and text boxes are different. Table 13.1 describes the PIF Editor text boxes that are the same for all three modes.

Table 13.1
The PIF Editor Text Boxes

Text Box	Use
Program Filename	Type the full path name and program name, including the file extension. Most programs end with EXE or COM. Batch files that run commands or start programs end with BAT.
	Examples:
	For WordPerfect 5.1, use C:\WP\WP.EXE.
	For 1-2-3 Release 2.2, use D:\123\123.EXE.

329

13

Table 13.1—(continued)

Text Box	Use
Window Title	Type the name you want to appear in the program window title bar.
Optional Parameters	Type any parameters you want added to the program when it starts. These are the parameters or arguments you might type after the file name when you start a program from the DOS prompt. Examples: /m-*macroname* starts the specified macro when WordPerfect 5.1 starts. /C puts Microsoft Word into character mode.
Start-up Directory	Type the full path name of the drive and directory where you want Windows to go when the program starts. If the program needs to locate additional files on start-up (as is true for 1-2-3), make sure that you indicate a start-up directory which is the same as the program's directory.

Editing Standard Mode PIF Files

Table 13.2 describes some of the more important PIF Editor settings for standard mode. The PIF Editor screen for standard mode offers additional settings beyond those described in table 13.1.

The PIF Editor screen for standard mode is slightly different from the screen for 386-enhanced mode.

330

Table 13.2
PIF Editor Settings for Standard Mode

Option	Use
Video Mode Settings	
Text	Select this option if the program uses only text. Memory is conserved.
Graphics/Multiple Text	Select this option if the program displays graphics. You will use this setting for most programs.
Memory Requirements Setting	
KB Required	Type the number of KB of memory recommended by the user manual for the program to operate without approximately 40 KB used by DOS. If you are unsure, start at the default setting of 128 and raise it in increments of 64 until the program works.

Reserve Shortcut Keys Settings

Select the Reserve Shortcut Keys check boxes for the shortcut keys you want to use in the program. When selected, these keys are reserved for the program's use and cannot be used by Windows. The shortcut keys and their current uses by Windows are the following:

Alt+Tab	Switches between programs.
Alt+Esc	Switches between programs.
Ctrl+Esc	Displays the Task List.
PrtSc	Copies the full screen to the Clipboard.
Alt+PrtSc	Copies the full screen to the Clipboard.

Other Settings	
No Screen Exchange	Select this option to prevent copying and pasting between non-Windows programs; more memory is made available.
Prevent Program Switch	Select this option to conserve memory; however, you must quit the program to return to Windows. Usually, this option is not selected.
Close Window on Exit	Select this option to close the window when you exit the non-Windows program.

13

331

Editing 386-Enhanced Mode PIF Files

The PIF file options for 386-enhanced mode appear in two dialog boxes: PIF Editor (for basic options) and Advanced Options. The basic PIF options are similar to those for standard mode. The advanced options fine-tune special features of the program for running in 386-enhanced mode. For more information on setting the advanced PIF features for 386-enhanced mode, see the Que book *Using Microsoft Windows 3*, 2nd Edition.

Table 13.1 described the text boxes and options common to the PIF Editor for both standard and 386-enhanced modes. Table 13.3 describes the basic options in the PIF Editor for programs running in 386-enhanced mode.

This PIF Editor screen contains basic options for 386-enhanced mode.

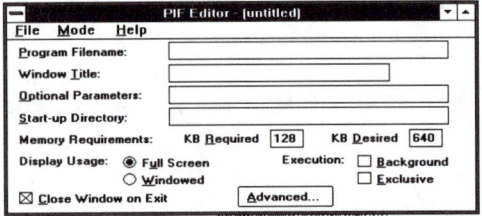

Table 13.3
PIF Editor Settings for 386-Enhanced Mode

Option	Use
Memory Requirements Settings	
KB **R**equired	Type the amount of conventional memory that must be free. Generally, use 128 KB; program manuals usually specify too much because they must include memory for DOS and drivers. Windows will not start the program if the KB **R**equired setting is not large enough. This setting does not limit the amount of memory the program receives. Use -1 to give the program all available conventional memory.

13

Table 13.3—(continued)

Option	Use
KB Desired	Type the maximum amount of memory you want the program to use, if memory is available. Usually, 640 KB is the maximum. Most programs use much less. Using a smaller setting conserves memory. Some programs run more efficiently with more memory. Use -1 to give the program as much memory as possible, but not more than 640 KB.

Display Usage Settings

Full Screen	Select this option to start the program in a full-screen display.
Windowed	Select this option to start the program in a window.

Execution Settings

These settings determine how a program shares processing power with other programs.

Background	Select this option to run the program while you are using another program.
Exclusive	Select this option to stop all other programs while this program is active. This option gives a program more computer power.

Other Settings

Close Window on Exit	Select this option to close the window when you exit the program.
Advanced	Choose the Advanced button to display the Advanced Options dialog box.

With the advanced options in 386-enhanced mode, you can modify a PIF file to get the best memory usage and performance from your non-Windows program. The advanced options are discussed in the Que book *Using Microsoft Windows 3*, 2nd Edition.

Changing Settings While Programs Are Running in 386-Enhanced Mode

If you are running Windows on an 80386 computer in 386-enhanced mode, you can change how non-Windows programs operate, even while they run.

13

To change settings for a program running in 386-enhanced mode, follow these steps:

1. Click on the program's Control menu or press Alt and then the space bar to open the Control menu. Then choose the **Settings** command.

The Settings dialog box appears for the running program.

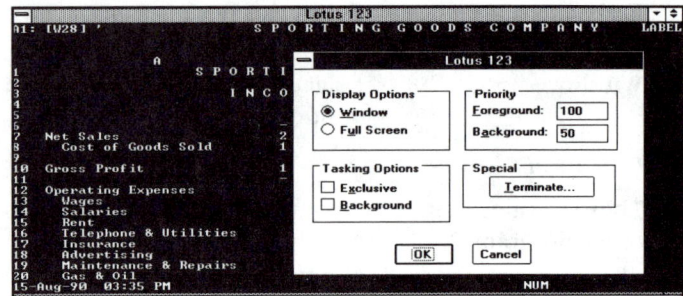

2. Select the option you want to change.

The options you can change while the non-Windows program is running in 386-enhanced mode are described in table 13.4.

**Table 13.4
Options You Can Change
While Programs Are Running
in 386-Enhanced Mode**

Option	Use
Display Options	
Window	Select this option to display the program in a window.
Full Screen	Select this option to display the program full screen.

Note: Press Alt+Enter to switch between full-screen and window operations while a program is running.

Tasking Options	
Exclusive	Select this option to dedicate computer power to the active non-Windows program. Windows programs continue to run if the non-Windows program is in a window.
Background	Run this program in the background when other programs are active.
Priority Options	
Foreground	Increase this number for more computer power to the active program. Use a setting from 1 to 10,000.
Background	Increase this number for more computer power to the inactive program and less power to the active program. Use a setting from 1 to 10,000.
Special Option	
Terminate	Choose this option when you cannot quit the program in any other way. This option closes the program and gives you the chance to return to Windows and save open files in other programs. You should close the other programs after saving their files and then restart your computer with Ctrl+Alt+Del. With this option, you can lose data you are working on in the program being terminated.

13

Summary

In this chapter, you learned how to start non-Windows programs, control them, switch between them, and fine-tune their operations. You learned also how to use the PIF Editor to change settings in PIF files, which determine how Windows works with non-Windows programs.

13

Some of the most important points covered in the chapter are the following:

- Windows can run multiple non-Windows programs simultaneously in 386-enhanced mode. In real or standard mode, non-Windows programs that are not active are put on hold.

- Windows will run most non-Windows programs with its default PIF file settings.

- You can switch between programs by either pressing Ctrl+Esc and selecting a program from the Task List, or by pressing Alt+Tab to cycle through programs.

- You can change operating settings while running in 386-enhanced mode by pressing Alt and then the space bar, choosing the Settings command, and entering new settings in the dialog box.

Don't forget that you can run Windows and non-Windows programs together. This capability enables you to work with multiple programs and to share data between them. You learned in Chapter 8 how to copy and paste data between programs; with some Windows programs, you can automatically read and translate files from non-Windows programs, such as 1-2-3, WordPerfect, and dBASE. To learn how to share data from multiple programs, read Chapter 14, "Integrating Programs."

Integrating Multiple Programs

One of the most useful features of Windows is its capability to run multiple programs and to share or exchange data between them. Windows enables you to use different Windows programs together as though they were part of the same program. And non-Windows programs can copy and paste data to other programs, making it much less complicated to share data. By integrating programs and tasks, you can do your work faster, easier, and more accurately.

When you link Windows programs, you can work in new ways. For example, as you type a letter in Word for Windows, you can enter a name and address by selecting the name in the letter and then choosing a custom command on the Word menu. PackRat, a personal information manager designed for Windows, will find the correct address and insert it in the letter. You never see PackRat working. Word appears to find the address by magic. The macros that do these tasks come with PackRat.

14

Key Terms in This Chapter

Dynamic Data Exchange (DDE)	A feature of many Windows programs that enables programs to share the same data. When the data in the source program changes, the changes are automatically sent to the target program.
Link	The sharing of data between Windows programs that is performed with Dynamic Data Exchange (DDE). Documents within a Windows program can share data when they are linked.
Personal Information Manager (PIM)	A program that manages your personal information, such as agendas, calendars, to-do lists, phone numbers and addresses, and contact lists.

Budget and financial reports you create at the end of every month can be updated automatically. You can link numbers and charts from Excel into a professional word processor such as Word for Windows or Amí Professional. When you change numbers in the Excel spreadsheet, the numeric tables and charts in the report change.

Training materials and documentation are easy to create if you copy a program's screen into the Clipboard and then paste the information into the training document that you are composing in PageMaker, Word for Windows, or Amí Professional. The time required to develop your training materials is reduced significantly, and the file from any of these Windows programs can go straight to a Linotronic typesetting machine.

You can create high-quality presentation slides and overheads by linking data in Excel or Lotus 1-2-3 into the presentation maker called Microsoft PowerPoint. The slides or overheads you make can even be sent out by modem; you receive 35mm slides within 24 hours.

Windows makes non-Windows programs more productive also. For instance, you can use non-Windows programs under Windows to copy budget and report information from an accounting program or 1-2-3 spreadsheet. You can then paste that information into a WordPerfect document.

Accounting, auditing, and tax programs can be run in windows alongside Excel or 1-2-3. You can copy data from one program to another instead of printing and retyping the data.

1-2-3 spreadsheets can be linked into Excel spreadsheets, enabling you to consolidate your work or to enhance your 1-2-3 spreadsheet and chart printouts.

You can compile documents in Word for Windows that are created from links to 1-2-3 spreadsheets and charts, or from text from WordPerfect, WordStar, or MultiMate. Pressing the F9 function key updates the compiled document to reflect any changes in the sources.

14

Finally, you can link dBASE files to Q+E so that programs such as Excel and Word for Windows are linked to dBASE data files.

Understanding Types of Integration

You use the following types of integration with Windows and non-Windows programs:

- Copying and pasting text or graphics between programs
- Transferring text or graphics by saving the file from one program and converting the file for use in another program
- Linking text or graphics between Windows programs by using links created with Dynamic Data Exchange (DDE)

One of the easiest ways to transfer text or graphics between programs is to use the copy and paste procedures common to all Windows programs. You select the data to be copied from one Windows program, choose **E**dit **C**opy, switch to the other Windows program, position the insertion point, and choose **E**dit **P**aste. If you are working with non-Windows programs, additional steps are required, and you can copy and paste text only.

Note: To learn how to copy and paste text and graphics with Windows and non-Windows programs, refer to Chapter 8, "Using the Clipboard To Copy and Paste."

The most common method of exchanging data in non-Windows programs is to save the file from one program, exit the program, use a second program to convert the file's data and format, exit that program, and finally import the data into a third program. This method is used, for instance, by 1-2-3 with its Translate program, and by WordPerfect with its Conversion utility.

Windows programs have improved significantly on exchanging data by file. Most Windows programs read or save other file formats and automatically convert or translate the file as the programs read or save. For example, Excel reads and writes text files, 1-2-3 files, and dBASE files. Word for Windows automatically reads and writes files for common word processors such as WordPerfect, WordStar, MultiMate, and the IBM standard, DCA (RFT). PageMaker converts files from Word for DOS, WordPerfect, and other word processors. The translation process is invisible to you. Thus, you can easily use both the new generation of Windows programs and the old non-Windows programs in the same office.

Some Windows programs, such as Word for Windows, have the capability to include in their documents all or part of another program's document. In Word for Windows, for example, you can create a document that is composed of its own text as well as pieces of files from WordPerfect, 1-2-3, Excel, Word for DOS, or WordStar. These other files can be on disk. When you select the Word for Windows document and press the F9 function key, the entire document on-screen is updated to reflect the new data stored on the files on disk. Word for Windows automatically translates files that are different from its own format.

The greatest level of integration comes with Dynamic Data Exchange (DDE). DDE enables Windows programs to link data. When the data in one program changes, the change is sent to the program to which the first program is linked. The change can be sent automatically or when the operator requests an update. If you have a business solution requiring more than one program, and those programs need to act as a single integrated unit, you need to use DDE. For instance, you can continually analyze inventory quantities by linking Excel worksheets and charts, through the Q+E program, to an inventory database stored in dBASE files. When the inventory changes, Excel updates its analysis. Mainframe data can also be linked to Windows programs through DDE.

Copying, Pasting, and Linking Data

When you operate programs under Windows, you can copy information from one program and paste it into another program. Copying and pasting are described in detail in Chapter 8, "Using the Clipboard To Copy and Paste." When you learn how to copy and paste between programs, you will understand also how to create Dynamic Data Exchange links for many of the Windows programs that support DDE.

Copying and Pasting between Windows Programs

The procedure for copying and pasting between Windows programs is almost the same as for copying and pasting within the same program. Follow these steps:

1. Select the text or graphics you want to copy.
2. Choose the **E**dit menu and select the **C**opy command.

   Or if you want to capture the entire screen as a bitmap graphic image, press the PrtSc key. If you want to capture the active window as a bit-map graphic image, press Alt + PrtSc.
3. Switch to the other program by clicking on its Window, or by pressing Ctrl + Esc and selecting the program from the Task List.
4. Position the insertion point where you want the text or graphics to appear.
5. Choose the **E**dit menu and select the **P**aste command.

Note: Not all Windows programs are designed to accept pasted graphics. Some programs will accept only text or numbers.

Copying and Pasting between Non-Windows Programs

Non-Windows programs copy and paste differently in Windows, depending on the mode in which Windows is operating. When non-Windows programs are running in real or standard mode, you can copy only an entire text screen or graphics screen. When non-Windows programs are running in 386-enhanced mode, you can use the keyboard or mouse to select portions of a text screen to copy, or you can copy an entire graphics screen. Copying and pasting with non-Windows programs are described in Chapter 8, "Using the Clipboard To Copy and Paste."

Linking Windows Programs

Many Windows programs have the capability to link data. When the data in one of the programs changes, the corresponding data in the linked program changes also. This feature is called Dynamic Data Exchange or DDE.

DDE links are created in two ways. One method is as simple as using the Edit menu to copy and paste between two Windows programs. This method is so easy that you can use it as soon as you begin using a program. The second method uses a macro language to start, control, and end the DDE link between programs. The second method is more useful when the data exchange involves timed updates, communication programs, or links to mainframe data.

Here are a few of the programs that enable you to create links with the Edit Paste Link command or that come with ready-to-use macros:

Microsoft Excel, the worksheet, database, and chart program

Word for Windows, a professional word processor

Amí Professional, a professional word processor

Q+E, a query-and-edit tool for use with dBASE files

PackRat, a personal information manager

SuperBase 4, a relational database

If you are using two Windows programs that support DDE links created with Edit Paste Link, follow these steps to link the programs:

1. Start the two programs and activate the source program, which contains the data to be linked.

2. Select the data you want to link.

3. Choose the Edit menu and select the Copy command.

4. Activate the target program, which receives the data.

5. Position the insertion point where you want the linked data to appear.

6. Choose the Edit menu and select the Paste Link command.

7. Some programs display a dialog box asking how you want the data to be updated. You can choose to update whenever the source data changes, or only when the operator wants an update. (Updating on every change may slow down your programs.) Make a selection from this dialog box. Choose OK or press ⏎Enter.

Depending on the capability of the source and target programs, you can exchange graphics as well as text with DDE. Each program may have additional DDE features, such as the capability to edit existing links so that the source of data can be changed.

Some programs—for example, Word for Windows, DynaComm, Excel, and Q+E—can create and control DDE links through their macro languages. This capability enables a consultant or programmer to link Windows programs together so that they exchange data at specific times or under certain conditions. Mainframe data can even be downloaded and linked under DDE control.

Copying and Linking between Windows Programs

Many Windows programs can be linked together with Dynamic Data Exchange (DDE) so that changes in one program produce changes in another program. You can thus solve business problems that require multiple programs operating together.

Linking Word Processing Letters to a Personal Information Manager

One way in which Windows can improve productivity is to link a personal information manager, such as PackRat, to a word processor, such as Word for Windows. Because both are Windows programs, PackRat can pass data to a Word for Windows letter while you are typing the letter.

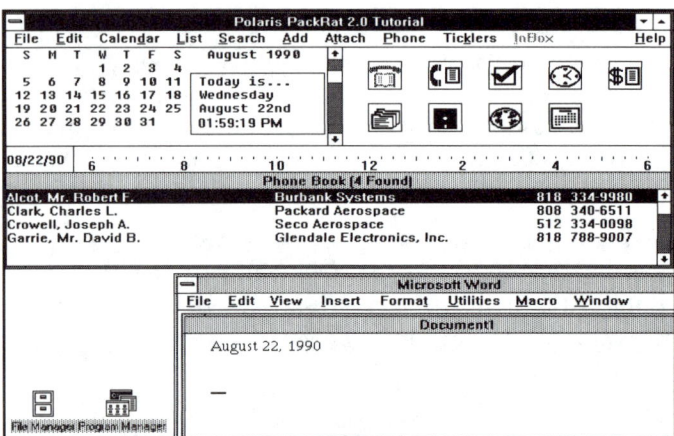

Personal information managers (PIMs), like PackRat shown in the upper window, store your personal information.

PIMs are designed especially to handle personal priority lists, agendas, phone books, and address files. Such programs can contain many unrelated notes that you can retrieve by looking for key words within the notes.

PackRat comes with a set of macros that you can load into Word for Windows. When the macros are loaded, they automatically attach themselves as new commands in the Word for Windows menus. These new commands enable you to stay in Word for Windows and retrieve information from PackRat. For example, you can generate form letters in Word for Windows from a selected group of names and addresses in PackRat.

The following example shows you how a forgotten name and address can be retrieved from PackRat and automatically inserted into the letter you are typing in Word for Windows.

To insert a name and address that is stored in PackRat into a Word for Windows letter, follow these steps:

1. Position the insertion point in Word for Windows where you want the name and address to appear.

2. Choose the **Insert** menu and select the Find Name in **Pack**rat command. (This is a custom Word for Windows command that comes with PackRat.)

3. In the dialog box that appears, enter the search criteria that you remember about the person. If you remember only the last name, type it in the dialog box. In this example, type **Alcot**.

4. Choose OK or press ⏎Enter.

5. The name and address are retrieved from PackRat's phone book and inserted and formatted in the Word for Windows letter.

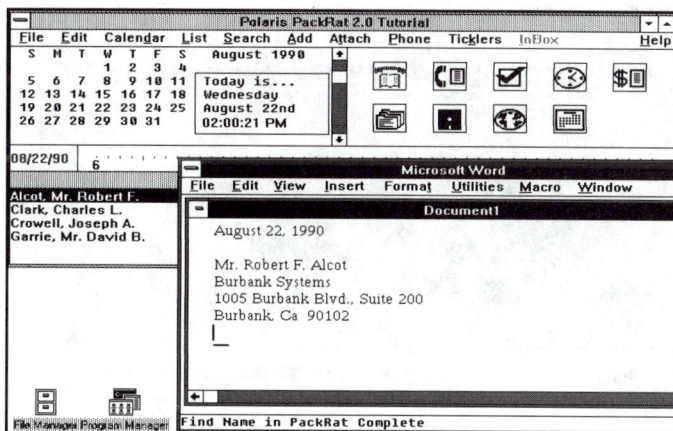

PackRat uses its phone and address lists to fill in the address for the Word for Windows document.

14

Copying Worksheet Data from Excel into Word for Windows

A frequent data exchange with Windows programs is copying Excel worksheet data or charts and pasting them into Word for Windows or Amí Professional. Copying data prevents wasted effort in retyping, eliminates the possibility of typing incorrect numbers, and produces a more professional report with tables, charts, and illustrations integrated into the text body.

Note: When you paste Excel worksheet data into some Windows programs, each cell is pasted in as a cell in a table. In other Windows programs, such as Windows Write, each cell is pasted in as text separated by tabs. To align data separated by tabs, select the rows of data and then create new decimal or right tab settings. If quotation marks appear in the data, use a search-and-replace command to replace them with nothing.

When you paste Excel data into Word for Windows, it builds a table to hold the data. You can format the cells, cell contents, and borders in a Word for Windows table just as you would in Excel.

Follow these steps to copy worksheet data from Excel and paste it into Word for Windows to produce a table of data that is not linked to the worksheet:

1. Activate the Excel worksheet.
2. Select the cells to be copied.

14

Note the selected cells in Excel before the copy operation.

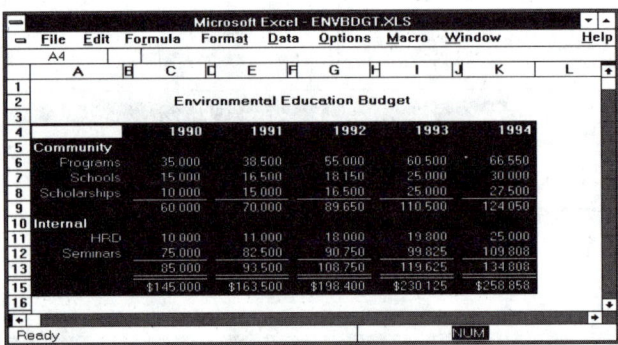

3. Choose the **Edit** menu and select the **Copy** command.
4. Activate Word for Windows.
5. Position the insertion point in the document where you want the data in the cells to appear.
6. Choose the **Edit** menu and select the **Paste** command.

The Excel worksheet data appears as a table in Word for Windows.

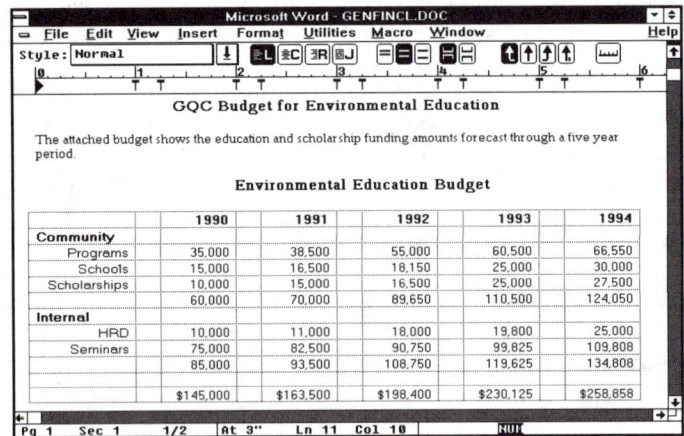

This table contains numbers and text just as if they had been typed into Word for Windows. Because the **P**aste command was chosen instead of Paste Link, the data is not linked to Excel. (The edges of cells in the table are shown in gray when you choose the **V**iew P**r**eferences command and select the Table **G**ridlines option.)

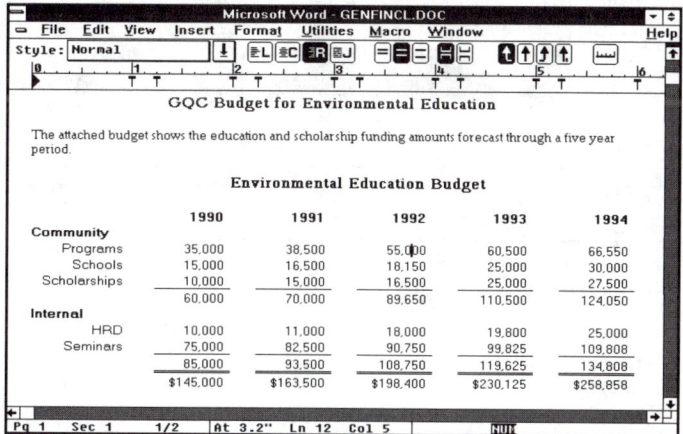

You can use the Format **T**able command to format tables with printable outlines, double lines, borders, and shadows.

Copying Excel Charts into CorelDRAW

You can copy and paste charts or graphics from one Windows program to other Windows programs for additional graphic enhancement or changes. For example, you can copy and paste a chart from Excel into Paintbrush to add simple shadings in bars. Or you can copy the chart into CorelDRAW or Micrografx Designer for extensive artistic enhancement. CorelDRAW and Micrografx Designer are professional art and design programs that add touches to a graph, such as logos, additional text fonts, and gradient shaded backgrounds.

To copy an Excel chart and paste it into CorelDRAW, follow these steps:

1. Display the Excel chart in the active window.

2. Choose the **C**hart menu and select the Select **C**hart command.

3. Choose the **E**dit menu and select the **C**opy command to copy the entire chart into the Clipboard. A dashed line, the *marquee*, appears around objects that are copied into the Clipboard.

347

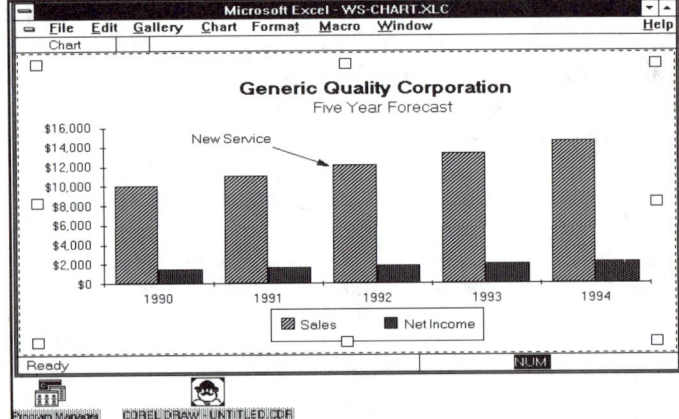

Because this entire chart has been selected, it is enclosed by a marquee.

14

4. Start or activate CorelDRAW.

5. Choose the **E**dit menu and select the **P**aste command to paste the chart into CorelDRAW.

Use the professional art capabilities of CorelDRAW to select and change any object on the chart. Each object on the chart—such as a column, an arrow, or a string of text—is a separate object and can be stretched, rotated, resized, or colored. You can also paste in your corporate logo, add clip art from the extensive clip-art libraries that come with CorelDRAW, or add a shaded and colored background. The CorelDRAW logo is shown at the top right of the Excel chart's preview display.

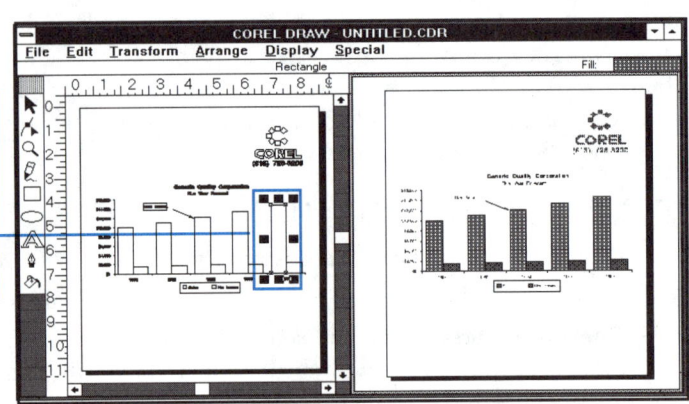

You can see how the rightmost column has been selected because of the square *handles* at each of its corners.

Linking Excel Data and Charts into Word for Windows

You can link Excel worksheet data and charts into Word for Windows. Several methods are available. You can create links with the **Edit Paste Link** command, use an Include field that reads data from the Excel file on disk, or use macro commands to control DDE transfers.

To copy Excel worksheet data or a chart and to link it into a Word for Windows document, using the Paste Link command, follow these steps:

1. Display in the active window the Excel worksheet data or chart.

2. Save the worksheet data or chart with a file name that the link will use to identify the worksheet or chart.

3. Activate the worksheet data or chart you want to link.

4. Select the worksheet cells you want linked. For a chart, choose the Chart menu and select the Select Chart command.

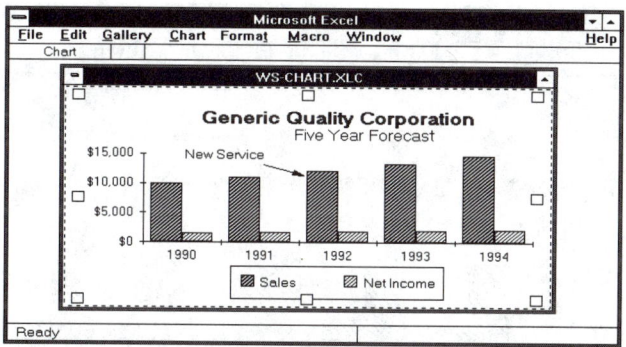

The square handles and dashed marquee show that the entire chart has been selected.

5. Choose the **Edit** menu and select the **Copy** command to copy the data or chart into the Clipboard.

6. Start or activate Word for Windows.

7. Position the insertion point in the document where you want the data or chart to appear.

8. Choose the **Edit** menu and select the **Paste Link** command.

349

9. From the dialog box that appears, select the **Auto Update** check box if you want the Word document to be updated automatically whenever the Excel data or chart changes. Then choose OK.

If you do not select the **Auto Update** check box, you can manually update a link by selecting the linked data in Word and pressing the F9 key.

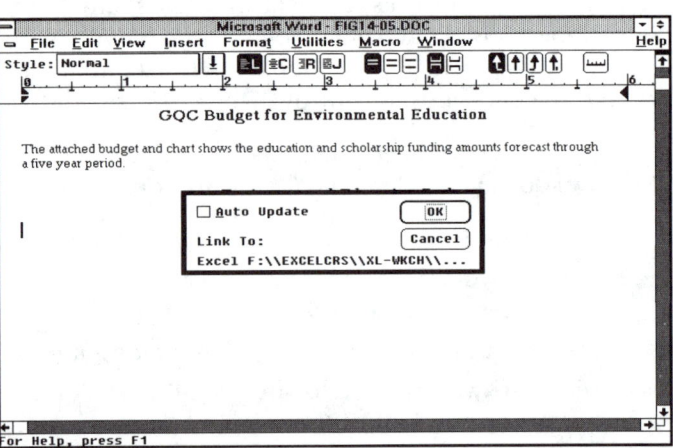

The linked data or chart appears in the Word document.

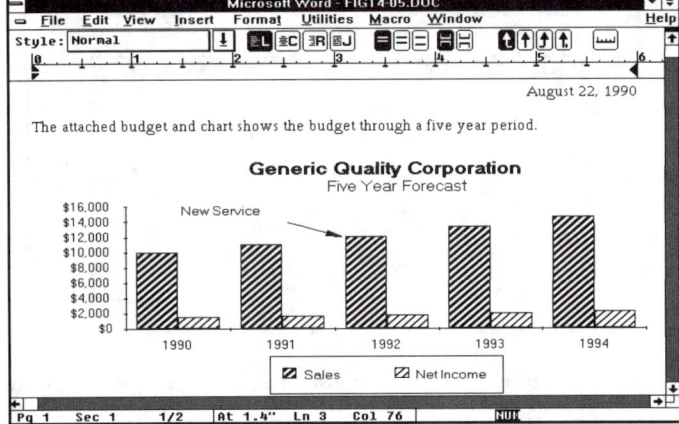

If you later change the file name of the source worksheet or chart in Excel, you will need to change the linked file name in the Word for Windows document. You can see and edit this file name by scrolling in the Word document to the linked data or chart, and then choosing the **View Field Codes** command. Edit the file name you see in the {DDE} or {DDEAUTO} field code to reflect the new name of the Excel file.

Copying and Linking between Non-Windows and Windows Programs

Windows programs and non-Windows programs can exchange data in two ways: you can manually copy and paste data between the programs, or you can use a common file format that both programs understand. Some Windows programs, such as Word for Windows, can also link to non-Windows files like those of 1-2-3 and WordPerfect. When you press a key, the Word document updates all links to files from non-Windows programs. You can therefore use Word for Windows to create dynamic documents that are updated when you choose.

14

Copying and pasting data with non-Windows programs are easier when Windows is operating in 386-enhanced mode. Because programs can be running in windows in 386-enhanced mode, you can easily switch between programs, as well as select portions of the screen to copy and paste into another program.

Note: Non-Windows programs handle multiple lines of pasted data differently. The difference is caused by how the program deals with the carriage return at the end of a line. For example, if you paste multiple lines of data into 1-2-3, all the lines are pasted into the same spreadsheet cell; each line is entered over the top of the previous line. You should therefore paste cells one at a time in 1-2-3. WordPerfect, however, accepts multiple lines of data as expected. Each line of data is pasted into a new line in the WordPerfect document.

Creating Training Materials and Documentation with PageMaker

Windows presents you with an excellent set of tools for creating training materials and documentation. In Windows, you can simultaneously run the software you want to document and the Windows software used to create the documentation. Pressing the Print Screen key, as described in Chapter 8, "Using the Clipboard To Copy and Paste," puts a snapshot of the screen into the Clipboard. You can then paste the screen shot into Windows composition software, such as PageMaker, Word for Windows, or Amí

Professional. This technique is useful for documenting Windows or non-Windows software.

The following technique describes how to capture a 1-2-3 screen and paste it into PageMaker:

1. Start 1-2-3 and retrieve the spreadsheet you want to document.

2. Start the Windows software that you are using to write documentation. (In this example, the page-layout software PageMaker is used.)

3. Activate the 1-2-3 program. If it is running in a window in 386-enhanced mode, press Alt + ↵Enter to expand 1-2-3 to full screen.

4. Capture an image of the 1-2-3 screen by pressing PrtSc. The image is stored in the Clipboard. (This step captures the screen text. If the program is any Windows program or a non-Windows graphics program, the screen is captured as a graphic.)

5. Activate the PageMaker window. Position the insertion point where you want the captured screen to appear.

6. Choose the Edit menu and select the Paste command. The 1-2-3 screen text appears in PageMaker as though typed.

7. If the spreadsheet columns do not correctly align, select the pasted 1-2-3 text and change the font to Courier, a nonproportional typeface. The columns of 1-2-3 text will then be aligned.

Windows enables you to use the software you are documenting as you write the documentation.

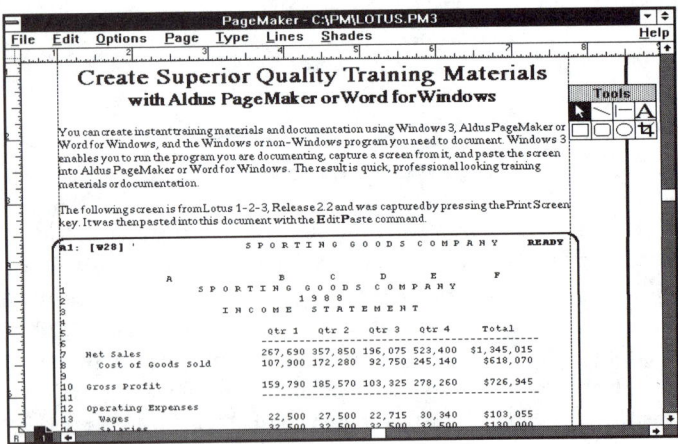

Text captured from non-Windows programs may not align when pasted into Windows programs because non-Windows programs use nonproportional typefaces, in which each character is the same width. Most Windows programs use proportional typefaces like those used in typesetting. To align the text pasted from a non-Windows program, change the font of the pasted text to a nonproportional typeface like Courier, or use tabs to realign columns.

If you paste a graphic screen image into PageMaker, Word for Windows, or Amí Professional, the image appears as a picture that can be resized or cropped. These Windows programs also enable you to draw lines and borders around screen images. The resulting documentation can be sent to a normal printer for printing, or to a file for printing on a Linotronic typesetter.

14

Linking 1-2-3 Spreadsheets into Excel Worksheets

If you are using Windows, you are probably using Excel. However, others in your work area may be using 1-2-3.

Because Excel can read and write 1-2-3 spreadsheets and read 1-2-3 charts, you can use Excel to link 1-2-3 sheets into Excel to consolidate data or to enhance 1-2-3 printouts and charts.

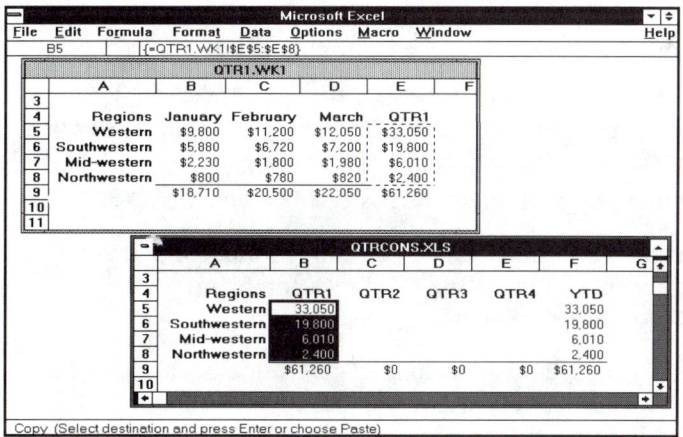

Use Excel to link or consolidate 1-2-3 spread-sheets. In this example, the 1-2-3 spread-sheet file is QTR1.WK1.

353

You can create and save only the links that go from 1-2-3 spreadsheets into Excel worksheets. Links that exist directly between 1-2-3 spreadsheets will be lost when those spreadsheets are saved again to disk.

If you want to link 1-2-3 spreadsheets into an Excel worksheet, follow these steps:

1. Activate Excel.
2. Choose the **File** menu and select the **Open** command.
3. Change the file name pattern to *.WK? and choose OK so that you can see the 1-2-3 file names.
4. Select the 1-2-3 spreadsheet you want to link. If the spreadsheet has attached graphs, you will be asked whether they should be converted.
5. Repeat steps 2 through 4 until all 1-2-3 spreadsheets are open in Excel. (Excel reads them automatically. You do not have to do any conversion.)

While 1-2-3 spreadsheets are open (on-screen or hidden), they can be linked into Excel worksheets. To link an open 1-2-3 spreadsheet into an Excel worksheet, follow these steps:

1. Activate the 1-2-3 spreadsheet so that it is the topmost document in Excel.
2. Select the cell or range of cells you want to link.
3. Choose the **Edit** menu and select the **Copy** command.
4. Activate the Excel worksheet that will receive the linked data.
5. Select the cell in the Excel worksheet that is at the top left corner of the area in which you want the linked data to appear.
6. Choose the **Edit** menu and select the **Paste Link** command.

If you later rename the 1-2-3 spreadsheet, you can reconnect the link by opening the linked sheets and using the **File Links** command with the **Change** button to reconnect the sheets.

Note: When you save your 1-2-3 spreadsheet, Excel automatically saves the spreadsheet in 1-2-3 format. Excel cannot save its enhanced charts in 1-2-3 format because 1-2-3 has no equivalent. If you enhanced the 1-2-3 spreadsheet with Excel's formatting power or if you used formulas or functions that are not available in 1-2-3, the enhancements will be lost when the spreadsheet is saved as a 1-2-3 file. If you want to keep the formatting and the extra features, save the file in Excel format by choosing the **File Save As** command, choosing the **Options >>** button, and selecting the **Normal** format. Then save the file with the same name or a different name.

Copying 1-2-3 Spreadsheet Data into WordPerfect

14

You can use Windows to copy data from a non-Windows program, such as 1-2-3, into a non-Windows word processor, such as WordPerfect. Using Windows can save you time by preventing errors caused by retyping financial data into the non-Windows word processor. You can copy numeric data from an accounting screen, a 1-2-3 screen, or a database screen, and then paste the data into a word processing document.

To copy data from 1-2-3 (or from another non-Windows program that displays data in a text screen) and paste the data into WordPerfect (or another word processor), follow these steps:

1. Start both programs in Windows.

2. If you are running in 386-enhanced mode and the programs are not in windows, activate each program and press `Alt`+`↵Enter` to place each program in a window. The copy and paste operations are therefore easier.

3. Activate the 1-2-3 spreadsheet or non-Windows program from which you want to copy data.

4. If you are running in real or standard mode, press `PrtSc` or `Alt`+`PrtSc`. This copies the entire text screen.

   If you are running in 386-enhanced mode with the program in a window, position the mouse at the top left corner of the text you want to copy, and then drag the mouse down and to the right to select the text you want copied. Click on the 1-2-3 window's Control menu icon. Choose the **Edit** command and select the **Copy** command from the menu that appears.

355

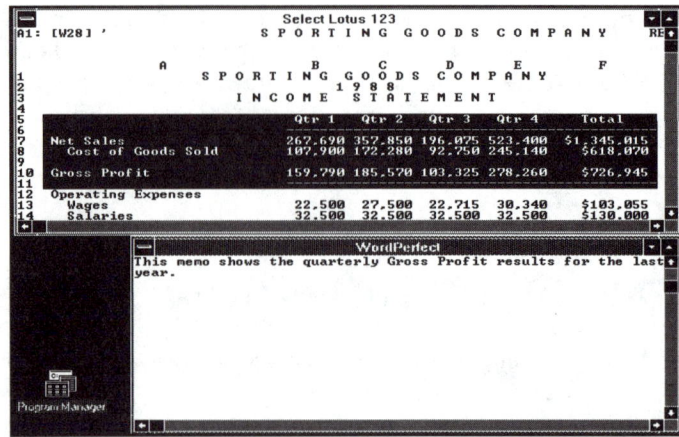

14

Selected text shows in inverse video in a non-Windows program running in a window.

5. Activate WordPerfect or the non-Windows word processor into which you want to paste the data.

6. Position the program's cursor where you want the data to appear.

7. If you are running the program full screen, press Alt + Esc to minimize the program to an icon. Press Alt and then the space bar to open the icon's Control menu; then choose the **Paste** command.

   Or if you are running the program in a window in 386-enhanced mode, click on the Control menu icon and choose the **Paste** command.

8. If you pasted in text that you copied with PrtSc, you may have to edit out unwanted lines of information.

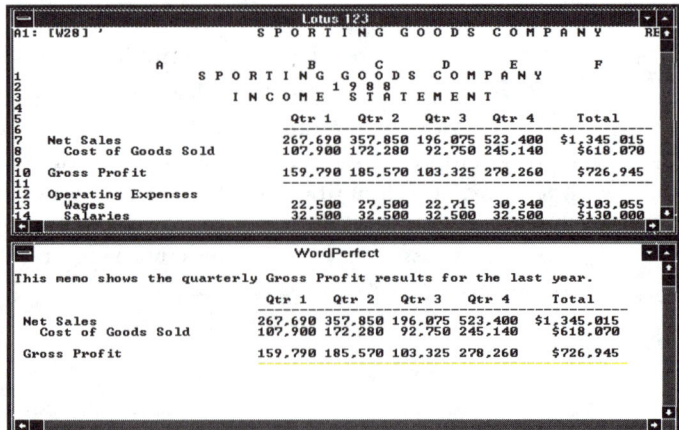

The selected data is copied from a 1-2-3 worksheet and pasted into a WordPerfect document just as though the data were typed.

Sharing Data from Old and New Windows Programs

Some Windows programs (Windows 2.X and earlier) may run only in real mode. Yet you may also use programs that run only in Windows 3. Copying and pasting data between the old and new Windows programs may present a problem. There is a solution, however.

You can copy and paste data between a program running in Windows 3 and an older program designed for Windows 2.X by following these steps:

14

1. Type **win /r** at the DOS prompt to start the program in real mode.

2. Start the Windows 2.X program that contains the data to be copied. Copy the data to the Clipboard, using one of the methods, as described in Chapter 8, for non-Windows programs.

3. Open the Main group window in the Program Manager and start the Clipboard. To save the copied data to a file, choose the **File** menu and select the **Save** command. Note the file name and directory of the saved file.

4. Exit the program and Windows.

5. Restart Windows by typing **win** at the DOS prompt to start the program in standard mode if you have an 80286 computer, or to start the program in 386-enhanced mode if you have an 80386 computer.

6. Open the Main group window in the Program Manager and start the Clipboard.

7. Choose the **File** menu and select the **Open** command to open the file in which you saved the copied data. The data should appear in the Clipboard's window.

8. Start the Windows 3 program and open the document to receive the data.

9. Position the insertion point or cursor in the document, choose the **Edit** menu, and select the **Paste** command.

Summary

An important feature of Windows is that multiple programs can work together and share data. Windows programs can be linked together so that data passes between them automatically or under operator control. You or a consultant can thus build business systems that were never before possible. Non-Windows programs such as 1-2-3, WordPerfect, and dBASE can use Windows to operate simultaneously. And data from these programs can easily be copied and pasted from one program to another.

14

The most important points covered in this chapter are the following:

■ You can use Windows to copy and paste fixed text and numbers between all Windows and non-Windows programs. Use the **Edit Copy** command to copy the selected data, and the **Edit Paste** command to insert the data.

■ You can easily link many Windows programs together so that they pass data automatically. You can copy data from one program and paste the data into another program with the **Edit Paste Link** command. Remember, though, that if the file name of the source data file is changed, the Windows program will not know where to find the data when the next update occurs.

■ You can use macro commands to link many Windows programs so that they operate as if they were one program. Some programs, such as Q+E for dBASE links, or PackRat for personal information data, come with macros that do this linking. For custom systems, you may need to hire a consultant or programmer.

For more information on how to copy and paste between Windows and non-Windows programs, refer to Chapter 8, "Using the Clipboard To Copy and Paste."

If you are using non-Windows programs and you want to increase their performance, make sure that you read Chapter 13, "Running Non-Windows Programs," to learn how to create PIF files for non-Windows programs.

Installing Windows 3

The Windows Setup program guides you through installing Windows. The Setup program displays screens with directions for inserting disks and making selections; you also can quit and start over if necessary. This appendix covers installing, testing, and starting Windows.

Before You Install Windows

For Windows to operate correctly, your hardware and software must meet certain requirements:

- IBM Personal System/2, Personal Computer AT, COMPAQ Deskpro 286, or a compatible computer that uses an 80286 processor or any 80386 or 80486 processor
- 640K or more of memory
- VGA or EGA graphics cards, or graphics cards with proprietary Windows drivers
- A hard disk with 6M to 8M of available storage
- At least one 1.2M or 1.44M floppy disk drive
- MS-DOS 3.1 or higher

Optional equipment supported by Windows includes the following:

- A mouse (highly recommended)
- Most printers
- Hayes-compatible modems for communications
- Major networks

When you install Windows, it checks to see what equipment you have installed and tries to determine the equipment's manufacturer and type. Windows is usually correct, but you should verify the list it presents, especially if you use clone equipment. To speed the installation process, make a list of the following information before you install Windows:

A

- The drive and directory name that you want to contain Windows.
- Manufacturer and model number of your computer. If you cannot determine your exact computer model and your computer has an MCA bus, choose an equivalent IBM model. If your computer has an EISA bus, choose an equivalent COMPAQ model. Most clone computers having an EISA bus.
- Type of display adapter.
- Manufacturer and model number of your printer.
- Printer port(s) for connecting your printer(s).
- Printer communication information if you are using serial printers connected to a COM port or if you are using a modem. Include baud rate, number of bits, stop bits, and parity. Find this information in your printer or modem manual, from your dealer, or from the manufacturer.
- Mouse manufacturer and type (if you have a mouse).
- Type of keyboard.
- Type and version of the network you are on (if you are connected to one). Your system administrator can help with this information.

If you are uncertain of the manufacturer or type of equipment you use, check your manuals or sales receipts, or call your dealer or corporate personal computer support line.

Before you install Windows, you need to make sure that you have 6M to 8M of storage available on your hard disk. Use the DIR command to find your available storage. You do not have to install Windows on drive C. You can put it on any drive.

Note: You can check the amount of hard disk space you have with the CHKDSK command from the DOS prompt. Although Windows enables you to run DOS commands from within Windows, never run the CHKDSK command with a /F argument—CHKDSK /F—while Windows is running. Doing so will cause Windows' temporary work files to be destroyed. If that happens, you may lose the data you were working on, and you may have to reinstall Windows. Running the CHKDSK /F command directly from the DOS prompt is OK, however, if Windows is not running.

Installing Windows

A

After you have made a list of your equipment, you are ready to install Windows. Follow these steps:

1. Protect your original disks from change. On 1.2M (5 1/4-inch) diskettes, put a write-protect tab (an adhesive plastic patch) over the square notch on the disk's edge. On 1.44M (3 1/2-inch) diskettes, slide open the write-protect tab (a square sliding button).

2. Insert the Setup Disk (disk 1) into diskette drive A or B.

3. Type **A:** if the diskette is in drive A, or **B:** if the diskette is in drive B. Then press `↵Enter`.

4. Type **setup** and press `↵Enter`.

   A welcome screen is displayed, explaining what the Setup program does.

5. Follow the directions given by the Setup program.

If you need help during setup or if you need additional information about the options available to you, press the F1 key for Help. A Help screen specific to the current point in the Setup program is displayed. Watch the bottom of the screen for which keys to press to receive more help or to return to the Setup program. If you are unfamiliar with installing programs, you may feel more comfortable reading the Help screens before you continue.

During installation, you are asked where you want to install Windows. The default or automatic choice is this:

    C:\WINDOWS

You can edit this path name so that Windows is installed on a different hard drive or directory. To edit, press the arrow keys to move from character to character, the Del (Delete) key to delete to the right, the Backspace key to delete to the left, and the typing keys to type characters.

A

Operating the Setup Menus

If you have not used Windows or a mouse before, you may not be familiar with how to make choices from the Setup screens with the mouse or the keyboard. You can review these techniques by skimming Chapter 3's discussion on operating Windows programs.

If you have a mouse, you can make choices from Setup menus by moving the mouse so that the tip of the on-screen pointer is on a menu name, and then clicking the left mouse button. When the menu pulls down, click the mouse pointer on the name of the command you want. To edit text, click the pointer at the location in the text where you want the cursor to appear. (When inside text, the mouse pointer's appearance changes from an arrowhead to an I-beam. The I-beam is not the typing cursor. The I-beam simply shows where the typing cursor will be when you click the left mouse button.) Once you have positioned the flashing cursor, you can use the Del key to delete characters to the right, and the Backspace key to delete characters to the left. Or you can insert new characters by typing them. Click on the Continue or OK button to continue with Setup.

If you are using the keyboard, choose a menu by pressing the Alt key and then typing the underlined letter that appears in the menu name. Select a command from the pull-down menu by typing the underlined letter in the command's name. When you are presented with a group of round option buttons, look to see whether the name of the group has an underlined letter. If there is an underlined letter, press Alt followed by that letter to select the group. Move the selection between buttons by pressing the arrow keys. When you need to edit a name or text, hold down the Alt key as you press the underlined letter for that text box. A flashing cursor, called the *insertion point*, appears in the box. Move the insertion point with the left- or right-arrow keys; then use the Del key to delete characters to the right, use the Backspace key to delete characters to the left, or type to insert new characters at the insertion point. Press Enter to choose the Continue or OK button.

The installation program now checks to see what hardware you are using and what international language the keyboard and DOS are set for. Review the list of settings that Windows displays; the settings are usually correct. If you want to make changes to the list, follow the directions at the bottom of the screen to make the changes.

Once the initial part of Setup is complete, you enter the Windows environment and see the Windows background display. While in this environment, you can use the mouse or the keyboard to choose from menus or to edit text entries. Don't forget to press Help (F1) if you have questions.

You will be asked to insert additional diskettes as you complete steps. Insert them as the Setup program requests and then follow the instructions on-screen.

Windows also asks whether it can make changes to the AUTOEXEC.BAT and CONFIG.SYS files. These files are read by DOS when you start your computer. They tell DOS and Windows how to configure memory and where different programs are located. To run Windows, you may want these files altered. You will be given three choices:

- Windows can make all the changes for you; copies of the old files will be saved to backup files.

- Windows will show you two windows. One contains the original file; the other contains the changed file. You can edit or accept the new file and replace the original, or save the new file with a different name.

- Windows will skip all modifications. You must make the necessary changes to AUTOEXEC.BAT and CONFIG.SYS manually before Windows will run optimally. These changes are discussed in text files with the TXT extension found in the WINDOWS directory.

You are now given a chance to install printer and plotter drivers. Drivers tell software how to interact with a printer or plotter. You need to have a driver that is made for your printer or plotter if you want to get the best of its capabilities. You do not have to install printer or plotter drivers at this point although it is a convenient time. You can install drivers later, using the Control Panel, as described in Chapter 6, "Customizing Your Work Area."

Select the printer or plotter drivers you want from the scrolling list of printers on-screen. Set the printers you want to use most frequently to Active status. Don't forget to click the Help button in the lower right corner or press Help (F1) from the keyboard if you need help.

You can have only one active printer on a serial (COM) or parallel (LPT) port at a time. If you have two printers that normally operate from the same COM or LPT port, set one of the printers to Inactive status. If you later need to change printers, you can change their Active or Inactive status while you are running a program.

After selecting the printers you will use, you must configure each one. Configuration settings tell Windows which port the printer is attached to, paper orientation (vertical or horizontal printing), paper size, number of copies, font cartridges, and so on. These settings can be changed later from a program's printer setup command or from the Control Panel. Don't forget to use the help information that's available by pressing Help (F1).

When you have finished installing printers, Windows asks whether you want it to search your hard disk for Windows or DOS programs. If you choose this option, Windows makes a list of all programs on your hard disk. You are given an opportunity to put the names of these programs into a special group window. Each program will be represented by a small picture. These pictures, called *icons*, make starting a program easy. You should probably select the programs you recognize and have them put into a group. You can add or remove programs in a group window at any time after Windows is installed. Procedures for using group windows are described in Chapter 4, "Grouping Programs and Documents."

At the end of the Windows installation, you are given an opportunity to read files that Setup copied into the WINDOWS directory. You can read the files from the installation program when it asks you to, or you can complete the installation of Windows and read the files by using any word processor. The Notepad program, a small word processor that comes with Windows, is convenient for reading these information files. The names of the files are the following:

README.TXT

NETWORKS.TXT

PRINTERS.TXT

SYSINI.TXT

WININI.TXT

If you read these files during setup, they are displayed through the Notepad program. To exit Notepad when you are finished reading a file, click on the File menu and then on the Exit command. Or from the keyboard, press Alt, F, and X.

Note: If you are installing Windows on a network, read the NETWORKS.TXT file or call Microsoft before completing installation. Windows works with a wide range of networks, but some networks require updated software. Most network companies are releasing these updates free of charge. Because your network may need an update or may need commands changed to accommodate Windows 3, be sure to read the NETWORKS.TXT file.

When you have finished installing Windows, three large buttons appear: **R**eboot, **R**estart Windows, and **R**eturn to **D**OS. The selections you made during setup do not take effect until you restart your computer by rebooting it. To choose **R**eboot, click on that button or type R.

Rebooting restarts your computer without turning off the power. Memory is erased and DOS is reloaded. The AUTOEXEC.BAT and CONFIG.SYS files are reread, which configures your computer with the selections you made during setup. If you chose not to let Windows Setup modify AUTOEXEC.BAT and CONFIG.SYS, Windows may not run correctly even after you reboot. Check the TXT files in the WINDOWS directory for information on how to change your AUTOEXEC.BAT and CONFIG.SYS files if you are changing them manually.

Once you have rebooted, follow the information in Chapters 1 and 2 to start Windows, learn operating procedures, and quit Windows.

Installing Unlisted Printers

If you are unable to locate a compatible printer driver from the same manufacturer, Windows offers a temporary solution. One of the choices for a printer driver is Generic/Text Only. Using the Generic/Text Only printer driver enables you to print text and numbers on most printers. However, you will not be able to print with special capabilities, such as underline, bold, or graphics.

Check with the Microsoft telephone support line and your printer manufacturer for a printer driver for your printer, or for a compatible driver.

Windows has over 140 printer drivers available. When you receive a printer driver to match your equipment, you can install the driver without reinstalling Windows. Use the Control Panel to add the new printer driver. The procedure is described in Chapter 6, "Customizing Your Work Area."

Running Windows after Installation

A

At the DOS prompt, `C:>`, you can type **win** and press Enter to start Windows in the most efficient mode for your processor and memory configuration. You can force Windows to start in one of the other operating modes to meet a certain operating condition, such as operating Windows 2.X programs. For more information on the capabilities of these modes and how to start Windows in a specific mode, refer to Chapter 1, "An Overview of Windows."

If the screen goes blank when you start Windows, you may have installed Windows with an incorrect graphics adapter. To fix this problem, repeat the installation. Turn off your computer, restart it, and repeat the installation process, specifying a different graphics adapter.

If Windows starts but your mouse does not work, you may have a serial mouse yet you configured a printer to use the same serial port, COM. To fix this problem, reconnect the mouse to a different COM port and restart Windows, or refer to Chapter 6 for instructions on using the Control Panel to change the printer to a different COM port. You will need to use keystroke operations until the mouse works.

Changing the Setup after Installation

Once Windows is operating correctly, you can make modifications to the way Windows is installed without reinstalling the entire Windows program. Occasionally, you may want to change the installation. At times, you may have a portable computer running Windows. When you are on the road, you'll need to use the plasma or LCD screen in the portable, but when you are at the office, you'll want to use a high-resolution color monitor. Instead of reinstalling Windows to get the new video driver, you can use the Windows Setup program to switch between the drivers you will be using. Windows Setup is useful also when you buy and attach a new keyboard or mouse, or when you attach your computer to a network.

366

The Windows Setup program is located in the Main group window of the Program Manager. If you need to change the setup after installation but aren't familiar with Windows, go through Chapters 1 and 2 to learn how to operate Windows menus and dialog boxes. To change the setup of the display, keyboard, mouse, or network after Windows is installed, follow these steps:

1. Activate the Program Manager and then activate the Main group window.

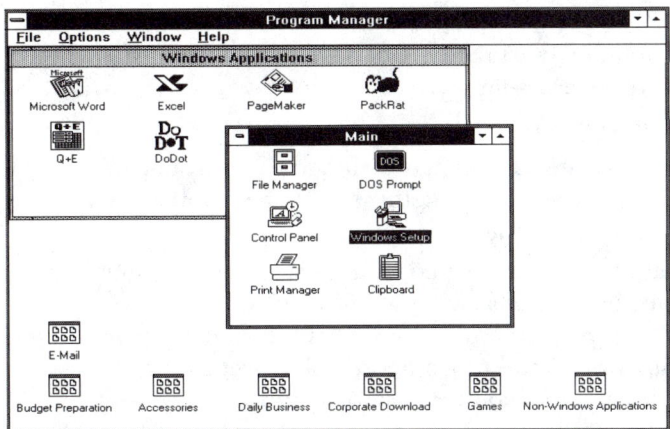

The Program Manager with the Main group window shown.

2. Choose the Windows Setup program item icon.

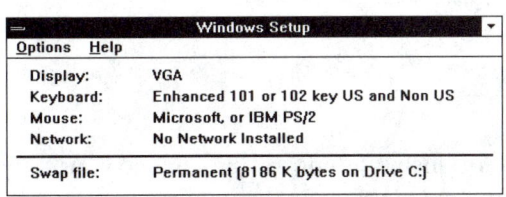

The Windows Setup dialog box displays the current installation's settings for display, keyboard, mouse, and network.

3. from the Windows Setup dialog box, choose the **Options** menu and select the **Change System Settings** command.

From the Change
System Settings
dialog box, you
can change in-
stallation settings
without reinstall-
ing Windows.

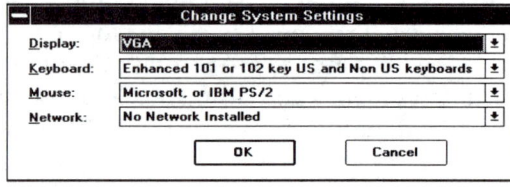

4. Select the pull-down list of the setting you want to change by clicking on the related down-arrow icon. Or press (Alt)+*letter* to select the list, and then press (Alt)+(↓) to pull the list down.

5. Select from the pull-down list the type of device you want installed by clicking on it, or by pressing (↑) or (↓).

6. Choose OK or press (↵Enter).

7. If a special driver is required, you may be asked to insert one of the original Windows diskettes or a diskette sent by the manufacturer of your display, keyboard, mouse, or network.

8. Once the new setup has been created, you must restart Windows. You are given the choice of restarting Windows or returning to DOS. If you need to change hardware—such as attaching a new keyboard or mouse, or connecting a new display—return to DOS, make the new connection, and then restart Windows.

If Windows or a Windows program does not behave correctly after changing the installation, check the Windows Setup dialog box to see whether you have the correct settings. Return to the original settings if necessary or reinstall Windows if appropriate.

Summary

This appendix should help you install Windows and change your Windows installation when you change hardware. Now that you have installed Windows, you may want to begin with Chapters 1, 2, and 3 to get an overview of Windows and to learn why Windows is valuable to any personal computer user. In the early chapters, you also learn the fundamentals of operating all Windows programs, as well as how to start and exit the program.

Summary of Windows Commands

This appendix summarizes all the Windows commands covered in this book. To use this reference material, look in the left-hand column for the task you want to perform. In the column to the right of each task listing are the keyboard and mouse commands for performing that task.

Operating Windows

Task	Keyboard	Mouse
Select program icon	Alt+Tab	Click on icon
Select program window	Alt+Tab	Click on window
Open a window	Select icon and press Enter	Double-click on icon
Start a Windows or Non-Windows program, or open a Windows accessory program	Select icon and press Enter	Double-click on icon
Quit a program	Alt, space bar, **Close**	Double-click on program Control icon, top left
Switch between programs	Alt+Tab	Click on window
Display Task Manager	Ctrl+Esc; or Alt, space bar, **Switch To**	Double-click on desktop
Move a program window	Alt, space bar, **Move**	Drag title bar
Move a document window	Alt, hyphen, **Move**	Drag title bar
Resize a program window	Alt, space bar, **Size**	Drag borders
Resize a document window	Alt, hyphen, **Size**	Drag borders
Minimize a program window to an icon	Alt, space bar, **Minimize**	Click on Minimize icon, top right
Minimize a document window to an icon	Alt, hyphen, **Minimize**	Click on Minimize icon, top right
Maximize a program window to full screen	Alt, space bar, **Maximize**	Click on Maximize icon, top right
Maximize a document window to full screen	Alt, hyphen, **Maximize**	Click on Maximize icon, top right
Restore a program to a window	Alt, space bar, **Restore**	Click on Restore icon, top right
Restore a document to a window	Alt, hyphen, **Restore**	Click on Restore icon or use keystroke if icon not available

B

370

Operating Programs

Working with Commands

Task	Keyboard	Mouse
Select a menu command	Alt, underlined menu letter, underlined command letter	Click on menu, click command

Working with Dialog Boxes

Task	Keyboard	Mouse
Move between areas in dialog box	Tab or Alt+underlined command letter	Click on selection
Select button in dialog box	Tab, arrow key	Click on selection
Select check box in dialog box	Tab, space bar	Click on selection
Select text box in dialog box	Tab, type	Click in box, type
Choose command button in dialog box	Select and press space bar	Click on command
Choose OK button	Enter	Click on OK
Choose Cancel button	Esc	Click on Cancel

Getting Help

Task	Keyboard	Mouse
Get help	Alt, **Help**	**Help** menu

B

371

Working with Documents

Task	Keyboard	Mouse
Start a new document	Alt, **File**, **New**	**File** menu, **New** command
Open an existing document	Alt, **File Open**	**File** menu, **Open** command
Close a document	Alt, **File**, **Close**	**File** menu, **Close** command
Save a document	Alt, **File**, **Save**	**File** menu, **Save** command
Save and name a document	Alt, **File**, Save **As**	**File** menu, Save **As** command

B

Printing

Task	Keyboard	Mouse
Print a document	Alt, **File**, **Print**	**File** menu, **Print** command
Select a printer	Alt, **File**, **Printer Setup**	**File** menu, **Printer** Setup command

Using Command Program Commands

Task	Keyboard	Mouse
Exit the program	Alt, **File**, **Exit**	**File** menu, **Exit** command
Undo most recent edit	Alt, **Edit**, **Undo**	**Edit** menu, **Undo** command
Cut a selection to the Clipboard	Alt, **Edit**, **Cut**	**Edit** menu, **Cut** command
Copy a selection to the Clipboard	Alt, **Edit**, **Copy**	**Edit** menu, **Copy** command

372

Task	Keyboard	Mouse
Paste a selection from the Clipboard	Alt, **Edit**, **P**aste	**Edit** menu, **Paste** command
Select text	Shift+move insertion point	Press, hold, and drag over selection

Using the Program Manager

Working with Group Windows or Icons

Task	Keyboard	Mouse
Select a group window or icon	Ctrl+F6 or Ctrl+Tab	Click on group window or icon
Move a group window or icon	Alt, hyphen, **Move**, arrow, Enter	Drag title bar with mouse
Arrange group windows	Alt, **Window**, **Cascade** or **Tile** or **Arrange Icons**	Drag with mouse
Activate a group window	Ctrl+Tab	Click on group window
Quit Windows	Alt, **File**, **Exit Windows**; or Alt+F4	Double-click on program Control icon, top left
Arrange icons if window changes	Alt, **Options**, **Auto Arrange**	**Options** menu, **Auto Arrange** command
Shrink Program Manager to icon when a program starts	Alt, **Options**, **Minimize on Use**	**Options** menu, **Minimize on Use** command
Arrange windows in cascade	Alt, **Window**, **Cascade**; or Shift+F5	**Window** menu, **Cascade** command
Arrange windows side by side	Alt, **Window**, **Tile**; or Shift+F4	**Window** menu, **Tile** command
Arrange icons in a row	Alt, **Window**, **Arrange Icons**	**Window** menu, **Arrange Icons** command

B

373

Summary of Windows Commands

Task	Keyboard	Mouse
Select and open group window	Alt, **Window**, **1** or **2** or **3** (and so on)	Window menu, **1** or **2** or **3** (and so on)
Add a group window	Alt, **File**, **New**, **Program Group**	File menu, **New** command, Program Group
Close a group window	Activate group window, Alt, hyphen, **Close**; or Ctrl+F4	Double-click on group Control icon

Working with Program Items

Task	Keyboard	Mouse
Select a program item	Press arrow keys	Click on program item
Copy a program item	Select, Alt, **File**, **Copy**	Select, **File** menu, **Copy** command
Move a program item	Select Alt, **File**, **Move**	Drag with mouse
Delete a program item	Select, Alt, **File**, **Delete**	Select, **File** menu, **Delete** command
Change description or name	Select program item, Alt, **File**, **Properties**	Select program item, **File** menu, **Properties** command
Start program	Select program item and press Enter	Select program item, **File** menu, **Run** Command; or double-click on program item

Using the File Manager

Operating the File Manager

Task	Keyboard	Mouse
Move between drive icons and Directory Tree	Tab	Click on drive icon or window
Move selection between drives	Left or right arrows	Click on drive icon
Open selected drive	Enter	Double-click on drive icon
Select and open a specific drive	Ctrl+letter	Double-click on drive icon
Close the File Manager	Alt, **File**, **Exit**	Double-click on program Control icon

Working with the Directory Tree in the File Manager

Task	Keyboard	Mouse
Select any directory	Up or down arrows	Click on directory
Open selected directory into a window	Enter	Double-click on directory icon
Select the first subdirectory in currently selected directory	Right arrow	Click on desired subdirectory
Select the directory containing current subdirectory	Left arrow	Click on desired directory
Select previous directory	Up arrow	Click on desired directory
Select next directory	Down arrow	Click on desired directory
Select previous directory, same level	Ctrl+up arrow	Click on desired directory

B

375

Summary of Windows Commands

Task	Keyboard	Mouse
Select next directory, same level	Ctrl+down arrow	Click on desired directory
Select directory one screen up	PgUp	Click on desired directory
Select directory one screen down	PgDn	Click on desired directory
Select root directory	Home	Click on root directory
Select last directory	End	Click on desired directory
Select next directory beginning with *letter*	*letter*	Click on selection
Collapse the selected directory	Hyphen (-); or Alt, **Tree**, **Collapse Branch**	Click on folder with hyphen (-)
Expand the selected directory by one level	Plus (+); or Alt, **Tree**, **Expand One Level**	Click on folder with plus (+)
Expand selected directory to all levels	Asterisk (*); or Alt, **Tree**, **Expand Branch**	**Tree** menu, **Expand Branch** command
Expand all branches	Ctrl+* (asterisk); or Alt, **Tree**, **Expand All**	**Tree** menu, **Expand All** command
Create a new directory	Alt, **File**, **Create Directory**	**File** menu, **Create Directory** command

Working with Files in the File Manager

Task	Keyboard	Mouse
Start a program	Select, Enter	Double-click on program or file icon
Select adjacent files	Shift+arrow keys	Shift+Click on files to select

Task	Keyboard	Mouse
Select nonadjacent files	Ctrl+arrow, space bar to select	Ctrl+Click on file to select
Select all items	Ctrl+/ (slash); or Alt, **File**, **Select All**	Click on first file, Shift+Click on last file
Deselect all items	Ctrl+\ (backslash); or **File** menu, **Deselect All**	Click on one file
Print a selected text file	Alt, **File**, **Print**	File menu, **Print** command
Associate a file with a program	Alt, **File**, **Associate**	File menu, **Associate** command
Search for a file	Alt, **File**, Searc**h**	File menu, Search command
Move selected file(s) or a directory	Alt, **File**, **Move**	Select and drag a directory on same disk (Alt+Drag to a different disk)
Copy selected file(s) or a directory	Alt, **File**, **Copy**	Select and drag to another disk (Ctrl+Drag to the same disk)
Delete a selected file or directory	Alt, **File**, **Delete**	File menu, **Delete** command
Rename a selected file or directory	Alt, **File**, Re**name**	File menu, Re**name** command
Change a selected file's attributes (read only, hidden, archive, system)	Alt, **File**, Change Attributes	File menu, Change Attributes command

B

Working with Diskettes in the File Manager

Task	*Keyboard*	*Mouse*
Copy contents of a diskette	Alt, **Disk, Copy Diskette**	**Disk** menu, **Copy Diskette** command
Create/change disk volume label	Alt, **Disk, Label Disk**	**Disk** menu, **Label Disk** command
Format a diskette	Alt, **Disk, Format Diskette**	**Disk** menu, **Format Diskette** command
Format a diskette for start-up	Alt, **Disk, Make System Diskette**	**Disk** menu, **Make System Diskette** command

Working with a Network in the File Manager

Task	*Keyboard*	*Mouse*
Connect computer to a network	Alt, **Disk, Connect Net Drive**	**Disk** menu, **Connect Net Drive** command
Disconnect computer from a network	Alt, **Disk, Disconnect Net Drive**	**Disk** menu, **Disconnnect Net Drive** command

Using File Manager Options

Task	*Keyboard*	*Mouse*
Display confirmation box for "dangerous" actions (such as deleting a directory)	Alt, **Options, Confirmation**	**Options** menu, **Confirmation** command
Display item names in lowercase	Alt, **Options, Lower Case**	**Options** menu, **Lower Case** command
Display status bar	Alt, **Options, Status Bar**	**Options** menu, **Status Bar** command
Minimize File Manager to icon when you start a program	Alt, **Options, Minimize on Use**	**Options** menu, **Minimize on Use** command

378

Controlling File Manager Windows

Task	Keyboard	Mouse
Arrange overlapping windows	Alt, **Window**, **Cascade**	**Window** menu, **Cascade** command
Arrange tiled windows	Alt, **Window**, **Tile**	**Window** menu, **Tile** command
Update contents of displayed windows	Alt, **Window**, **Refresh**	**Window** menu, **Refresh** command
Close all the directory windows	Alt, **Window**, Close **All Directories**	**Window** menu, Close **All Directories** command
Activate a window	Alt, **Window**, #Window name	**Window** menu, #Window name command

Using the Print Manager

Pausing or Canceling a Print Job

Task	Keyboard	Mouse
Temporarily stop printing	Alt, **Pause**	Click on **Pause** button
Restart a paused print	Alt, **Resume**	Click on **Resume** button
Cancel a print job	Alt, **Delete**	Click on **Delete** button

Controlling Printer Priority

Task	Keyboard	Mouse
Give the program high priority; the program runs faster	Alt, **Options**, **Low Priority**	**Options** menu, **Low Priority** command

Task	Keyboard	Mouse
Give the program and printer equal priority; the program and printer run equally	Alt, **Options**, **Medium Priority**	**Options** menu, **Medium Priority** command
Give the printer high priority; the program may slow down	Alt, **Options**, **High Priority**	**Options** menu, **High Priority** command

Controlling Printer Alert Messages

Task	Keyboard	Mouse
Always alert you when your printer needs attention	Alt, **Options**, **Alert Always**	**Options** menu, **Alert Always** command
Beep and flash if your printer needs attention but the Print Manager is inactive	Alt, **Options**, **Flash if Inactive**	**Options** menu, **Flash if Inactive** command
Ignore printer messages	Alt, **Options**, **Ignore if Inactive**	**Options** menu, **Ignore if Inactive** command

Displaying Information in the Print Manager

Task	Keyboard	Mouse
Display time and date a file was sent to the printer	Alt, **View**, **Time/Date Sent**	**View** menu, **Time/Date Sent** command
Display size of files waiting to print	Alt, **View**, **Print File Size**	**View** menu, **Print File Size** command

Closing the Print Manager Program

Task	Keyboard	Mouse
Close the Print Manager program	Alt, Options, Exit	Options menu, Exit command

Using Write

Using Pagination

Task	Keyboard	Mouse
Set page breaks	Alt, File, Repaginate	File menu, Repaginate command

Working with Pictures

Task	Keyboard	Mouse
Move a picture	Alt, Edit, Move Picture	Edit menu, Move Picture command
Resize a picture	Alt, Edit, Size Picture	Edit menu, Size Picture command

Searching for Text

Task	Keyboard	Mouse
Look for a word or phrase	Alt, Search, Find	Search menu, Find command
Look again	Alt, Search, Repeat Last Find	Search menu, Repeat Last Find command
Change a word or phrase	Alt, Search, Change	Search menu, Change command
Go to a certain page number	Alt, Search, Go To Page	Search menu, Go To Page command

B

Character Formatting

Task	Keyboard	Mouse
Remove all character formatting	Alt, Character, Normal	Character menu, Normal command
Bold the selection	Alt, Character, **Bold**	Character menu, **Bold** command
Italicize the selection	Alt, Character, **Italic**	Character menu, Italic command
<u>Underline</u> the selection	Alt, Character, **Underline**	Character menu, Underline command
Superscript the selection	Alt, Character, **Superscript**	Character menu, Superscript command
Subscript the selection	Alt, Character, **Subscript**	Character menu, Subscript command
Change a font	Alt, Character, **1 or 2 or 3**	Character menu, **1 or 2 or 3** command
Reduce the size of text	Alt, Character, **Reduce Font**	Character menu, **Reduce Font** command
Enlarge text	Alt, Character, **Enlarge Font**	Character menu, **Enlarge Font** command
Change the font	Alt, Character, **Fonts**	Character menu, **Fonts** command
Select a point size for type	Alt, Character, **Fonts**	Character menu, **Fonts** command

Paragraph Formatting

Task	Keyboard	Mouse
Remove all paragraph formatting	Alt, **Paragraph,** Normal	**Paragraph** menu, Normal command
Align a paragraph to the left	Alt, **Paragraph,** **Left**	**Paragraph** menu, Left command
Center a paragraph	Alt, **Paragraph,** **Centered**	**Paragraph** menu, Centered command

Task	Keyboard	Mouse
Align a paragraph to the right	Alt, **Paragraph, Right**	**Paragraph menu, Right command**
Align a paragraph left and right	Alt, **Paragraph, Justified**	**Paragraph menu, Justified command**
Single-space a paragraph	Alt, **Paragraph, Single Space**	**Paragraph menu, Single Space command**
Add extra half space between lines	Alt, **Paragraph, 1 1/2 Space**	**Paragraph menu, 1 1/2 Space command**
Double-space a paragraph	Alt, **Paragraph, Double Space**	**Paragraph menu, Double Space command**
Set paragraph indents	Alt, **Paragraph, Indents**	**Paragraph menu, Indents command**

Document Formatting

Task	Keyboard	Mouse
Add a header	Alt, **Document, Header**	**Document menu, Header command**
Add a footer	Alt, **Document, Footer**	**Document menu, Footer command**
Add automatic page numbers	Alt, **Document, Header or Footer**	**Document menu, Header or Footer command**
Display a ruler	Alt, **Document, Ruler On**	**Document menu, Ruler On command**
Set tabs	Alt, **Document, Tabs**	**Document menu, Tabs command**
Set margins	Alt, **Document, Page Layout**	**Document menu, Page Layout command**

B

Using Paintbrush

Using the Paintbrush Tools

Task	Keyboard	Mouse
Select toolbox, line-width box, or palette	Tab	Click on selection
Select tool, line, color, or shade	Arrow, Ins	Click on selection

Task	Select This Tool	Mouse Action
Select an object		Press, hold, drag around object, release
Select an area		Press, hold, drag across area, release
Create an airbrush effect		Press, hold, drag across screen, release
Type text		Click, type
Change foreground color to background color		Press, hold, drag across to change
Change all colors to background color		Press, hold, drag across screen
Fill a shape with color or shade		Select fill color, point, click
Paint a brushstroke		Select color, press, hold, drag to paint
Draw a curved line		Press, hold, drag, release; press, hold, pull sides
Draw a straight line		Press, hold, drag, release
Draw a filled box		Select fill, press, hold, drag, release

B

384

Task	Select This Tool	Mouse Action
Draw an unfilled box		Press, hold, drag to opposite corner, release
Draw a filled rounded-corner box		Select fill, press, hold, drag, release
Draw an unfilled rounded-corner box		Press, hold, drag to opposite corner, release
Draw a perfect square		Hold Shift, draw as usual
Draw a filled circle or oval		Select fill, press, hold, drag, release
Draw an unfilled circle or oval		Press, hold, drag, release
Draw a perfect round circle		Hold Shift, draw as usual
Draw an unfilled polygon		Press, hold, drag; repeat to each corner; double-click
Draw a filled polygon		Select fill, press, hold, drag; repeat to each corner; double-click

Choosing Different Line Widths

Task	Select from the Line-Width Box	Result
Choose a thinner or wider line	Any line width	Line, brush, and eraser strokes are this width

B

Choosing Different Colors and Shades

Task	Select from the Palette	Result
Choose a fill color or shade	Any color or shade	Filled objects are filled with this color or shade
Paint with a color or shade	Any color or shade	Painted objects are this color or shade

Setting Up Margins, Headings, and Footers

Task	Keyboard	Mouse
Create margins, headers, or footers	Alt, **File**, **Page Setup**	File menu, Page Setup command

Controlling Your View of the Screen

Task	Keyboard	Mouse
Zoom in for a close-up view	Alt, **View**, **Zoom In**; or Ctrl+Z	View Menu, Zoom **In** command
Zoom out if you are zoomed in	Alt, **View**, **Zoom Out**; or Ctrl+O	View Menu, Zoom **Out** command
View just the picture, with no tools or palette	Alt, **View**, **View Picture**; or Ctrl+C	View Menu, **View** Picture command
Cancel View Picture	Enter	Click

B

Changing the Appearance of Text

Note: The changes apply to the current block of text only.

Task	Keyboard	Mouse
Change the font	Alt, **Font**, select any listed font	**Font** menu, select any font
Change the text size	Alt, **Size**, select any bold size	**Size** menu, select any bold size
Bold the current text	Alt, **Style**, **Bold**; or Ctrl+B	**Style** menu, **Bold** command
Italicize the current text	Alt, **Style**, Italic; or Ctrl+I	**Style** menu, Italic command
Underline the current text	Alt, **Style**, Underline; or Ctrl+U	**Style** menu, Underline command
Outline the current text	Alt, **Style**, Outline	**Style** menu, Outline command
Add a shadow to the current text	Alt, **Style**, Shadow	**Style** menu, Shadow command

B

Manipulating Selected Areas

Note: Select area to be manipulated with the Scissors or Pick tool before you choose these commands. The **Pick** menu becomes available after you select the area to be affected.

Task	Keyboard	Mouse
Flip an object left to right	Alt, **Pick**, Flip **Horizontal**	**Pick** menu, Flip **Horizontal** command
Flip an object upside down	Alt, **Pick**, Flip **Vertical**	**Pick** menu, Flip **Vertical** command
Invert an object's color or shade	Alt, **Pick**, Inverse	**Pick** menu, Inverse command

Summary of Windows Commands

The following commands switch between on and off each time the command is chosen:

Task	Keyboard	Mouse
Clear original area when you shrink, grow, or tilt it (choose this command first)	Alt, **Pick**, **Clear**	**Pick** menu, **Clear** command
Enlarge or shrink an object	Alt, **Pick**, **Shrink+Grow**, Ins+arrow to draw a rectangle to hold pasted area. Rectangle determines new size.	**Pick** menu, **Shrink+Grow** command; then drag to draw a rectangle to hold pasted area. Rectangle determines new size. (Hold down Shift to keep it proportional.)
Tilt an object	Alt, **Pick**, **Tilt** Ins+arrow to tilt selected area	**Pick** menu, **Tilt** command; then drag to tilt selected area

Changing the Brush Shape

Task	Keyboard	Mouse
Paint with a different brush shape	Alt, **Options**, **Brush Shapes**; then arrow and Enter	**Options** menu, **Brush Shapes** command; then click on the shape you want

B

Using the Recorder

Recording, Saving, and Playing Back Macros

Task	Keyboard	Mouse
Record a macro	Alt, **Macro**, Re**c**ord, **S**tart; then Ctrl+Break to stop recording	**M**acro menu, Re**c**ord command, **S**tart button; click on Recorder icon to stop recording
Save a macro	Alt, **F**ile, Save **A**s	**F**ile menu, Save **A**s command
Open a Recorder file in order to use the macros it contains	Alt, **F**ile, **O**pen, select file	**F**ile menu, **O**pen command, select file
Replay a macro contained in an open Recorder file	Select macro, Alt, **M**acro, **R**un; or press shortcut key from Windows program	Select macro, **M**acro menu, **R**un command

B

Index

Using Microsoft Windows 3, 2nd Edition

Ron Person & Karen Rose

Excellent introduction to Windows basics! This easy-to-understand text contains **Quick Start** tutorials, technical tips, and a Windows software applications directory.

Order #1054
$22.95 USA
0-88022-509-2, 500 pp.

MS-DOS QuickStart, 2nd Edition

Developed by Que Corporation

The visual approach to learning MS-DOS! Illustrations help readers become familiar with their operating systems. Perfect for all beginning users of DOS—through Version 4.0!

Order #1205
$19.95 USA
0-88022-611-0, 400 pp.

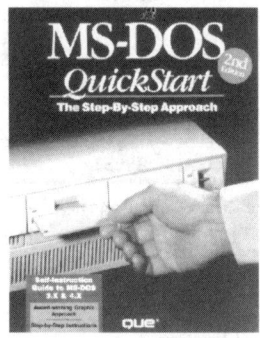

Excel QuickStart

Developed by Que Corporation

Excel QuickStart takes readers step by step through basic Excel operations—including spreadsheets, databases, and graphs —with more than 100 two-page illustrations. Covers both IBM and Macintosh.

Order #957
$19.95 USA
0-88022-423-1, 400 pp.

Using Word for Windows

by Ron Person & Karen Rose

Quick Start tutorials, a special **Troubleshooting** section, and a tear-out menu map give this text top value! Helps users capture the potential of word processing in the powerful Microsoft Windows environment. Begins with basic functions and progresses into advanced desktop publishing features.

Order #886
$22.95 USA
0-88022-399-5, 500 pp.

Free Catalog!

Mail us this registration form today, and we'll send you a free catalog featuring Que's complete line of best-selling books.

Name of Book _____

Name _____

Title _____

Phone ( ) _____

Company _____

Address _____

City _____

State _____ ZIP _____

Please check the appropriate answers:

1. Where did you buy your Que book?
   ☐ Bookstore (name: _____)
   ☐ Computer store (name: _____)
   ☐ Catalog (name: _____)
   ☐ Direct from Que
   ☐ Other: _____

2. How many computer books do you buy a year?
   ☐ 1 or less
   ☐ 2-5
   ☐ 6-10
   ☐ More than 10

3. How many Que books do you own?
   ☐ 1
   ☐ 2-5
   ☐ 6-10
   ☐ More than 10

4. How long have you been using this software?
   ☐ Less than 6 months
   ☐ 6 months to 1 year
   ☐ 1-3 years
   ☐ More than 3 years

5. What influenced your purchase of this Que book?
   ☐ Personal recommendation
   ☐ Advertisement
   ☐ In-store display
   ☐ Price
   ☐ Que catalog
   ☐ Que mailing
   ☐ Que's reputation
   ☐ Other: _____

6. How would you rate the overall content of the book?
   ☐ Very good
   ☐ Good
   ☐ Satisfactory
   ☐ Poor

7. What do you like *best* about this Que book?
   _____
   _____

8. What do you like *least* about this Que book?
   _____
   _____

9. Did you buy this book with your personal funds?
   ☐ Yes   ☐ No

10. Please feel free to list any other comments you may have about this Que book.
   _____
   _____
   _____

— que —

Order Your Que Books Today!

Name _____

Title _____

Company _____

City _____

State _____ ZIP _____

Phone No. ( ) _____

Method of Payment:

Check ☐   (Please enclose in envelope.)

Charge My: VISA ☐   MasterCard ☐

American Express ☐

Charge # _____

Expiration Date _____

Order No.	Title	Qty.	Price	Total

You can **FAX** your order to **1-317-573-2583**. Or call **1-800-428-5331, ext. ORDR** to order direct.
Please add $2.50 per title for shipping and handling.

Subtotal	
Shipping & Handling	
Total	

— que —

NO POSTAGE
NECESSARY
IF MAILED
IN THE
UNITED STATES

BUSINESS REPLY MAIL
First Class Permit No. 9918   Indianapolis, IN

Postage will be paid by addressee

11711 N. College
Carmel, IN 46032

NO POSTAGE
NECESSARY
IF MAILED
IN THE
UNITED STATES

BUSINESS REPLY MAIL
First Class Permit No. 9918   Indianapolis, IN

Postage will be paid by addressee

11711 N. College
Carmel, IN 46032